GOVERNING LATIN AMERICA

Figure 1.1 Map of contemporary Latin America
Source: University of Texas Library (www.lib.utexas.edu)

GOVERNING LATIN AMERICA

Joe Foweraker
Todd Landman
Neil Harvey

polity

First published in 2003 by Polity Press in association with Blackwell Publishing Ltd

Editorial office:
Polity Press
65 Bridge Street
Cambridge CB2 1UR, UK

Marketing and production:
Blackwell Publishing Ltd
108 Cowley Road
Oxford OX4 1JF, UK

Distributed in the USA by
Blackwell Publishing Inc.
350 Main Street
Malden, MA 02148, USA

ISBN: 0-7456 2371-9
ISBN: 0-7456 2372-7 (pb)

A catalogue record for this book is available from the British Library and has been applied for from the Library of Congress.

Typeset in 10.5 on 12 pt Times New Roman
by SNP Best-set Typesetter Ltd., Hong Kong
Printed and bound in Great Britain by MPG Books Ltd, Bodmin, Cornwall

For further information on Polity, visit our website: www.polity.co.uk

▌ CONTENTS

List of Figures and Tables   vii

Introduction: Governing Latin America   1

PART I: AUTHORITY AND POWER   9

1   Authoritarianism and Democracy in Latin America   11
Founding state authority: nation-building and early modernization   12
Expanding state authority: divergent responses to mass politics   15
Reforming state authority: neoliberalism and delegative democracies   27

2   Latin America and the Democratic Universe   34
Defining democracy   35
Explaining democracy   37
Electoral vs. liberal democracy   40
Threats to democracy   44
Assessing democracy   54

PART II: ACCOUNTABILITY AND LEGITIMACY   57

3   Government and Citizens   59
Legitimacy, accountability, and participation in modern state formation   60
Legitimacy, accountability, and participation in Latin America   65
Neoliberalism, governments, and citizens   73

4   Constitutionalism and the Rule of Law   76
Political order   76
Constitutionalism and the rule of law   77
Human rights and Latin American governance   83
Forms and practices   91

PART III: REPRESENTATION, POLITICAL, AND SOCIAL RIGHTS   93

5   **Political Parties**   **95**
    Alphabet soup   95
    Political parties are not well rooted in their societies   97
    Political parties are patronage parties   99
    Political parties are undisciplined   101
    Political parties cannot be placed on a left–right continuum   103
    Political parties are populist   105
    Political parties are short-lived   107
    Political parties contribute to political stability   109

6   **Presidents, Legislatures, and Elections**   **111**
    Government and governability   111
    Presidentialism and governability in Latin America   112
    Explaining variations in governability in Latin America   113
    Classifying the democratic governments of Latin America   120

7   **Political and Social Rights**   **123**
    Defining political and social rights   124
    Mapping political and social rights   126
    Political rights, social rights, and democracy   140

PART IV: PARTICIPATION, CONTESTATION, AND CIVIL RIGHTS   145

8   **New Political Actors**   **147**
    Social movements and civil society   147
    The novelty of new political actors   149
    Impact of new political actors   156
    Future directions: global networks and NGOs   161

9   **Minority and Indigenous Rights**   **166**
    Minority and indigenous rights   167
    State formation: the denial of minorities   170
    Indigenous movements, land, and cultural identity   174
    Constitutional reform and indigenous rights   180

10 **Uneven Democratic Performance**   **190**
    The uneven performance of Latin American democracies   190
    Exploring uneven performance   192
    Demonstrating uneven performance   193
    Uneven performance and democratic transition   195
    Uneven performance and democratic consolidation   196
    Explaining uneven performance   197
    Uneven performance and the rule of law   199
    Putting the people back in democracy   200
    The future democratic performance of Latin America   202

Notes   204
References   214
Index   228

▌ FIGURES AND TABLES

FIGURES

1.1	Map of contemporary Latin America	*frontispiece*	ii
2.1	Liberal democracies, pseudo-democracies, non-democracies		43
2.2	Foreign debt of selected Latin American countries		53
4.1	Political and civil liberties in Latin America		90
7.1	Political rights and democratic transitions in Latin America, 1972–1995		128
7.2	Voter turnout in Latin America by year, 1945–1997		129
7.3	Voter turnout in Latin America by country, 1945–1997		130
7.4	Gross domestic product per capita in Latin America, 1975–1996		132
7.5	Income distribution in Latin America, 1989–1998		133
7.6	Comparative human development for Latin America, 1975–1999		135
7.7	Human development over time in Latin America, 1975–1999		135
7.8	Healthcare expenditure in Latin America, 1990–1994		136
7.9	Illiteracy rates in Latin America, 1970–1995		137
7.10	Expenditure on education in Latin America by country		137
7.11	Expenditure on education in Latin America, 1980–1998		138
7.12	Prevalence of undernourishment in Latin America, 1979–1998		139
7.13	Depth of hunger in Latin America		139

7.14 Support for democracy by country in Latin America,
      1995–2001   142
7.15 Support for democracy by year in Latin America,
      1995–2001   143
7.16 Human development and support for democracy in
      Latin America, 1998–2000   143
9.1   Minority protest in Latin America, 1980–1995   181
9.2   Minority rebellion in Latin America, 1980–1995   182
10.1 Democratic performance in Latin America
      (institutions and rights), 1970–1996   194

TABLES

2.1 Third wave democratic transitions in Latin America   41
2.2 Effective number of parties and ideological
     polarization   46
4.1 Status of selected international human rights
     instruments in Latin America, 1999   87
4.2 Status of Inter-American human rights instruments,
     1998   89
5.1 Examples of political parties in the Americas   96
6.1 Varieties of Latin American presidential democracies   121
7.1 Political rights and social rights   124
7.2 Women's suffrage in Latin America   127
9.1 Indigenous and black population in Latin America   175

INTRODUCTION:
GOVERNING LATIN AMERICA

In contrast to many textbooks on Latin American politics, *Governing Latin America* examines the region in terms of concepts and categories that are central to mainstream political science. In other words, it tackles the main topics of Latin American politics using tried and tested approaches in political science. It does not see Latin America as a separate political reality. Rather it seeks to "bring Latin America back into" comparative politics and to demonstrate that the governments of the region face the same or similar problems as governments elsewhere in the world. Although it is recognized that Latin America is historically and culturally specific (see chapter 1), we approach the region within a comparative perspective, both comparing countries within the region and comparing Latin America with other regions of the world. These regional and global comparisons throw into relief the principal challenges to the governments of the continent and reveal their linkages to international politics and international agencies. These agencies include governmental organizations like the United Nations, the World Bank and the International Monetary Fund, as well as non-governmental organizations, such as human rights groups, environmental groups, and other transnational advocacy groups.

In keeping with this brief, we do not provide a simple historical account of the politics of Latin America. On the contrary, we set out to analyze how government works, and how it responds to the problems of governance, whether institutional, political, social, or economic. *Government* is that set of specialized institutions for reaching collective decisions that have an impact on society as whole, while *governance* is the process of implementing these collective decisions and maintaining long-term political stability. Our analysis of government and governance in Latin America focuses on power and authority (chapters 1 and 2), accountability and legitimacy (chapters 3 and 4), representation, political, and social rights (chapters 5, 6, and 7), participation, contestation, and civil rights (chapters 8 and 9), and the quality of democratic government (chapter 10). It is this thematic focus that makes *Governing Latin America* different from the many textbooks composed of country-specific chapters. By maintaining this focus we are able to address the problems of governing Latin America in the common language of political science rather than adopting or crafting concepts that are particular to Latin America. Indeed, each chapter of the book addresses a core topic in comparative political science that could equally well be studied in North America or Europe, Africa, or Asia. At the same time, we are keen to explain our key concepts and categories as the argument advances, and careful to support our arguments with comparative evidence of different kinds. This brief introduction will serve to review the book's place in comparative politics, outline its organization, and sketch its main themes.

Latin America in comparative perspective

Why study Latin American politics today? Some commentators argue that comparative politics belongs in the past. In the 1960s and 1970s there were important debates over the causes, consequences, and relative merits of state-controlled versus market-based development, and democratic versus authoritarian solutions to problems of governance. But the collapse of the governments of the Soviet Union and its satellites in Central and Eastern Europe, and the demise of many authoritarian regimes in the capitalist world, have changed all that. Nearly all governments now subscribe in greater or lesser degree to liberal democratic values, and converge on a model of market economics, so there is no longer anything very important to compare. The "end of history" signals the end of comparative politics.

There is no doubt that the world has changed, but everything has not thereby become the same. The number of democratic governments in the world has certainly increased, but the quality of democratic government varies widely because of the persistence, severally, of oligarchic power, political corruption, legal impunity, and social exclusion. These are fundamental problems that continue to require comparative analysis. Thus, the democratic advances achieved in

Latin America are checked by challenges to the scope and consistency of democratic government. The spread of electoral politics is often undermined by violations of civil and minority rights. The promise of greater political equality often sits uneasily with widespread poverty and social distress. And although the democratic governments of Latin America have proved remarkably stable in the circumstances, this political stability is not completely assured – as recent government crises in Argentina, Colombia, and Venezuela remind us.

The large literature on democratization has responded to these persistent problems of democratic government. The initial focus on processes of transition from authoritarian to democratic rule has shifted to the difficulties of democratic consolidation, and, by extension, to a critical assessment of the quality of the new democracies. Consequently, there is now much talk of the growing number of "electoral," "illiberal," "façade," or "pseudo" democracies around the world. It is readily admitted that the quality of democratic government may be impaired by global economic pressures or by the constraints imposed by international actors like the International Monetary Fund. But although all Latin American governments suffer these pressures and constraints, they do not all do so in equal measure or in the same ways. Equally, there are – for example – violations of human rights in every country of Latin America, but some governments are clearly much better than others at dealing with the problem.

In sum, although the general problems besetting the democracies of the continent may be easy to discern, it is only a comparative perspective that can elucidate and explain the variable success of governments in responding to these problems.

In recent decades the study of Latin American politics has become increasingly concerned with (economic) interests, (social) identities, and (political) actors, whether individual or collective. Interests, identities, and actors all figure largely in this book. But our aim of explaining the diverse responses to the pressing problems of governing Latin America has also required a more traditional focus on legal frameworks, political institutions, and the organization of government itself. In this way we can compare the particular features of individual political systems while still reaching for general statements about political change and characteristic forms of political behavior. A comparative politics of Latin America should not seek to erase the political diversity of the continent, but rather draw on that diversity to achieve a better understanding of contemporary democratic government and the challenges it faces.

The organization and main themes of the book

The book begins by exploring the use of power and authority, two classical concerns of political science, in Latin America. Chapter 1 traces the different ways in which power and authority have operated since the time of Latin America's independence in the nineteenth century to the present day. It categorizes the region's characteristic forms of political rule and addresses the enduring question of all political inquiry of "who gets what when and how" (Lasswell 1950). It reviews the early caudillo governments, oligarchic democracies, personal dictatorships, populism and democratic pacts, military rule and bureaucratic authoritarianism, revolution and civil war in Central America, and dominant- and single-party states in Mexico and Cuba. It also considers the emergence of so-called "delegative" democracies in the context of neoliberal economic reform in the 1990s.

Chapter 2 develops these themes by examining Latin America's insertion into the new "democratic universe" that now comprises over 60 percent of the nation-states of the world. It does so by debating different conceptions of democracy, examining current explanations for the emergence of democracy over the period of the "third wave," defining the differences between "electoral" and "liberal" democracy, and highlighting the residual but often powerful threats to democracy in the region. Together the two chapters trace the different contours of power and authority and demonstrate that democratic governments in Latin America still have some way to go before either power or authority are fully subject to democratic controls.

Whether authoritarian or democratic, legitimacy is a key requirement for stable government since the rulers then exercise their authority with the broad acceptance of those they rule. The accountability of rulers to those they rule, on the other hand, is mainly associated with democratic government. Chapter 3 addresses accountability and legitimacy by investigating the relationship between government and citizens, while chapter 4 explores them in their contexts of constitutionalism and the rule of law. Starting with the theory and history of the relationship between government and citizens in Europe and North America, chapter 3 recounts how Latin American governments seek to legitimize their rule, how they are held accountable for their actions, and how citizens are able to participate in decision-making (or not). Chapter 4 shows that the history of constitutional rule in the region does not necessarily make it more hospitable to democracy, since the rule of law itself is often inconsistent and incomplete. Both authoritarian and democratic regimes in Latin America have sought legitimacy through appeals to constitutionalism and the rule of law. The difference today is that most Latin American governments have now subscribed to the international law of human rights through the legal instruments and apparatus of both the United Nations and the Organization of American States. Participation in international human rights regimes has raised the profile of constitutional guarantees and protections so that breaches in the rule of law – though still pervasive – are now more difficult to hide.

The third section of the book encompasses political representation, political rights, and social rights. Chapter 5 examines political parties as the universal means for aggregating and representing individuals and interests in democratic systems of government. It presents seven theses about political parties in Latin America in order to show the similarities and differences between party systems within Latin America and beyond it. Chapter 6 focuses on the formal structures of central government, which tend to follow the "separation of powers" model familiar from the United States. Although Latin America has adopted the pure presidential model of government, coupled with an electoral system of proportional representation (PR), there is still great variation across the continent in the overall degree of *governability*. This variation is explained by the size and strength of the president's support in the legislative assembly, differences in party systems, degrees of ideological polarization, and the executive's ability to forge enduring coalitions that can underpin legislative programs. Contrary to the prevalent and pessimistic evaluation of the presidential-PR model, contemporary democratic governments in Latin America have proved remarkably resilient, with only occasional instances of democratic decline or breakdown. Chapter 7 looks at the promotion and protection of political and social rights, and points up the tensions between them. Drawing on competing definitions of democracy outlined in chapter 2 it seeks to explain the persistent gap between an improving record of political rights, and the patchy, inadequate, and often deteriorating provision of social rights.

The final section of the book looks at the relationship between government and civil society in Latin America by focusing attention on participation, contestation, and civil rights. Chapters 8 and 9 investigate the participation of key political actors from civil society in the political system, both through formal channels of representation and through informal linkages between social movements and the state.

Equally, they examine the protections that civil rights offer (or not) to these same actors. Chapter 8 charts the rise of new political actors seeking redress for a wide range of grievances generated at the grassroots of society. It also investigates and illustrates the identities and political impact of several social movements and civil associations. Chapter 9 turns to the political status of minorities and the struggles for minority rights in Latin America. It looks at the plight of indigenous communities, in particular, and their attempts to secure political recognition. It has often proved difficult or impossible to escape the confines of the colonial legacy, or overcome contemporary prejudice and oppression.

The final chapter (and conclusion) assesses the contemporary governments of Latin America through the prism of democracy and its vicissitudes in the continent. It addresses the key question of the quality of democratic government, stated in terms of the comparative democratic performance of Latin America's governments. It demonstrates that this performance is uneven, with governments performing best in the electoral and institutional aspects of democratic politics, and worst in delivering civil, minority, and social rights. In doing so it provides a synoptic account of the insights into Latin American democracy generated throughout the argument of the book, as well as explaining the current pathologies of democracy in the continent.

Reading the book

In pursuing these themes the book does not make exclusive use of any particular approach in political science or any single paradigm of social explanation. So the argument moves untroubled between structures and actors, and between culturally rooted political behavior and rational calculation. But, as a matter of emphasis, it does pay rather less attention to economic and cultural explanations of government and government performance, and rather more attention to the political institutions and decision-making processes of government itself. This means that we remain sensitive to the cultural legacies of patrimonialism and clientelism, and to the structural constraints of neoliberal policy prescriptions, for example, while developing our analysis – severally – of political bargaining, elite pacts, the intersection of party systems and legislative politics, the institutional weakness of the rule of law, the trade-offs between political participation and government stability, and so forth. The result is a mainly political inquiry into the problems and opportunities of governing Latin America.

There are twenty-one republics in Latin America, with twenty-one distinct political realms, each one replete with political debate, deliberation, calculation, and strategic action. Just as there is no government without institutions, so there is no government without politics, including everything from policy-making to corruption. If it is difficult to describe the complexities of Latin American government in a book of this scope, it is probably impossible to describe the intricacies of its politics. So whether you encounter this text in a course on Latin America, or a course on comparative politics writ large, it should perhaps be complemented by further study and a closer focus on one or two country cases. Equally, the general statements drawn from the diversity of Latin American government might profitably be tested in the study of political systems beyond the continent. Whatever you decide, or whatever the task set by your professor, it may prove useful that each chapter of this book can stand alone in its treatment of a discrete topic. Yet, on a first reading, we would encourage you to take on the argument overall in the order it is presented.

PART I
AUTHORITY AND
POWER

1 | AUTHORITARIANISM AND DEMOCRACY IN LATIN AMERICA

How have governments ruled in Latin America? In this chapter we look at the main historical tendencies that have defined governmental power and authority in the region since the early nineteenth century. In doing so, we refer to three main problems that have faced all modern nation-states. These are: (1) the founding of state power in the face of external pressures and internal divisions; (2) the expansion of the state's authority in response to mass politics; and (3) the reform of the state in response to international changes and domestic politics.

Although power can be held by individuals and groups, in this chapter we are concerned with different types of governmental power. Until the modern period of nation-state formation, governmental power was often weak and had many contenders, such as rival states and regional fiefdoms. In Europe, the rise and gradual consolidation of governmental power was produced by similar processes, in particular the waging of war (which required the creation of standing armies and modern bureaucracies) and the transition from agrarian to industrial societies. In the process, individuals came to demand rights as members of nation-states, lending authority to government in exchange for protection of rights as citizens. This process has of course presented variations in the type of regimes which emerged and has therefore constituted an important issue in comparative politics (Moore 1966; Tilly 1998; Skocpol 1979).

When discussing the sources of governmental power, that is, what allows governments to govern in the way that they do, we are concerned with the question of authority. Comparativists have given a great deal of attention to the question of how governments gain, keep, or lose authority, distinguishing different kinds of relationships and interactions between governments, social classes, and individual citizens (Migdal, Kohli, and Shue 1994; Linz and Stepan 1978).

A common way of distinguishing between different kinds of authority is to compare democratic and non-democratic forms of government. Although, as chapter 2 makes clear, there is no single definition of democracy, it does imply some degree of free political competition for elected office, the constitutional protection of civil rights, and the removal of barriers to participation in public life. A key concept in this regard is that of legitimacy, which we discuss in chapter 3. Some governments are able to derive legitimacy from the regular holding of free elections, while others are not. The legitimacy of elected governments, however, may also be limited if democratic rights, such as civil liberties and freedom of the press, continue to be violated. Elections may also be insufficient instruments for addressing deep social inequalities and ethnic cleavages. It should also be noted that elections are not the only source of legitimacy. Governments may also appeal to nationalist sentiments or the personal charisma of individual leaders. In Latin America, governmental power and authority have sought legitimacy through both democratic and non-democratic means, to different degrees and at different moments in its history. It is to this history that we now turn.

Founding state authority: nation-building and early modernization

Constitutionalism and caudillo government

Despite the dominant tendency of authoritarianism in Latin American political history, the region has also been characterized by a long association with constitutional government. In fact, the achievement of national independence from European powers in the nineteenth century was accompanied in many Latin American countries by a political commitment to the republican form of government in which power would no longer derive from the divine will of kings, but instead from the will of the people. In this case, however, the "people" was defined narrowly to include the native-born (or "Creole") property-owning classes. Nevertheless, the rules of political competition were shaped by the constitutional republic, which stood in opposition to the monarchical basis of colonial rule. As a result, the various competing factions of the Creole elite had to continually appeal to the ideals of constitutionalism, if only to distinguish their political identity from that of the old colonial regime.

This appeal to constitutionalism makes sense in the context of early national independence. The builders of an independent nation could only succeed if they adopted a different model to that of their colonial predecessors. However, constitutional rules were rarely followed in practice. Most countries in the region experienced several decades of instability and civil war before the authority of central governments was recognized. The main source of conflict was between conservatives and liberals, the former supporting the Church and economic protectionism, the latter favoring a secular state and greater integration into the world market. Although the liberals emerged as the stronger faction, they were also obliged to negotiate pacts with their conservative rivals in order to establish stable governments. As a result, the early faith in constitutionalism was transformed into a preoccupation with governability and modernization, or "order and progress."

Constitutionalism did not necessarily imply support for liberal democracy. Instead, government in Latin America would appear democratic in form, but would be authoritarian in practice. Noting the parallels with ancient Rome, the Venezuelan writer Laureano Vallenilla Lanz (1870–1936) dubbed this form of government "democratic Caesarism" (Hale 1996: 177).

Many Latin American intellectuals lent weight to this argument. They were heavily influenced by "positivism," a philosophical current which argued that societies, like natural phenomena, could only be known through the scientific study of their inner workings. Drawing on what they saw as unassailable scientific knowledge, by the late 1890s most leaders and intellectuals pessimistically concluded that liberal democracy could not exist in Latin America. Disorderly and uncivilized societies were instead naturally predisposed to "caudillo government," and the best that could be hoped for was the rule of enlightened and competent caudillos who would work for national unity and material progress.[1]

In this formulation, the idealism of early constitutionalism was seen as an expression of the radical and egalitarian tendencies of the French Revolution. The belief that a written document could mold a society to its abstract ideals was something that European conservatives such as Edmund Burke had condemned as early as 1791 (Burke 1955). The new intellectual elite argued instead that societies are shaped by their historical customs and traditions, which, in the Latin American context, meant hierarchical and centralist forms of rule and an organic versus an individualistic conception of society. Conservative ideas came to dominate the region's governments in the period between 1870 and 1930, with profound implications for political development in subsequent decades. For these elites, the purpose of politics was not the promotion of abstract ideas such as liberty and equality, but rather the efficient operation of government in accordance with local tradition and the demands of economic modernization. "Conservative liberalism" became the preferred doctrine, one in which politics would be guided by the conservative values of authority and discipline, while economics would be guided by the classical liberal doctrine of private enterprise and limited government.[2]

Oligarchical democracies and personalist dictatorships

This conservative brand of liberalism did, however, permit the establishment of some of the formal institutions of democratic government. In Argentina, Chile, Uruguay, and Costa Rica, the holding of regular elections for presidents and congresses and the formation of political parties laid the basis for future democratic development. In these countries, elites rotated power and learned to compete for office through peaceful means. For some scholars, these "oligarchical democracies" were better prepared to face later pressures for expanding political participation, conceding gradual reforms that allowed for stability and continuity (Diamond, Linz, and Lipset 1989: 8–9; see also Dahl 1971). On the other hand, where elites effectively blocked electoral competition, as in Mexico under Porfírio Díaz, political reforms were won only after a period of polarization and social revolution.

In Central America and the Caribbean Basin, the consolidation of "conservative liberalism" was also encouraged by the actions of the US government. Throughout the nineteenth century the United States, invoking the myth of its "Manifest Destiny," sought to establish its own sphere of influence in the Western hemisphere.[3] At first this project advanced by territorial expansion, largely at the expense of Mexico. Later, the preferred strategy was to gain financial and commercial control of the region's economic resources. Between 1898 and 1934, the US intervened militarily on more than thirty occasions to support conservative oligarchies in Central America and the islands of the Caribbean (Smith 1996: 52–62). Although the official justification for these interventions was the "export of democracy," the real motives were economic and geopolitical. On the one hand, the US needed to open up new export markets for its surplus production of industrial goods. On the other, the US was determined to keep competing imperial powers out of the Western hemisphere.

Political instability and economic mismanagement were dangerous not because they threatened the US directly, but rather because they provided European powers with a strong pretext to intervene in the region. The US sought to avoid such a prospect by using military force to restore order in alliance with local conservative elites. At the same time, US banks were entrusted with control of customs houses in order to guarantee repayment of debts to European creditors. In this context, the US was also able to gain sole rights to build and operate the first transisthmian canal through Panama, which was completed in 1914. By the 1930s, with Europe embroiled in its own problems, the US represented the dominant imperial power in Central America and the Caribbean, although democracy was not among its list of exports. Instead, the most visible legacy of this period were the new National Guards, created and trained by the US army to maintain order once the marines withdrew. These forces would become central to the consolidation of personalist dictatorships in the region between the 1930s and 1950s. These regimes were tightly controlled by caudillos linked to wealthy elites. Examples of personalist dictatorships were the Somoza dynasty in Nicaragua until the Sandinista revolution of 1979, the rule of Rafael Trujillo in the Dominican Republic until his assassination in 1961, and the Duvalier family in Haiti until 1986. They were unwilling to make concessions to popular demands, nor were they able to provide for the stable transfer of executive power. As a result, they generated polarization and violent opposition, and retained control through repressive means.

Expanding state authority: divergent responses to mass politics

In most Latin American countries, the combination of "order and progress" led to the rapid growth of the primary export sector, which provided minerals and foodstuffs to meet the growing demand in Europe and the United States. One result of this process was the growth of urban-based middle- and working-class populations tied to the export economy. In some countries, particularly Argentina, Uruguay, and Southern Brazil, labor shortages were compensated by mass immigration from Europe. The changing social composition of Latin American societies and the emergence of liberal, socialist, and anarchist ideologies, led to a series of conflicts and reforms which gradually saw the expansion of state authority into more areas of political and economic life. In this section we review the different types of response to the challenge of mass politics in Latin America in the twentieth century. We also note the continued influence of the United States in the region's political history.

Liberal and populist responses

In Argentina, Chile, and Uruguay, the traditional landed oligarchies were challenged by the emergence of new political parties, organized labor movements and the growth of a sizeable middle class. Industrialization and urbanization created strong demands for greater political inclusion, leading to the initial democratization of these countries in the first half of the twentieth century (Rueschemeyer, Stephens, and Stephens 1992).

In Argentina, the Radical party mobilized middle-class and popular sectors in support of electoral reform and the expansion of the right to vote. This reform was won in 1912, allowing for the electoral victory of the Radical party in 1916 and its subsequent rule until it was overthrown by a military coup in 1930. Although the oligarchy resumed power for the following thirteen years, it was unable to prevent the reemergence of pressures for expanding political participation.

In Uruguay, a similar process of social mobilization and political reform was accompanied by the establishment of the first welfare state in Latin America in the 1910s. In this case, labor was incorporated via one of the traditional parties, the Colorados. In Chile, the early consolidation of oligarchical democracy in the mid-nineteenth century allowed for a longer experience with political competition than anywhere else in the region. As a result, opening the system to broader mass participation was achieved through limited concessions and social reforms. Like Uruguay, Chile embarked on a long period of virtually unbroken democratic rule until 1973.

Given its dependence on external trade, Latin America was severely affected by the crash of 1929 and the subsequent depression in Europe and North America. The political impact was to further weaken the traditional oligarchies and allow for the expansion of state authority in the economy and in organizing new bases of support among urban and rural labor. After 1930, the export-oriented model could no longer direct the national economy. Instead, a more inward-looking model was called for and various efforts were made to promote import-substitution industrialization (ISI). In this context, leaders sought new sources of legitimacy and many found the answer in "populism," a style of governing which combined a modern sense of nationalism, support for the state, and ideals of social justice (see chapter 3).

Populist leaders gained power during the 1930s and 1940s in Mexico, Argentina, and Brazil and generated many similar movements throughout the continent. The state took an active role in forming and regulating the confederations of labor unions, peasant organizations and business groups. This model of control, known as "corporatism," allowed some benefits to the more modern sectors of the economy, particularly industrial labor. For example, urban workers in Argentina provided the strongest base of support for the populist leadership of President Juan Domingo Perón between 1945 and his overthrow in a military coup in 1955. Despite the official proscription of his political party and the installation of new military regimes in 1966 and 1976, the Peronist movement has remained a significant, although changing, political force in Argentina to the present day. In the Argentine case, the corporatist organization of labor and business groups has often led to stalemates in which neither side is able to gain sufficient support for its project of national transformation. Such stalemates have impeded the consolidation of stable institutions that could mediate between conflicting interests. Instead, political impasses have tended to be broken by the intervention of the armed forces (in 1966–73 and 1976–82).

For populist regimes democracy was valued less for its formal procedures and more for the promise of bringing modernization to the mass of the population through an independent, national path. This entailed an evident danger in that populist politics might polarize societies already marked by deep socioeconomic inequalities (see pp. 67–70).

The populist experiments also coincided with the onset of the Cold War in the late 1940s. US involvement in Latin American politics became deeper and more widespread, extending beyond individual leaders or elite factions to penetrate virtually every area of domestic politics from the military to political parties and labor unions. The guiding rationale was the containment of the alleged threat of communism to the Western hemisphere. This policy inhibited the growth of democracy in Latin America. For example, in the brief period between the end of the Second World War in 1945 and the onset of the Cold War in 1947, democratic governments replaced authoritarian regimes in several countries of Latin America, including Brazil, Venezuela, and Guatemala. These new governments included nationalist reform-minded leaders, including members of broad-based socialist or communist parties. With fascism and authoritarian rule discredited, newly elected governments enjoyed a high degree of legitimacy. However, the logic of the Cold War led the US to undermine reformist democracies, most notably in 1954 when the CIA helped overthrow the democratically elected government of Jacobo Arbenz in Guatemala.

The US continued to strengthen anti-communist forces throughout the Americas in the wake of the Cuban revolution of 1959. US policy sought in vain to overthrow the Castro regime. It then concentrated on the avoidance of "another Cuba" in the hemisphere, at first seeking centrist alternatives to dictatorship during the Kennedy administration, before abandoning such hopes and settling for alliances with anti-communist regimes, despite their obvious lack of democratic credentials.

Elite-pacted democracies: Colombia, Venezuela, and Costa Rica

After the 1950s, only three Latin American countries were able to sustain unbroken democratic rule: Colombia, Venezuela, and Costa Rica. In Colombia, a decade-long war between supporters of the rival Liberal and Conservative parties, known as "la Violencia," was brought to an end when the leaders of the two parties established the National Front pact in 1958 that also allowed for the transition from military to civilian rule. This bipartisan (or consociational) pact resulted from elite fears of either protracted military rule or social revolution. It permitted the two main parties to alternate power and thereby exclude other political forces from influencing government. The pact lasted until 1974, during which time the presidency was alternated and other government positions were distributed between the two parties. After 1974, competitive presidential elections were resumed and the pact began to unravel, particularly in the face of increasing popular opposition and armed insurgency which were in part produced by the exclusionary nature of the National Front. Faced with a deep crisis of legitimacy and mounting guerrilla violence, Colombian elites accepted the need for far-reaching political reforms in the late 1980s (van Cott 2000b: 40–41).

In 1991 a Constituent Assembly was elected with the sole purpose of drafting a new Constitution in the hope that this would overcome widespread disillusionment with the political system and convince some guerrilla organizations to lay down their arms. Although the Constituent Assembly did allow for much broader participation of Colombian society, it was unable to break completely with the power of the two main parties or reduce the multiple forms of violence perpetrated by guerrillas, the armed forces, paramilitary organizations, and drug-traffickers. By the mid-1990s, the political system was still seen by most Colombians as corrupt and unresponsive to popular demands for such basic necessities as personal security and material well-being. The ruling Liberal party was also tainted by allegations that drug-traffickers had supported the successful electoral campaign of Ernesto Samper in 1994. His administration was unable to dispel these allegations and, in 1998, the voters chose the candidate of the rival Social Conservative party, Andrés Pastrana, for president. Pastrana was unable to fulfill his promise to achieve a peace accord with the guerrilla movements. Instead, violence continued unabated throughout his administration. Peace talks collapsed and, in the face of a new wave of kidnappings and bombings in 2002, voters gave their support for a more hardline approach advocated by presidential candidate Alvaro Uribe. Uribe, a former Liberal who ran on an independent ticket, received strong backing from the US government which, as part of its global "war on terrorism," agreed to support the Colombian military in its counterinsurgency efforts. In addition, Uribe proposed the creation of a "citizens' militia" to work alongside the armed forces in its battle with the guerrillas. Critics argue that this measure will lead to more violence and human rights abuses, thereby reducing rather than strengthening the democratic authority of the Colombian state.

In Venezuela, democratic rule was established in 1958 following a decade-long military dictatorship. Unlike Colombia, armed insurgency was defeated in the 1960s, and the political system was able to enjoy a greater degree of legitimacy, although it too became dominated after 1968 by two main parties, the center-left Democratic Action (AD) and the center-right Committee for Political Organization and Independent Election (COPEI). The system came under greater strain in the 1980s as it faced rising foreign indebtedness and declining prices for its main export commodity, oil. Austerity policies imposed by the AD government of Carlos Andrés Pérez in 1989 led to mass protests and riots, government repression, and two failed coup attempts. One of the coup leaders, Hugo Chávez, formed a new party with a large popular following and won the presidential elections in 1998, reformed the Constitution the following year, and retained control of the presidency in new elections held in 2000. Although mass participation has been achieved, democratic institutions have been weakened by the corruption of the traditional parties, and more recently by the centralization of power by the Chávez government. As a result, Venezuela has become highly polarized between supporters and opponents of Chávez, as manifested in a failed coup attempt in April 2002.

Costa Rica has been the exception of stable democracy in Latin America. The country benefited from its relative isolation during Spanish colonial rule. It did not develop the kind of unequal land distribution seen in other countries nor did it suffer the ravages of civil war in the post-independence period. Poverty tended to have a leveling effect on the entire population until the emergence of the coffee-exporting elite in the second half of the nineteenth century. Even this process of class formation occurred without the degrees of inequality experienced in other countries of the region. This was in part due to the shortage of labor, which had the effect of keeping wages relatively high. In these circumstances, elites followed the path noted above for oligarchical democracies. They first established the rules for political competition among themselves before opening up the system to mass participation. Despite the early establishment of electoral competition, however, Costa Rica also witnessed unstable military and civilian rule for most of the nineteenth century as rival elite factions sought to manipulate elections in their favor.

The expansion of the right to vote and the incorporation of the working class in the early twentieth century meant that elections gradually became more meaningful channels of political contestation. Social reforms were implemented as social democratic and populist leaders sought power on the basis of alliances with the popular sectors. At the same time, corruption and electoral fraud remained serious problems and led to the outbreak of civil war in 1947. The victorious National Liberation Army carried out significant reforms, including the writing of a new constitution, the establishment of an independent electoral tribunal and the abolition of the armed forces. It also transformed itself into a political party, the Party of National Liberation (PLN), and won power through clean elections in 1953. Since that time, Costa Rica has been a pluralist liberal democracy. The expansion of social welfare programs, the abolition of the armed forces, and broad commitment to electoral procedures help explain the consolidation of Costa Rican democracy in subsequent years. Since the 1980s, like most developing countries, Costa Rica has had to face external pressures to service its large foreign debt by privatizing state-owned corporations and cutting back on social services. The government was able to weather the crisis in the 1980s due to the financial support provided by the US, which attempted to enlist Costa Rica as a strategic ally in the war against the Sandinista government in neighboring Nicaragua. In addition, political elites have tended to negotiate the pace and scope of privatization and spending cuts with domestic actors, avoiding the kind of crisis that we noted for Venezuela (p. 19).

Rise and fall of bureaucratic-authoritarian states

Elsewhere in the region, populist and reformist governments failed to meet rising expectations of newly mobilized sectors and succumbed in the early 1960s to a new crisis of constitutional rule. This time it was the armed forces that would intervene to establish a new form of regime, first in Brazil in 1964, followed by Argentina in 1966, Chile and Uruguay in 1973, and Argentina again in 1976. Although the Brazilian regime maintained much of the formal apparatus of constitutional government and embarked on a process of political liberalization in 1974, elsewhere the 1970s saw the closing down of democratic institutions such as congress, political parties, independent labor unions and the media. This was not the first time that the armed forces had openly intervened in politics in Latin America. However, in previous decades such interventions were designed to back one faction of the civilian elite against another, with the intention of leaving office quickly. In contrast, the military coups of the 1960s and 1970s brought to power regimes with more ambitious projects. Their diagnosis was that populism and communism were threatening not only to the interests of economic elites, but also to national security. As a result, a new "bureaucratic-authoritarian" (BA) state emerged with the dual goal of reestablishing economic stability and political order (O'Donnell 1973, 1978).

In order to attract foreign investment, this form of regime sought to offer political stability through the suppression of internal dissent, involving the arrest and forced disappearance of thousands of political opponents, labor union leaders, community activists, students, and journalists. Important areas of the economy became effectively transnationalized as multinational corporations found a favorable environment for their investments, particularly in Brazil where a "Triple Alliance" of state, domestic, and foreign capital was formed. Economic decisions were brought under the exclusive control of military generals and pro-business economists, or "technocrats." However, the military regimes also kept strategic areas of the economy under state control. For this they could rely on the availability of cheap loans from international private banks to finance new large-scale mining industries and the construction of hydroelectricity dams. With the removal of populist and socialist leaders from the scene, the military regimes could also dismantle many of the social programs, which had provided patronage for politicians and basic needs for the poor.

By the mid-1970s, it appeared that a new governing alliance of military leaders, technocrats, and transnational corporations was consolidating itself. The alliance could also count on the support of the US government, which, as noted earlier, favored those regimes that supported its anti-communist foreign policy during the Cold War. However, the tensions within this alliance began to emerge in the latter part of the decade, leading to the return of democratic and constitutional government in the 1980s (O'Donnell 1979).

Several factors led to the unraveling of military rule. First, the high levels of borrowing during the 1970s could not last forever. Declining export revenues, mainly due to the onset of economic recession in the North, combined with rising interest rates to produce the foreign debt crisis in 1982. In such conditions, foreign investors began to distance themselves from military rulers who were seen as incapable of successful economic management. Second, internal rivalries among factions of the armed forces led some key officials to argue that the institution had become too politicized by its years in government, threatening its own unity and sense of purpose. In short, government was for civilians, and, with the threat from populist and socialist forces effectively contained, there was little to fear from a peaceful transition of power to an elected government. A third factor was that the international climate was becoming less friendly to military regimes and more conducive to democratization. In the US, the Carter administration (1976–80) took a more principled stance against human rights violations in Latin America, while events in Europe seemed to signal a shift in favor of democratization as Portugal, Greece, and Spain all underwent transitions from authoritarian rule in the 1970s.

Democracy was chosen by the political and economic elites not because of its intrinsic worth, but because it offered them a way out from the failed projects of military rule. Moderate sectors of these regimes, or "softliners," argued that more could be gained from a pacted transition with similarly moderate opponents than would be lost with the continuation of a weak, divided, and isolated military regime. The moderates won out and most transitions to democracy took the form of elite pacts rather than violent ruptures (see chapter 2; O'Donnell, Schmitter, and Whitehead 1986; Mainwaring 1992; Higley and Gunther 1992; Przeworski 1991).[4]

Dictatorship and democratization in Central America

After 1930, most Central American governments continued to be ruled by dictatorships that served the interests of elites linked to the agricultural export sector of the economy. These countries did not experience rapid industrialization or urbanization in a form comparable to Brazil, Argentina, or Chile. Political development was not accompanied by the rise of a modern state apparatus and mass political parties with strong bases of support in industrial unions. Political power was concentrated in the hands of a small group of influential families, such as the Somoza dynasty in Nicaragua, rather than in the more modern and institutionalized form of the populist or bureaucratic-authoritarian state.

In 1979 a popular revolution, led by the Sandinista Front of National Liberation (FSLN), succeeded in overthrowing the Somoza dictatorship in Nicaragua and embarked on an ambitious project of social transformation. Despite the Sandinistas' decision to cooperate with the private sector in the development of a mixed economy, the Reagan administration in the US sought to prevent what it deemed a "communist beachhead" in Central America. The US-backed counterrevolutionary force, or *contras*, failed to overthrow the FSLN but wreaked havoc on the economy and diverted scarce resources from the revolution's social programs to its defense budget. Elections in 1990 produced a shock defeat for the Sandinistas as an alliance of opposition parties capitalized on the war weariness of the general population and the desire for economic respite after a decade of war. The new government of Violeta Chamorro had few economic successes but did manage to steer a pragmatic course between *somocistas* and Sandinistas. The 1996 election of Arnoldo Alemán confirmed the shift away from Sandinismo to a more conservative, pro-market agenda. Unlike Chamorro, however, Alemán proved to be an example of the worst features of corrupt and centralized executive power. Even members of his own party distanced themselves from his actions which included the offer of tax breaks to legislators in exchange for their votes in congress. The FSLN took advantage of this situation by winning local elections in 2000, but were unable to regain the presidency. In November 2001, the electorate chose another Liberal party candidate, Enrique Bolaños, who promised to run a clean government and respond to social needs.

In El Salvador, a decade of civil war (1979–89) produced an impasse between the two major contenders, the armed forces and the Farabundo Martí National Liberation Movement (FMLN). By the end of the decade, faced with a decline of US support for the war, Salvadorean elites looked for a negotiated solution and in 1992 all parties to the conflict signed a peace agreement that called for demilitarization, the gradual restructuring of the armed forces, and the transformation of the FMLN into a political party. As in Nicaragua, elections led to a decline in ideological polarization, but also to a high degree of disengagement from the political system as people focused primarily on their economic survival, which was increasingly tied to the informal economy or migration to the United States.

In Guatemala, a resurgence of guerrilla activity in the late 1970s was concentrated in the mainly indigenous region of the western highlands. Between 1980 and 1982 the Guatemalan military carried out a scorched earth operation against the Indian villages, with the goal of eliminating potential support for the armed struggle. Hundreds of communities were destroyed and thousands killed or forced to flee into neighboring Mexico. In 1983 an internal coup within the armed forces brought a different faction to power and advocated a less overtly repressive strategy toward the conflict. Recognizing the changing international climate, the new military leaders sought a pacted transition to democracy with moderate civilian leaders in which the military would retain full control of internal security, including counterinsurgency operations. A new constitution was approved in 1984, opening the way for the election of a civilian president the following year and, by 1987, the initiation of peace talks with guerrilla leaders. Although the peace process took much longer than in El Salvador, accords were finally completed in 1996. Despite the establishment of civilian government in Guatemala, human rights abuses persist and past violations remain unpunished. One clear indication of the gap between democratic rhetoric and reality was the assassination of Bishop Juan Gerardi in April 1998, just two days after he formally presented the final report of the Recovery of Historical Memory Project (REMHI), which demonstrated the army's responsibility for the vast majority of human rights abuses and atrocities committed during Guatemala's civil war (Ogle 1998).

Dominant and single-party rule: Mexico and Cuba

Although Mexico has had an unbroken history of civilian rule since the 1920s, it has until recently been a dominant-party state. This is due to the almost complete control that the Institutional Revolutionary Party (PRI) exercised over every branch and level of government. However, cracks in this system began to appear in the 1960s as newly mobilized urban sectors demanded greater political freedoms and an end to corruption. The most significant opposition was mounted by university students who called for autonomy from government control as well as a broad range of economic, social, and political reforms. In 1968 the government used troops to suppress this movement, killing hundreds of unarmed student demonstrators at a rally in downtown Mexico City. Public outrage at this act led subsequent governments to make gradual political reforms that allowed for greater pluralism with the intention of bolstering the regime's legitimacy.

Of more immediate value for the PRI in the 1970s were the increasing revenues from oil exports, as well as the availability of international loans. Mexico's state-led development model was based on an authoritarian political system in which patronage, corruption, and occasional repression were the norm. But massive capital flight, a dramatic fall in oil prices, and higher interest rates on Mexico's $100 billion foreign debt, combined to send the economy into recession and forced the government to declare a moratorium on debt payments in August 1982.

After 1982 the Mexican government began implementing austerity policies recommended by the International Monetary Fund (IMF) in exchange for the rescheduling of debt payments over a longer period. At the same time, the government abandoned its traditional state-led development policy, embracing instead "neoliberal" economic theory (see p. 27), which favors private enterprise and free markets. Mexico implemented one of the most orthodox neoliberal reform programs in Latin America. The administration of Carlos Salinas de Gortari (1988–94) was responsible for a rapid process of trade liberalization with the goal of increasing the competitiveness of Mexican firms and of gaining access to the lucrative US market. This policy culminated in the negotiation of the North American Free Trade Agreement (NAFTA) with the US and Canada in 1993. Despite warnings that, without adequate transition measures, free trade could wipe out many small- and medium-sized businesses Salinas pushed forward with supreme confidence in the merits of neoliberal theory.

This style of policy-making was characteristic of the neoliberal era in which executives and their economic teams of technocrats were effectively insulated from political dissent. In the Mexican case, it was also facilitated by a long history of centralization of decision-making in the presidency. Despite the rise of opposition parties and the gradual consolidation of a multiparty system, the legacy of presidentialism prevented any serious discussion of neoliberalism and NAFTA.

Economic crisis and reform were accompanied by the increasing strength of parties opposed to continuation of PRI rule. In 1997 the PRI lost its traditional majority in the federal Chamber of Deputies. It also lost in the first direct election for Mexico City's mayor, which went to the candidate of the center-left Party of the Democratic Revolution (PRD), Cuauhtémoc Cárdenas. The center-right National Action Party (PAN) strengthened its representation in congress and by 1999 held the governorships of several of the most industrialized states in northern and central Mexico. In 2000 the PRI was finally defeated in presidential elections. The PAN candidate, Vicente Fox Quesada, won 43 percent of the vote, eight points more than the PRI candidate Francisco Labastida Ochoa. Fox promised to bring change to the political system by attacking corruption, increasing efficiency, and promoting high levels of economic growth. However, his first two years in office were disappointing as little impact was made on any of these fronts and the Mexican economy contracted as a result of the recession in the United States. Fox also maintained the same macroeconomic policies that he inherited from the Zedillo adminis-tration. Politically, however, Mexico is no longer a dominant-party state. Its long, slow process of democratization has produced a com-petitive party system at the national level, although authoritarian enclaves continue to exist at sub-national levels (Cornelius, Eisenstadt and Hindley 1999).

The problems facing democratization in Cuba stem from that country's revolution against the US-backed Batista regime in 1959. Although many other problems have arisen in the subsequent four decades, the relationship between the US government, the Cuban exile community in the US, and the regime of Fidel Castro still shapes the prospects for democracy in Cuba. The Cuban revolution repre-sented the only successful armed insurgency in the region until the Sandinistas seized power in Nicaragua two decades later. The Castro regime produced great advances in education, literacy, health, and general welfare. However, the government established a single-party state, maintained strict control over political dissent, and became increasingly dependent on aid from the Soviet Union. Cuban foreign policy in the 1960s and 1970s became more active in supporting national liberation movements in Africa and Latin America, leading to costly commitments that began to sap the economy in the 1980s. The disintegration of the Soviet Union in 1989–91 threw Cuba into a deep crisis, as revenues from subsidized sugar exports collapsed and forced the government to search for alternative sources of interna-tional investment while attempting to maintain the goals of the revolution.

The 1990s saw a hardening of the regime's position towards oppo-sition groups as it responded to increasing threats from the Cuban exile community in Miami. Believing that Cuba would soon follow the path of other communist states, the anti-Castro lobby, organized as the Cuban American National Foundation (CANF), hoped for additional support from the US government to finally topple Castro and install a new government in Havana. Eager for votes (and campaign funds) from CANF supporters in southern Florida and New Jersey, US presidential candidates sought to outbid each other in their commitment to tightening a thirty-year-old trade embargo against the island. In 1996, President Clinton signed into law the "Cuban Liberty and Democratic Solidarity Act," better known as "Helms-Burton" after the two senators who sponsored the bill. The most controversial element of the new bill was that it would allow individuals to sue, in US courts, entities suspected of "trafficking" in properties which the Cuban government confiscated after the 1959 revolution. This meant that virtually any employee or shareholder of any foreign company doing business with Cuba would be liable to such action. The measure was clearly designed to discourage foreign investments in Cuba and had a marginal impact in this regard. However, the greater impact was on the continued reluctance of the Cuban government to open up the political system as long as the US embargo persists.

Reforming state authority: neoliberalism and delegative democracies

Debt crisis and structural adjustment

Democratic government is today present in varying degrees in most Latin American countries. Given the history of the region's political development, this represents an important shift, although many limitations remain. Among these are the negative impacts that economic crisis, structural adjustment, and social exclusion are having on the participation (or inclusiveness) dimension of democracy in the region.

The debt crisis which broke in the early 1980s not only brought an end to military rule. It also marked the end of state-led economic development. Faced with massive fiscal deficits and the sudden decline in international lending, Latin American governments were obliged to adopt a new model based on the "neoliberal" doctrine of promoting private enterprise and free markets. The reference to liberalism was economic rather than political, favoring the unfettered pursuit of individual self-interest in open and competitive markets. This doctrine is often traced to the eighteenth-century economist Adam Smith, whose ideas were used by the emerging bourgeois capitalist class in challenging the institutional constraints of feudalism, monarchy, and the Church. Economic liberalism gained supremacy with the laissez-faire policies of nineteenth-century British capitalism. However, unregulated capitalism led to cyclical crises of over-production and underconsumption, culminating in the crash of 1929 and the subsequent worldwide depression of the 1930s. Between 1930 and the 1970s, economic liberalism lost its dominance to a variety of alternatives in which the state was given a central role. In Latin America, state-led development was politically supported by populist coalitions until the onset of military rule in the 1960s and 1970s. Although some military regimes (notably Chile) began the shift to neoliberalism as early as 1975, most could continue to count on external borrowing to maintain a significant presence for the state until the debt crisis hit in 1982.

It was the debt crisis that allowed for critics of state-led development to argue more forcefully for a return to the main assumptions of economic liberalism. The main institutions responsible for implementing this shift in Latin America were the World Bank and the International Monetary Fund (IMF), which receive most of their funding from the advanced industrialized countries. Together with the US government, large private banks, and transnational corporations, these multilateral institutions consolidated the dominance of neoliberalism over all alternatives during the 1980s and 1990s. High-level support for this model, dubbed the "Washington Consensus," made it virtually impossible for a debtor country to choose any other path of national development. Although some countries sought to resist the immediate imposition of Structural Adjustment Programs (SAPs), their attempts were usually unsuccessful and often exacerbated existing problems. By the end of the 1990s, the "Washington Consensus" reigned supreme throughout the Americas, despite the mostly negative assessments of its impact on wages, social conditions, and income inequality (Bulmer-Thomas 1996; Green 1995; Peeler 1998: 148–53).

Although the precise content of neoliberal reforms tended to vary between countries, in general they sought to restore macroeconomic stability through a reduction of fiscal deficits and promotion of private investment. This meant a severe contraction of the public sector in most Latin American countries, the privatization of state-owned corporations, deregulation of key sectors of the economy, trade liberalization through the removal of tariffs on imported goods, and suppression of wage demands in order to control inflation. Although critics of neoliberalism denounced the fact that the negative costs of adjustment policies fell disproportionately on the poor, the lack of a politically viable alternative left the Washington Consensus virtually unchallenged at the national level. This does not mean that Latin Americans passively accepted neoliberal reforms. Popular grassroots movements mobilized throughout the 1980s and

1990s to resist job losses and falling wages caused by privatization and deregulation. In some cases, neoliberal reforms have provoked wide-scale riots, as in the Dominican Republic in 1984, Venezuela in 1989, Argentina in 1993 and 2001, and Peru in 2002. The Indian uprising in Chiapas, Mexico, in 1994 was also designed to draw attention to the social exclusion of indigenous farmers who are unable to compete in newly liberalized markets. More commonly, unionized employees in state-owned firms have mobilized against privatization plans, while students have resisted fee increases and cuts in public education.

As we have noted, the adoption of neoliberal policies coincided with the return of elected government in most Latin American countries. This political transition was clearly more complex than a simple reflection of shifting economic doctrines. However, the enormity of the debt crisis and the absence of alternative sources of capital clearly limited the range of macroeconomic policies for transitional democratic governments. Popular expectations that democracy would lead to greater social justice were frustrated by adverse economic conditions. Although there were no successful attempts by the military to retake power, the new democracies remained vulnerable to social and economic instability.

In the main, the values of democracy and constitutional government were accepted by a broader range of political actors than ever before. However, economic restructuring of the type envisioned by the IMF and World Bank required the demobilization of important sectors of civil society, particularly the more independent and oppositional labor unions. The most significant example of this was the Bolivian government's repression of a 1985 strike to resist privatization of the mining sector. The defeat of the Bolivian unions facilitated the imposition of IMF orthodoxy under three successive governments. The establishment of pacts between the three main political parties did allow for greater stability than in neighboring Peru and Ecuador, but this stabilization tended to exclude significant sectors of the population from decision-making. Nevertheless, neoliberal policies did bring down inflation from over 8,000 percent in 1985 to 11 percent by 1987, allowing the various elite factions to deepen the process of privatization over the subsequent decade, without significant opposition from the weakened labor movement (Peeler 1998: 144–5).

In fact, during the 1990s many observers noted the hollow quality of formal democratic procedures (Markoff 1997; Petras and Morley 1992; Silva 1999). This was exemplified by the declining appeal of traditional parties and the election of presidents who proclaimed themselves as "national saviors." By attacking parties and interest groups, these new leaders appealed to the sense of urgency created by hyperinflation, increasing poverty, and social disorder. In these cases elections were seen more as a plebiscite to provide a single leader with absolute power, rather than as a means of representing a broad range of opinions and projects.

Delegative democracies: Peru and Argentina

By the early 1990s the new democracies of Argentina and Peru had not succumbed to military coups. They were instead taken over by elected executives for whom the constitutional framework of congress, the judiciary, and the party system were simply obstacles in the path of national recuperation. Political scientist Guillermo O'Donnell named this type of regime "delegative democracy," contrasting it with "representative democracy" (O'Donnell 1994). Whereas the latter is built on horizontal accountability between firmly embedded democratic institutions, delegative democracy did its best to avoid accountability and by its actions obstructed or undermined much needed institution-building in new democracies.[5] The flow of political power did not pass through key institutions that enjoyed widespread consensus, but rather was concentrated in the president and his immediate economic and internal security advisers. Government became detached not only from the majority of the population, but also from those very institutions that could give it cohesion, legitimacy, and continuity.

It is important to note that delegative democracy was not simply the result of short-term calculations, nor was it purposefully imposed as the preferred model by outside actors. Instead, it corresponded to a deeper structural problem in many Latin American countries, and revealed in a dramatic fashion the legacies of authoritarianism.[6] For O'Donnell, only Chile and Uruguay escaped this scenario, precisely because of their longer and more continuous democratic history. In practical terms, this meant that new democratic presidents in these two countries have had to negotiate important economic measures with congress and interest groups. This allowed both countries to avoid the types of disruptions and severe economic crises that plagued Peru and Argentina where presidents were freer to rule through decree measures (*decretismo*). Moreover, delegative democracy and *decretismo* had the effect of further eroding public trust in public institutions and elected officials, as manifested in higher rates of abstentionism and rejection of politicians.[7]

In Peru and Argentina, delegative democracies were instituted during the 1990s. At the start of the decade, Presidents Alberto Fujimori and Carlos Menem, respectively, were able to bring hyper-inflation under control, but not without inflicting a heavy cost in terms of higher unemployment, greater income inequality, and crumbling public services. In Peru, inflation ran at over 7,000 percent in 1990, the year that Fujimori was elected president. Although he campaigned on a fairly populist platform, he soon reversed position and advocated the orthodox IMF package of neoliberal reforms: privatization of state-owned corporations, job cuts in the public sector, deregulation, trade liberalization, and wage controls. Unable to win approval for his proposals from opposition deputies, Fujimori resorted to a "self-coup" in April 1992, dissolving congress and calling for new elections for a constituent assembly.

Despite initial protests, Fujimori was able to count on the support of the armed forces and leading business associations, as well as an effective media campaign. A new pro-Fujimori assembly was elected and, in 1993, passed constitutional amendments that allowed for presidential reelection, while expanding the powers of the executive over all other branches of government. These new measures gave Fujimori a freer hand in implementing his neoliberal package. The short-term results were positive as foreign investors were attracted to the Peruvian stock market, resulting in a 12 percent increase in economic growth in 1994. This performance allowed Fujimori to be easily reelected in 1995, although voter turnout was much lower, reflecting a growing disenchantment with the formal channels of political participation.

The institutionalization of Fujimori's rule was also assisted by the army's campaign against the Maoist guerrilla organization, Shining Path, whose leader, Abimael Guzmán, was captured in September 1992. The decline in guerrilla activity was clearly a relief to many Peruvians who had endured unprecedented levels of insecurity during the 1980s as a result of the war between Shining Path and the armed forces.

Fujimori's second term was in marked contrast to the first and a weakening economy led to a decline in his popularity. By 1997 his approval ratings in polls had fallen to under 20 percent, the lowest figure since his appearance on the political scene in 1990. His alliance with the armed forces was also seen as severely constraining democratization and most Peruvians viewed his style of government as dictatorial. The military was given a more expansive role in dealing with social problems such as crime and drug-trafficking, leading to an increase in human rights abuses and less accountability to civilian institutions. This increasing reliance on the armed forces led some observers to call this type of regime a militarized or "guardian" democracy (McSherry 1998). Fujimori sought to extend his rule for a third term and used fraud to claim victory in elections held in 2000. A broad-based opposition movement, led by defeated candidate Alejandro Toledo, forced Fujimori from office in 2001, allowing for new elections and Toledo's victory the same year.

Delegative democracy followed a similar path in Argentina. As the candidate of one of Latin America's classical populist parties, the Peronists, Carlos Menem could count on the backing of popular sectors, particularly the labor movement. The first democratic government that succeeded the military regime in 1983 was led by the Radical party of Raúl Alfonsín. This government had inherited a large foreign debt and economic recession, but tried to avoid imposing the orthodox IMF structural adjustment package, fearing that the social costs would destabilize the new and fragile democracy. However, Alfonsín's government failed to control spiraling inflation, which reached 4,923 percent in 1989, the year that Menem came to power.

Like Fujimori, Menem immediately reversed his position, replacing populism with neoliberalism. To bring inflation under control, he quickly moved to suppress wages, control the labor unions, open up the economy to cheaper imports, cut social spending, and privatize state-owned corporations. Most significantly, the government established parity between the peso and the dollar. While this allowed Argentina to increase imports and thereby reduce inflation in the short term, it also created a large trade deficit that became difficult to finance as the decade wore on. By 1994 inflation was down to 3.6 percent, enabling Menem to deflect criticisms of his authoritarian style and disregard for democratic procedure. Like Fujimori, Menem was also able to win support for a constitutional amendment allowing for his reelection in 1995. However, his popularity also declined in his second term as the economy began to reveal serious structural problems, particularly the country's vulnerability to sudden withdrawal of foreign investment, rising indebtedness, and declining government revenues. Rising unemployment and education cuts led to widespread protests by students and youth, as well as significant electoral defeats for Menem's party in the 1997 congressional elections. The Peronists finally lost power when the opposition Radical party and Front for a Country in Solidarity (Frepaso) formed an alliance for the presidential election in 1999.

The Radical party President Fernando de la Rúa, however, continued to implement the same economic policies, provoking further discontent among not only the poor majority but also large sectors of the middle class. Declining wages and rising unemployment were exacerbated in 2001 by a rapid increase in capital flight which depleted the country's foreign reserves to such an extent that, by the end of the year, the government imposed limits on the amount any individual could withdraw from their bank accounts, provoking wide-spread street protests by middle-class residents of the largest cities. The mounting protests led to the resignation of de la Rúa in late December 2001. The largest party in congress, the Peronists, regained control of the presidency following intense negotiations with the Radicals, but immediately became embroiled in a bitter internal dispute over which of its several factions would rule until new elections could be held. On the positive side, party leaders and legislators were able to overcome the political crisis through peaceful negotiations, demonstrating the potential for democratic consolidation in the future. However, given the growing public hostility toward the political establishment, parties need also to show that they are capable of responding to economic and social demands of the population.

The above discussion reveals some important lessons for understanding the problems facing government in the region today. Power and authority have been wielded in different ways during Latin America's modern history. In this chapter we have noted the early development of caudillo government, oligarchical democracies, and personalist dictatorships. These regimes were forced to respond to pressures to broaden the arena of political participation. Some countries were able to accommodate such pressures through democratic reforms. In other cases, revolution and populism provided new channels for the incorporation of popular actors. In the post-1945 period, populist regimes often gave way to military interventions and the establishment of new, exclusionary forms of authoritarian rule. The return to democracy in most of the region has not eliminated authoritarian practices, as seen in the case of delegative democracies. The historical trajectories outlined above are therefore important when assessing the prospects for democracy in the region today.

2 | LATIN AMERICA AND THE DEMOCRATIC UNIVERSE

With the 1989 democratic elections in Brazil and Chile, all Latin American countries, with the exception of Cuba, had elected constitutional governments, marking a significant transformation in the region away from long periods dominated by military authoritarianism. Since these two elections, no elected government has been successfully overthrown by violence in the region except for Ecuador, which suffered a three-day military intervention and democratic restoration in January 2000 (see chapter 9).[1] Five presidents in the region, of whom the most notable were Fernando Collor de Mello in Brazil and Carlos Andrés Pérez in Venezuela, were removed from office through legitimate and constitutional means, while in Argentina a further four resigned during the financial crisis of 2002. Moreover, for the first time in seventy years, the Mexican Institutional Revolutionary Party (PRI) was defeated in the 2000 federal elections, marking an important milestone in that nation's prolonged period of political liberalization. These transitions from authoritarian rule make the region an important component of the "third wave" of democratization (Huntington 1991), which had begun in Portugal in 1974 and quickly spread to Spain, Greece, Latin America, and other authoritarian countries in Africa, Asia, and Eastern Europe. This global spread, pace, and process of democratization meant that by the end of the twentieth century, there were over 120 "formal" democracies comprising approximately 60 percent of the total independent countries in the world (Diamond 1999: 28).[2]

Thus, after almost two centuries as independent states, the countries of Latin America now comprise a new democratic universe, joining other states on the world democratic stage. This chapter considers the degree to which the democracies in Latin America have established effective institutions and practices for stable democratic governance, and examines persistent problems in the region that threaten such governance. In the post-transition period, all the states in the region adopted (or readopted) presidential regimes with proportional electoral systems and independent judiciaries, where some states are federal (e.g. Mexico and Brazil) and others unitary (e.g. Chile and Peru). There has also been an effort to adopt systems for ensuring better accountability, transparency, and access to information in the civil bureaucracies that comprise the state apparatus. As we will see, threats to democracy in the region include problems with institutional design (tense executive–legislative relations, party fragmentation, and weak judiciaries), militaries with reserve domains of power, the presence of "uncivil" movements, and the persistence of social exclusion. Before considering these important dimensions of the democratic universe, it is first necessary to define democracy and outline popular explanations for its emergence in the region.

Defining democracy

There are many competing definitions and "models" of democracy that both *describe* and *prescribe* formulas for democratic governance in the modern world. Definitions range from procedural and political democracy to substantive and social democracy, while the models of democracy include such forms as classical democracy, republicanism, liberal democracy, and direct democracy (Held 1996: 5). Each definition rests on assumptions about fundamental interests and conflicts in society, the ways in which they ought to be mediated, and the types of social and political outcomes that ought to be achieved. Procedural and political definitions of democracy tend to concentrate on the minimal conditions needed for democratic resolution of conflicts and decision-making on key areas of public policy. Social definitions of democracy tend to focus on the substantive outcomes of democratic decisions, such as the fair distribution of income, broad provision of economic and social welfare, and a general commitment to egalitarianism. Overall, these definitions are committed to the notion of government as comprising the free participation of citizens in decision-making over matters of public concern.

Let us explore these definitions further. Procedural and political definitions of democracy establish minimal conditions that uphold our concept of democracy *as a form of governance*, while methodologically, a procedural and political definition of democracy allows for a broad set of comparisons to be made across Latin America. Such a definition of democracy has three "critical dimensions" identified by Hartlyn and Valenzuela (1994: 100–1): contestation, constitutionalism, and inclusiveness (or participation). Contestation embodies the notion of uncertain peaceful competition among groups in a democratic society, whose essence is the "acceptance of the legitimacy of the political opposition ... and ... the right to challenge incumbents." Constitutionalism guarantees the full legal protection of basic political and civil rights of the citizenry in a given polity, and establishes the rules that "define and restrict the powers of governmental authorities." Inclusiveness is the expansive capacity of the polity to include all adult groups in the competition for power regardless of "property, literacy, gender, race, or ethnicity." It is also possible for countries to uphold these ideals to a greater or lesser degree, making democracy a concept that is continuous, rather than an all or nothing affair (see Przeworski and Limongi 1997; Przeworski, Alvarez, Cheibub, and Limongi 2000: 14–18).

A social definition of democracy, on the other hand, establishes programatic outcomes of the democratic process that ought to be realized through a legislative agenda pursued by various governments over long periods of time. Such outcomes include the establishment of a welfare state, with broad provisions of resources in the areas of health, education, and welfare. In contrast to the procedural definition of democracy, which many see as comprising those features that are *intrinsic* to democracy, a social definition of democracy comprises those features that are *extrinsic* to democracy. Without the political and civil rights or the necessary political institutions outlined in the procedural definition of democracy above, a political system would not qualify in any minimal sense as a democracy. Yet, it is entirely possible for a non-democratic regime (i.e. one that does not have such fundamental rights and institutions in place) to realize broad social goals. For example, the Castro regime in Cuba has invested heavily in health and education, but does not have an open political system with alternating power, a competitive party system, and the protection of political and civil rights.

Methodologically, it is more difficult to make intraregional and interregional comparisons of social democracy since the outcomes of social policy are a function of long-term processes of socioeconomic development and the fiscal capacity of governments to fund the necessary programs. In subsequent chapters we do provide standard measures of socioeconomic development and social welfare to provide some comparative perspective on the Latin American social condition. This book concentrates on a procedural definition of democracy, and what we will see is that Latin America has experienced various forms of democracy, which have tried to guarantee the protection of basic rights, establish meaningful political institutions, and realize important social goals. However, there remains great variation across the region in the degree to which countries have been successful in so doing. It is this variation in experience that problematizes democracy in Latin America, leading to the articulation of different demands, the emergence of different social and political groups, the outbreak of political crises, and recurrent challenges to democratic stability.

Explaining democracy

Having defined democracy in these terms, it is necessary to consider the ways in which comparative politics has sought to explain the emergence and maintenance of democracy in the region. Broadly speaking, there are three dominant theoretical perspectives that offer different accounts of democratization in Latin America, namely modernization, transition, and transformation. Modernization focuses on large socioeconomic processes and the development of political values supportive of democracy. Transition theory examines the strategic interaction between key actors within the authoritarian regime and the opposition at the moment of transition. Democratic transformation theory analyzes the changing power relations between groups in civil society and the authoritarian state over a prolonged period of struggle. While each account focuses on a different aspect of the making of democracy, together they should not be seen as mutually exclusive, but complementary. Let us consider these accounts in more depth.

Modernization

One popular perspective used to explain the origins and maintenance of modern liberal democracy is *modernization theory*, which emphasizes the economic determinants of democracy. Modernization theory argues that as nations pursue economic development through high levels of savings and investment, the consequent development of social infrastructure and institutions, urban middle classes, and political culture leads to the installation of democratic forms of rule. The development of the social infrastructure and institutions encourages social and spatial mobility, while the emerging urban middle classes espouse a set of values and patterns of identification that favor liberal democracy. In this way, democracy is seen as <u>the final culmination</u> of social processes brought about by economic modernization (Przeworksi and Limongi 1997). On balance, statistical comparisons of large samples of countries, including those from Latin America, demonstrate a positive and significant relationship between high levels of economic development (e.g. per capita gross domestic product) and democracy (Rueschemeyer, Stephens, and Stephens 1992). Although these analyses do not test explicitly the complex set of social processes outlined by modernization theory, they do confirm a strong association between wealth and democracy at the global level. One interpretation of this strong positive association is that economic development causes democracy (see Helliwell 1994; Burkhart and Lewis-Beck 1994), while another interpretation is that wealthy democracies tend not to collapse (Przeworski and Limongi 1997; Przeworski, et al. 2000). If the analysis is repeated for Latin American countries only, however, the results of such global analyses cannot be upheld. Comparing seventeen countries from the region over the period 1972 to 1995 shows that no such relationship exists between economic development and democracy (Landman 1999). These results suggest that in order to understand democratization in Latin America, factors other than socioeconomic development must be taken into account.

 Transition

A second perspective that accounts for democratization in Latin America, particularly during the third wave, is *transition theory*, which focuses on the strategic interaction between key actors in the authoritarian regime and the leaders of the main forces of opposition (O'Donnell, Schmitter, and Whitehead 1986; Przeworski 1991). In this perspective, these key actors are assumed to pursue their interests in a rational manner so as to maximize their preferences with regard to the political system. Typically, the analysis focuses on the interaction between hardliners (*duros*) and softliners (*blandos*) in the authoritarian regime on the one hand, and between moderates and radicals in the opposition on the other. These two types of interactions are modeled as a "game" played between elites, where hardliners seek continued authoritarian rule, softliners seek alliances with the moderates in the opposition, and radicals seek open confrontation with the authoritarian regime. The impulse for democratization comes from the softliners and moderates, who calculate that the benefits of a move towards liberal democracy through mutual agreement far outweigh the costs of continued authoritarianism. It is possible, however, that no such agreement can be reached, where the political situation either continues with authoritarian rule and repression or violent confrontation and possible civil war. In this perspective, liberal democracy is only one political outcome of many that depends on the types of interactions that occur between dominant elites in society, where fledgling democratic institutions require the continued political support of such softliners and moderates. In comparative perspective, such accounts have been provided for the experiences of democratic transition in Spain (1975), Poland (1980–90), Chile (1988–90), Venezuela (1958), Colombia (1958), and Costa Rica (1948).

Transformation

While the account offered by transition theory captures some of the dynamics involved in the recent period of democratization in Latin America, it fails to address other important factors. *Democratic transformation theory* examines broader patterns of power relations within society and how consequent political struggles can transform elements within the political system to bring about sustained democratic rule (Rustow 1970; Foweraker and Landman 1997; see also chapter 10). This perspective demonstrates that in Latin America, an early consolidation of state power, labor mobilization for political inclusion, and the development of two dominant political parties paved the way for "initial" democratization during the first half of the twentieth century (Rueschemeyer, Stephens, and Stephens 1992: 79–154). For the latter period of democratization that began with Peru in 1978, this perspective argues that democratization is the direct result of prolonged political struggle between labor and other social movements on the one hand, and the authoritarian state on the other. In this account, social mobilization tends to precede the moment of democratic transition, while a period of democratic "habituation" after the transition is required for democracy to become a viable form of rule.

While some may see these three theoretical perspectives as offering mutually exclusive accounts of democratization in Latin America, it is important to understand that each focuses on different aspects of that process without completely ignoring the insights of the other. First, modernization theory is vague about the role of elites and individual decision-making, while emphasizing large socioeconomic processes and the emergent values supportive of democracy. Second, transition theory assumes that socioeconomic conditions may shape the preferences and constrain the choices of dominant actors during a moment of democratic transition, and concedes that increased mobilization threatens the stability and legitimacy of the authoritarian regime. Third, democratic transformation theory accepts that new social groups form out of the contradictions and antagonisms associated with economic modernization, and examines how the relations between such groups and the authoritarian state transform the political system toward democracy. Cracks in the authoritarian regime may encourage mobilization as much as increased mobilization may encourage softliners and moderates to pursue some form of democratic accommodation. Finally, it is important to emphasize that all three accounts seek to explain the same outcome: stable liberal democratic rule. The nature and quality of this form of rule in Latin America is now discussed.

Electoral vs. liberal democracy

In describing the nature and quality of Latin American democracy in this new period, it is important to emphasize the great strides that have been made in the region with respect to the peaceful transfer of political power between civilians. Our procedural definition of democracy includes the principle of contestation, in which different political interests, aggregated and articulated through political party organizations, compete freely through periodic and regularly scheduled elections. Since all the countries have presidential systems, these elections determine the ways in which parties occupy both the legislative and executive branches of government. It is typical in such systems to have the presidential term "interrupted" by elections for all or a portion of the legislative branch. In addition, federal systems hold elections for both the national and state governments. Thus, the cycle of elections that complement the democratic transitions in Latin America began with Peru's transition in 1978, and has expanded in number and across geographical space, as more countries became democratic. Between the Peruvian transition and 2000, there have been fifty-two presidential elections in those countries that experienced democratic transitions (see table 2.1), while there has been an equal number of elections for national legislatures, and numerous elections for offices at the state and other sub-national levels of government.

The promise of electoral victory has also led to the formation of new political parties (e.g. the Workers' Party in Brazil), the resurrection of old parties (e.g. the Christian Democrats in Chile and the Peronist party in Argentina), and the possibility of new governing

Table 2.1 Third wave democratic transitions in Latin America

Country	Mode of democratic transition	Year	Presidential elections up to the year 2000	(number in final column)
Argentina	Military defeat in Falklands/Malvinas War	1983	1983, 1989, 1995	3
Bolivia	Elite bargain	1982	1982, 1985, 1989, 1993, 1997	5
Brazil	Gradual transition controlled by the military	1985	1989, 1994, 1998	3
Chile	Plebiscitary defeat of General Pinochet	1988	1989, 1993, 1999/2000	3
Ecuador	Elite bargain	1979	1979, 1984, 1988, 1992, 1996, 1998	6
El Salvador	Military controlled, externally mediated peace process	1984	1984, 1989, 1994, 1999	4
Guatemala	Externally mediated peace process	1985	1985, 1990, 1995, 1999	4
Haiti	Popular revolt and US observation	1990	1990, 1995, 2000	3
Honduras	Elite concession and US intervention	1980	1982, 1985, 1989, 1993, 1997	5
Mexico*	Opposition National Action Party defeats Institutional Revolutionary Party	2000	2000	1
Nicaragua	Revolution and new elections	1990	1990, 1996	2
Panama	US overthrow of Manuel Noriega	1989	1994, 1999	2
Paraguay	Stroessner ousted by military, new elections	1989	1993, 1998	2
Peru	Elite bargain	1978	1980, 1985, 1990, 1995, 2000	5
Uruguay	Elite bargain	1984	1984, 1990, 1994, 1999	4

Total presidential elections during the Latin "third wave"   52

*Mexico has had regular elections for President every six years since 1934, but not until 1994 was there a reasonable chance that the opposition would win, which it did in 2000.

Sources: Landman (2000: 152–3); Calvert and Calvert (1993: 205–23); Cammack (1996); The Political Database of the Americas (www.georgetown.edu/pdba/)

coalitions between the executive and legislature to initiate and implement important public policy (see chapter 6). Even though periods of democratic transition were often accompanied by large-scale popular mobilization, the impulse for such mobilization can disappear after the moment of transition, while political party organizations become the main form of political representation in the new democratic period (see chapter 8 this volume; Foweraker 1995). Party systems have varied within the region across two important dimensions: (1) the degree to which they are institutionalized and (2) the level of ideological polarization between and among different parties. An institutionalized party system has four important characteristics: stable interparty competition, parties with stable roots in society, the acceptance of parties as institutions for determining who governs, and party organizations with stable rules and structures (Mainwaring and Scully 1995: 1). Party polarization refers to the ideological "distance" between political parties on the left–right spectrum (Mainwaring and Scully 1995: 2). On balance, Latin American party systems with low levels of institutionalization in multiparty systems that have high levels of ideological polarization produce problems of governance that may threaten the stability and maintenance of democratic rule (see p. 46 and chapter 6 this volume; Landman 2000: 190).

The presence of regular elections and the development of party systems partially fulfill our first criteria of a procedural democracy. For example, Mexico has conducted regular elections since the administration of Lázaro Cárdenas in the 1930s and has a multiparty system, yet until at least 1994 these elections were not seen as competitive. Until 1994, there was no real expectation that an opposition party could defeat the Institutional Revolutionary Party (PRI). In the 1976 federal elections, the main opposition party, the National Action Party (PAN) did not field a candidate, while as late as 1988 allegations of electoral fraud tainted the electoral process. In the 1994 election, the PRI won a narrow margin of victory, while the state level saw an increasing number of victories for both the PAN and the other main opposition party, the Party of the Democratic Revolution (PRD). Only with the 2000 federal elections has the PAN been able to defeat the PRI at the polls. Thus, in order to realize a system of real contestation, regular elections must be freely competitive and fairly conducted.

Beyond these more salient aspects of democracy, our procedural definition of democracy also includes the principle of constitutionalism, which is meant to protect the rights of citizens from unnecessary incursions by the state, as well as the rights of minorities from the rule of the majority (see chapters 4 and 10). Holding free and fair

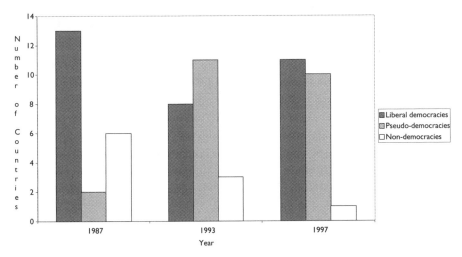

Figure 2.1   Liberal democracies, pseudo-democracies, non-democracies
Source: L. Diamond (1999) *Developing Democracy: Toward Consolidation*. Baltimore: Johns Hopkins University Press, 33

elections suggests that most countries have been able to guarantee political rights, such as the right to association, expression, and assembly, but evidence from Latin America on civil rights demonstrates continued violations, such as torture, arbitrary detention, and extrajudicial killings. This presence of elections and exercise of political rights alongside the persistent violation of civil rights highlights the "electoral fallacy" of those commentators and policy-makers who equate elections with democracy. Indeed, this difference between *electoral* democracy and *liberal* democracy has led others to characterize the region as having "pseudo-democracies," or "partial democracies" still in need of reform in order to guarantee the full protection of civil rights (see Cammack 1996; Diamond 1999). Figure 2.1 depicts the number of liberal, pseudo-, and non-democracies for different years in Latin America. Across the three time periods, the number of non-democracies has declined dramatically, while the number of pseudo-democracies has risen, effectively displacing the number of liberal democracies. Thus, by 1997, the figure shows that there are eleven liberal democracies, ten pseudo-democracies, and one non-democracy (i.e. Cuba) in the region. It has been argued that the persistence of the gap between electoral and liberal democracy in Latin America is due to severe institutional failure, creating conditions that have been variously described as low-intensity democracy, democracy by default, poor democracy, empty democracy, hybrid regimes, or delegative democracy (Diamond 1999: 34; cf. O'Donnell 1999a). Together, these terms embody a certain concern about the persistence of threats to democracy, to which the discussion now turns.

Threats to democracy

After recognizing the many achievements of the new democratic era in Latin America, it is important to consider important threats to democracy that remain. Such threats appear in very different places. First, despite successful democratic transition, the promulgation of new constitutions, and the (re)establishment of democratic institutions, *the design of these institutions themselves may threaten democratic stability.* The key institutional problems include high levels of executive–legislative conflict, political party fragmentation and ideological polarization, and weak judiciaries. Second, the elite bargains that were struck often included moderate solutions that allowed militaries of the authoritarian period certain "reserve domains" of power and immunity from prosecution for past crimes. Third, certain pathologies of liberal democracy and civil society have meant that "uncivil" movements of the left and right have been able to find space for their violent and politically destabilizing activities. Finally, the period of democratic transition has been accompanied by a set of neoliberal economic reforms and implementation of structural adjustment programs (SAPs) that have further marginalized certain groups and led to high rates of social exclusion that have effectively limited participation in the political system. Let us consider these four threats to democracy.

Institutional design

All the Latin American democracies have presidential institutional arrangements and proportional electoral systems, a combination that can increase executive–legislative conflict. Separate elections for the executive and legislative branches give a popular mandate to rule, even though it is possible for different political parties to control these different institutions. A strong popular identification with the figure of the president backed up with electoral support invests tremendous power in that office, while members of the legislature also claim to represent "the people." Dual popular mandates thus create a tension between the two branches. This tension is exacerbated since proportional electoral systems tend to produce party systems with more than two parties, leading to the frequent occurrence of minority presidents. Minority presidents are those who have won the office, but whose party representation in the legislature is small. For example, Fernando Collor de Mello in Brazil won the runoff election for President in 1989, but his political party, the National Renovation Party (PRN), had only 7 percent of the seats in the legislature.

The combination of dual electoral mandates and minority presidents can lead to serious legislative impasses, where presidents find it difficult or impossible to pass legislation. In some cases, such tension can lead some presidents to seek "extra-constitutional" means to carry out their measures, where they far exceed the powers stipulated in the national Constitution. In other cases, presidents may seek radical reform of their national Constitutions to give themselves more power. Indeed, with the support of the military, President Fujimori of Peru closed the national congress in 1992 and wrote a new Constitution that gave him increased powers. In the past (e.g. 1964 Brazil), such extra-constitutional action has led to disaffection with civilian presidents among certain sectors, military intervention to expel the president, and the implementation of authoritarian rule (see Cohen 1987; Stepan and Skach 1994). While military intervention is uncommon in the new democratic period, it is entirely possible that continued executive–legislative strain could produce coalitions, on the one hand, between the military and conservative sectors of society, or on the other hand, between the military and radical sectors with the desire to overthrow democratic institutions.

The presidential model is also meant to have strong "horizontal accountability" between the branches of government, where the actions of the president are accountable to the legislature and the judiciary possesses the authority to resolve any conflicts between them (Anglade 1994: 248). The existence of such horizontal accountability is meant to prevent demagoguery, as well as guarantee the full protection of individual rights. Historically, however, judiciaries in Latin America have been quite weak relative to the legislative and executive branches, owing to poor financial resources and the permeation of state institutions by powerful political interests. Lack of financial resources means that proper legal procedures cannot be carried out and that the protection of individual civil rights is precarious at best, while oligarchic power in the nineteenth century and neopatrimonial power in the twentieth century means judges are susceptible to political pressure. Such political influences on judicial power threaten the substantive meaning of democracy, since under

Table 2.2   Effective number of parties and ideological polarization

Number of parties	Ideological polarization			
	Low	Moderately low	Moderately high	High
1.8 ≤ N < 2.4	Paraguay (2.2) Costa Rica (2.4)	Colombia (2.1)	Mexico (2.2)	
2.5 ≤ N < 2.9		Argentina (2.7)		
3.0 ≤ N < 3.9			Venezuela (3.0) Uruguay (3.0) Bolivia (3.9)	Peru (3.8)
N ≥ 4.0			Chile (4.7) Ecuador (5.8)	Brazil (5.7)

democracy the rule of law is meant to limit the actions of the individuals who inhabit the offices to which they have been elected.

Finally, the countries in the region have adopted proportional electoral systems, which may produce multiparty systems with high degrees of party polarization. Presidential systems with proportional electoral systems and high levels of multipartism reduce the size of possible partisan support for the president within the legislature. Such a combination can limit executive–legislative agreement across key areas of public policy, and make effective governance problematic (Jones 1995: 78). If this low level of legislative support for the executive is combined further with ideological polarization of the political parties, then the problems of securing executive–legislative agreement and providing effective governance becomes more acute. Table 2.2 compares the effective number of political parties and the degree of their ideological polarization for twelve Latin American countries across various periods of democratic rule (Mainwaring and Scully 1995: 30–1). The table shows that Venezuela, Uruguay, Bolivia, Peru, Chile, Ecuador, and Brazil have the largest number of effective political parties and the highest degree of ideological polarization. In practical terms, this combination of multipartism and ideological polarization means that in these countries democratic governance is made more difficult since there is the possibility of increased executive–legislative conflict. In some cases, such conflict has led to military intervention (e.g. Brazil in 1964, Chile in 1973, and Ecuador in 2000), and in other cases it has led to "extra-constitutional" behavior of presidents seeking to concentrate their own power, as in Peru under President Fujimori and Venezuela under President Chávez (see chapter 4).

Military reserve domains of power

Most of the countries of Latin America that form part of the new democratic universe emerged from prolonged periods of military rule, and thus face serious challenges from the ways in which civil–military relations affect the process of democratization. On the one hand, if governments in the new democracies seek to exert too much civilian control over the military, they may risk military coups, barracks revolts, and indiscipline in the short term. On the other hand, if they do not seek changes in the relative power of the military, they risk long-term problems of democratic legitimacy and stability (Zagorski 1992: 59–60; Fitch 1998: 134). Militaries have maintained large areas of authority and capacity after the period of authoritarian rule, especially in those countries that had been ruled by a hierarchical military, which may impose certain "reserve domains" on the new democracy (Linz and Stepan 1996: 67–8). Such hierarchical militaries were most prevalent in the authoritarian periods of Argentina (1966–73; 1976–83), Brazil (1964–85), Chile (1973–90), and Uruguay (1973–84). The militaries in these countries want to preserve their institutional integrity, certain privileges such as immunity of officers from civilian trial, substantial budgets, discretion over issues of national security, and "pet" projects such as nuclear weapons programs (see Zagorski 1992: 55–8).

The key challenge for the new democracies is thus to exert democratic control over military autonomy while demonstrating that the costs of democracy are less than the costs of future military intervention (Fitch 1998: 135; see also Hunter 1997). Given this difficult balance, how have some countries in the region fared in reducing the power and legacy of their respective militaries? In Argentina, both the Alfonsín administration (1983–9) and Menem administration (1989–99) faced strong opposition from certain elements of the military despite its defeat in the Falklands/Malvinas war with the United Kingdom in 1982. There were three revolts during the Alfonsín administration and one revolt during the Menem administration, all of which were organized by a group of disaffected members of the military calling themselves the *carapintadas* (or painted faces). The main issue concerned the degree to which the new democratic government would investigate human rights abuses that had occurred during the authoritarian period. Through a general amnesty and careful negotiation, President Menem was able to lower the overall tension between civilians and the military, and ultimately establish the political subordination of the military to democratic governance. In similar fashion, the new democratic government in Uruguay established a *de facto* amnesty that, despite the continued tension over past human rights abuses, has led to a period of coexistence between civilians and the military (Zagorski 1992: 89–91).

Since the military had a large role in Brazil's prolonged transition from authoritarian rule (1974–85) and committed fewer gross human rights abuses than the military governments in neighboring Chile, Argentina, and Uruguay, the tension with civilian leaders has been much less. The first civilian President José Sarney (1985–9) was ostensibly chosen by the military, while the succeeding Presidents Fernando Collor de Mello (1989–94) and Fernando Henrique Cardoso (1994–2002) have had some success in redirecting military activities, downsizing military budgets, and cancelling large-scale projects. Like Uruguay, Brazilian civilians have maintained a peaceful coexistence with the military (Zagorski 1992: 87–9). In Chile, civil–military relations have been less tense than in Argentina despite General Pinochet's aspirations for establishing a "protected democracy" with the 1980 Constitution, which preserved wide-ranging authority for the military and created favorable conditions for political forces on the right (see chapter 4 this volume). Like Argentina and Uruguay, the new democratic governments in Chile had to confront the legacy of human rights abuses committed under the Pinochet regime. President Patricio Aylwin (1989–93) established a Truth Commission to investigate past abuses and established the Commission on Reparation and Reconciliation to provide financial compensation for victims of human rights abuses and their families. While the Truth Commission published all known extra-judicial killings and disappearances (over 3,000 in total), a standing decree law precluded from prosecution all acts committed by military personnel before 1978 (Fitch 1998: 156–7). Aylwin's successor, Eduardo Frei (1994–9), had a delicate task balancing the interests of a highly autonomous and proud military institution with the needs of democratic governance. On balance, "the armed forces remain a defiant authoritarian enclave" in Chile whose civilian support has waned over the course of the new democratic period (Fitch 1998: 159).

What are the general patterns across these examples of civil–military relations in these four countries? First, the militaries have made "tactical" retreats, but have not yet given up the pretensions associated with national security doctrine and the so-called "new professionalism" that has characterized their institutions since the 1950s (Zagorski 1992: 91). Second, senior military leaders have professed nominal allegiance to democratic procedures and overall obedience to democratic authority (Zagorski 1992: 92). Third, democratic governments have been successful in downsizing military budgets and cancelling key military projects. Fourth, despite the increase in civilian control over the militaries in these countries, there remains individual and institutional recalcitrance to accept civilian democratic authority, as well as tension and unease between civilian and military leaders with respect to the institutional and professional integrity of the armed forces.

Outside these countries with hierarchical military institutions, such as Peru and Ecuador, militaries still perceive themselves as the ultimate guardians of the state in times of crisis (Fitch 1998: 146). Throughout the 1980s in Peru, the military was charged with quashing the *Sendero Luminoso* guerrilla group (Shining Path), which led to an enhanced role for the military after its period of direct rule from 1968 to 1980. The military enjoyed unprecedented autonomy in combating subversion, which led to human rights violations that have continued beyond the capture of Sendero's leader in 1992 and extended well into the 1990s. Yet in 1995, the Peruvian congress passed a general amnesty for all security personnel accused or convicted of human rights abuses (Fitch 1998: 149). Moreover, Fujimori's *autogolpe* (self-coup) and subsequent political and constitutional gamble was made possible through explicit support of the Peruvian military, where its authority and power supplied the necessary force to shut down congress and reformulate the rules of the game. In neighboring Ecuador, the military has consolidated a higher degree of professional autonomy than it achieved during earlier periods of civilian rule and in January 2000, along with support from indigenous groups, fomented a restorative coup ousting President Jamil Mahuad and putting President Gustavo Noboa in his place.

In short, democratic transition has removed Latin American militaries from direct occupation of the government; however, their political presence and influence remains significant for the new democracies. While not perceived as an immediate threat to democracy, civilian governments have had to (and still must) remain sensitive to the institutional integrity and legitimacy of the military. Such sensitivity requires a balance between normative concerns over past abuses and the political contingencies of the moment, where perceived threats within the military as an institution may yield to further interventions in the future. In addition, it is possible that powerful leaders within militaries may use the institution as a platform for their own political ambitions. It is telling that Hugo Chávez, one of the leaders of the military coup attempts against Carlos Andrés Pérez in Venezuela in 1992, became the democratically elected President after a short stint in prison for his anti-democratic behavior. Militaries have receded into the background for the moment, but new democracies must remain vigilant of their possible resurgence, while at the same time creating conditions under which militaries will gain respect for the democratic order.

Uncivil movements and political violence

Civil society is composed of voluntary associations and organizations that represent a variety of interests not directly related to economic production or governmental activity, but nonetheless involve significant relationships among individuals as they interact in the "public sphere." Thus, civil society includes social clubs, guilds, local community groups, parent organizations, popular organizations, and social movements. As chapter 8 shows, such organizations in Latin American civil society include human rights advocates, feminist and women's movements, indigenous peoples' organizations, urban social movements, gay and lesbian organizations, environmentalist movements, independent labor unions, small farmers' associations, artistic and cultural collectives, alternative media, church groups, student movements, and non-governmental organizations (NGOs). These organizations have across various countries and time periods in the region struggled for specific goods, rights, fuller political participation, and an expanded sense of citizenship, as well as contributed to democratic transitions themselves (Foweraker and Landman 1997).

But civil society also has organizations and movements with different sets of goals and that employ different means to achieve them. Leigh Payne (2000) has called such organizations and movements "uncivil movements" since they seek to destabilize fragile democracies in pursuit of their own ends. They engage in violence against other social movements and democratic governments through kidnapping, murder, destruction of property, coups, and coup attempts. They seek to eliminate competition from their adversaries, and expand political power for an exclusive sector of the population. Like "civil" social movements, they use identity and symbolic politics and unconventional political strategies, and they straddle the divide between societal autonomy and integration by participating in the political system through existing forms of interest inter-mediation (Payne 2000: 3). Unlike civil movements, they engage in violent political action against their government or adversaries within civil society (Payne 2000: 220–1). Since they target adversaries in civil society and ultimately seek power within political institutions, such movements represent pathologies of both civil society and democracy. Unlike their civil counterparts who broadly support the idea of democracy, but seek to deepen it or transform it, uncivil movements threaten democratic stability and erode civil society, particularly in countries where both are relatively weak.

Examples of uncivil movements in Latin America include paramilitary organizations in Colombia and Argentina, the Shining Path in Peru, the Rural Democratic Union (UDR) in Brazil, the National Republican Alliance (ARENA) in El Salvador, the counter-revolutionaries (*Contras*) in Nicaragua, the Revolutionary Front for the Advancement and Progress of Haiti (FRAPH), and the Bolívar Revolutionary Movement (MBR-200) in Venezuela. It is difficult to sustain such violence for long periods of time, since the original threats that legitimated the movements may have disappeared, the contradictory logic of the movements themselves may have eroded their support, or the sheer magnitude of their violent acts has discredited them. The transitional countries in Latin America have tended to give such movements unintended support by capitulating to their demands, while the consolidated democracies in the region sought to discredit them through investigations and prosecutions (Payne 2000: 240–2). Like civil–military relations, the relationship between democratic governments and uncivil movements is a difficult balance: not taking them seriously may lead to their penetration of democratic institutions, while overreacting to them may lend credence to their cause and strengthen their power.

Poverty and social exclusion

Following Mexico's moratorium on paying its foreign debt obligations in 1982 and the emergence of the debt crisis more generally in Latin America, international financial institutions such as the World Bank and the International Monetary Fund developed policies to stabilize and restructure the faltering economies in the region. Based on inferences drawn from the successful economic experiences in South Korea, Taiwan, Singapore, and Japan, these policies concentrated on the degree to which state intervention in the economy had led to low, stagnant, or negative growth rates, high inflation, unstable currencies, and balance of payments problems. Broadly understood as *neoliberalism*, the policies that emerged in these financial institutions were based on free market ideas of neoclassical economics, and combined the extension of further loans to troubled Latin economies with the imposition of certain policy prescriptions for macroeconomic stabilization and structural adjustment. In the short term, macrostabilization was meant to alleviate hyperinflation, while in the long term, structural adjustment programs (SAPs) were meant to make economies more efficient in the allocation of their basic goods and services. By 1983, three-quarters of all Latin American countries were under IMF-supervised structural adjustment programs, while by the end of the 1980s, the remaining countries in the region fell under similar programs (Brohman 1996: 134).

Typically, macrostabilization involves a series of measures meant to tackle hyperinflation, including increased control on bank credit, government deficits, wage increases, and the removal of price controls. The absence of control over such areas of the economy can lead to large government spending deficits that are financed through increased levels of credit or money supply, which can result in rapid inflationary pressures. Imposition of the controls through "shock" programs can successfully stop such hyperinflation. Structural adjustment programs, on the other hand, seek to improve the overall allocation of goods and services through liberalizing foreign exchange and import controls, devaluing the exchange rate, opening the economy to increased levels of direct foreign investment, and privatizing large state-owned enterprises. Neoliberals argued that closed, regulated, and publicly financed economies with overvalued exchange rates ultimately promoted inefficiencies that led to poor growth and development. By implementing the structural adjustment prescriptions, neoliberals argued that such stagnant economies would make long-term efficiency gains from the free market allocation of goods and services.

The record of these policies is mixed for Latin America. On the one hand, macrostabilization policies have worked to alleviate problems with hyperinflation in countries such as Argentina and Peru, but did little to combat chronic inflation in countries such as Brazil, which have had to implement a series of revaluations and economic reforms. The longer-term structural adjustment programs have been successful in Pinochet's Chile, but largely unsuccessful in other countries of the region. On balance, there have been a large number of negative (and partially unintended) consequences to these programs since they attack artificially high wages, artificially low prices, and overvalued exchange rates. Cutting wages and raising prices for basic goods hurts those with low incomes, and devaluing exchange rates

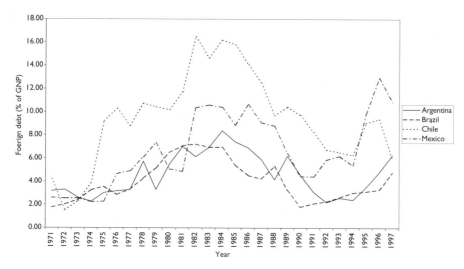

Figure 2.2 Foreign debt of selected Latin American countries
Source: World Bank 1999

makes imports more expensive and cuts the revenues generated by
exports, while the system of loans continues to expand the foreign
debt obligations of recipient countries. Figure 2.2 shows external debt
as a proportion of gross domestic product for Argentina, Brazil,
Chile, and Mexico for 1971–97, where it is evident that debt obligations have been on the increase after a dip in the mid-1980s.

This combination of economic subordination of low-income
groups and high indebtedness of national governments that limits
social spending means that structural adjustment programs have
in many cases had the opposite effects to those originally intended.
These effects are partly due to the insensitivity of the international
financial institutions to the nature of the state in Latin America and
the region's vulnerability to price and quantity fluctuations in the
primary export sector, as well as neglect of key problems of development, including income distribution, poverty alleviation, and access
to basic needs (see Stiglitz 2002). Thus, the negative consequences of
structural adjustment programs in Latin America include increased
levels of social polarization and rising social costs. The social costs
include job losses in labor-intensive industries, decreases in real
wages, increases in the cost of basic goods, reduced access to social
services, and cutbacks in government-sponsored social programs. In
addition to increased class polarization, structural adjustment pro-

grams have heightened tensions within other social relations, such as those based on gender and ethnicity (Brohman 1996: 165). By 1990, roughly 46 percent of all Latin Americans lived in poverty, a figure that has increased since the early 1970s, which means that the region has not successfully combated poverty but has aggravated it (O'Donnell 1999a: 195).

Taken together, the high social costs and increased societal polarization brought about in part by the implementation of structural adjustment programs erode and undermine democracy, since political participation is limited by increasing levels of social exclusion. Our third dimension of procedural democracy is participation, which is meant to extend to the largest number of adult citizens within a given country. However, *legally equal* citizens may be *socially unequal* and therefore may not enjoy the same level of political participation in real terms as others in the political system. Moreover, poverty may limit citizens' access to justice and may lead to violations of civil rights, since proper legal defense and due process of the law is unattainable for those without the financial means (see chapter 4). For the advanced industrial democracies in the world, the worst contradictions and consequences of free markets have been alleviated through the development of welfare states (Donnelly 1999). Even though neoliberalism emerged in Reagan's America and Thatcher's Britain, the scaling down of the state has never fully eradicated the welfare system. Thus, while there are patterns of social exclusion and subordination in such well-established democracies, the basic level of support facilitates a greater degree of political participation. In contrast, Latin American countries have a weaker tradition of welfarism, which contributes to the continuation of social exclusion and restricted forms of democratic participation.

Assessing democracy

This chapter has presented a democratic "balance sheet" for Latin America as the region has emerged from a prolonged period of undemocratic governance. Like any balance sheet there are positive and negative aspects to the democratic record for this period. The positive aspects include the installation of electoral democracy, the reestablishment of party politics, and successive years in which the region has seen the continued and regular peaceful transfer of power between civilians. The negative aspects include the persistence of a large gap between electoral and liberal democracy, the recurrence of executive–legislative conflict, strong presidentialism and delegative democracy, weak judiciaries and rule of law, reserve domains of power for the military, uncivil movements and political violence, and the persistence of poverty and social exclusion. These negative aspects of the Latin American democratic universe suggest that the region has many challenges ahead to achieve stable democratic governance. Giving more strength to judiciaries will provide greater horizontal accountability and more effective rule of law. Establishing greater civilian authority over the military and developing greater support for democratic institutions within the military will limit the chances of future intervention. Finally, more just distribution of income and greater investment in education, health, and welfare will reduce the misery of large sectors of the Latin American population while increasing their ability for meaningful political participation (see chapter 7).

PART II
ACCOUNTABILITY
AND LEGITIMACY

3 | GOVERNMENT AND CITIZENS

The possibilities and obstacles facing democracy in Latin America are closely tied to the kinds of relations established between rulers and ruled, that is, between government and citizens. This is one of the classical problems of political theory and comparative politics, particularly with regard to modern democracy. The meaning of "democracy" itself is derived from the combination of two words of the ancient Greeks: *demos* (the people) and *kratos* (to rule). In democracy, the people and the act of ruling are united, not separated, as in other political regimes. However, the way in which *demos* and *kratos* are united varies greatly from one place to the next (including within the European and North American democracies). In fact, exactly *how* people rule in their own name is a central question for the comparative study of democracy.

As noted in the previous chapter, there are several models of democracy that have been advocated and instituted in different places and times. In order for any of these models to function effectively, there are some basic requirements that must be present. These include free and fair elections, the full legal protection of the civil and political rights of all citizens, and the inclusion of all adult groups as participants in political life. These requirements are rarely met in practice in any country, but they do provide a basic conceptual framework for orienting democratic thought and action. Within this framework we can identify at least three main problems that affect the relationship between government and citizens: legitimacy, accountability, and participation. This chapter discusses each of these concepts and relates them to historical patterns of government–citizen relations in Latin America.

This chapter is divided into three parts. The first discusses the concepts of legitimacy, accountability, and participation in modern nation-states. The second traces the evolution of each of these concepts in Latin America's modern political history. This section ends by noting the reemergence of democracy and citizenship as the key elements for building governmental legitimacy in the 1980s and 1990s. In the third part, we discuss the implications of neoliberalism for government–citizen relations in Latin America.

Legitimacy, accountability, and participation in modern state formation

Much of the debate concerning the prospects for democracy in the world today revolves around the capacity of governments to uphold democratic ideas in the face of numerous pressures. In general terms, this involves the development of democratic values and institutions which gain broad popular acceptance and support, are open to public scrutiny, and which encourage rather than discourage citizen participation in political life. In the case of many Latin American countries, it can be argued that the first stage of the transition from authoritarian to democratic government was largely completed during the 1980s and early 1990s. These new democracies were then challenged by the complex task of consolidation. We believe that a useful way of comparing democratization at this point is to focus on the related problems of legitimacy, accountability, and participation. These terms can be seen as three indispensable elements of a democratic polity.

One of the enduring questions of political science is precisely what makes government legitimate. How is the authority of the governors accepted as legitimate by the governed? In other words, when is government accepted as *legitimate* government? Given that all societies have created some form of political organization, from ancient cities to nation-states and transnational institutions, it is understandable that the question of legitimacy has been close to the heart of both academic inquiry and political action.

In this regard, the emergence and consolidation of the nation-state in nineteenth-century Europe has exercised a great deal of influence over modern theories of legitimacy. The philosophical roots of Western political thought can be traced to the Enlightenment philosophers who sought to explain the profound social, economic, and religious transformations of eighteenth-century Europe in terms of the emergence of rational individual subjects who, equipped with the advances of scientific knowledge, demanded freedom from the shackles of social convention and tradition. In Europe, the targets of Enlightenment thinking were the monarchs, religious authorities, and oligarchies that based their rule on the feudal order. The legitimacy of such institutions, as well as their entire worldview, was rooted in the uncontestability of religious tradition, ascriptive categories such as caste or social status, and "natural hierarchy." In Spanish America, the more liberal leaders of independence movements would draw on this Enlightenment critique by challenging the very legitimacy of the monarchy's claims to rule.

However, there is a crucial difference between the European and Latin American experiences of state formation, at least in its initial stages. In Europe, state formation was largely driven by war and associated fiscal pressures, leading to the expansion of a large bureaucracy capable of ensuring the extraction of revenues from the citizens. This meant that the nation-state in Europe required effective control of the national territory (Weber 1956; Tilly 1998).[1] In contrast, in Latin America, early efforts at state formation were driven by integration into the world market in the latter quarter of the nineteenth century. Fiscal revenues were dependent on the primary export sector, usually located near to ports or mining enclaves. The elites which led this process sought alliances with local elites to achieve some measure of control over the national territory, leading not to the bureaucratization of the state (as in Europe), but its patrimonialization, that is, the dominance of government institutions by prominent families and personalistic leaders. Later stages of state formation involved other processes and actors. War, revolution, and mass politics created new institutions that became central to national development: the armed forces, political parties, and interest groups. Nevertheless, these actors often incorporated earlier forms of political behavior in new institutional forms. Such an outcome produced at least two effects that can still be seen in the region today: the pervasive use of patronage in government – citizen relations, and the incomplete extension of state authority across national territory. The prevalence of patrimonial forms of state power affect the possibility of consolidating the basic requirements of democracy in Latin America, particularly with regard to the rule of law (see chapter 4; Foweraker and Landman 1997).

State formation also entailed the public acceptance of new identities as members of new nations. Nationalism provided the basis for how citizens saw themselves and each other as part of the same collectivity. Since it was impossible for an individual to know all other citizens, the propagation of nationalist myths (facilitated by the printing press and road building) allowed for the mental construction of nations as "imagined communities" (Anderson 1983). In Latin America, we again find the incomplete reach of such myths, due to the lack of national integration and the isolation of large areas and populations from the centers of political and economic power. Nevertheless, in the twentieth century, violent social upheavals created new nationalist myths in several countries, allowing for a greater penetration of state institutions across national territories.

Theorists of state formation also expressed some ambivalence about the rise of modern bureaucracy and the centralizing tendencies of national integration. Although, for Max Weber, the legitimacy of modern states was indeed distinctive because of its rational-legal foundations, this moment represented new dangers. While celebrating the advances of modern forms of governmental power, Weber also warned that modern states may turn into "iron cages" in which rationality goes "too far," turning government into a bureaucratic machine capable of too much rationality and efficiency. With its legitimacy assured through legal and rational modes of societal integration and governmental intervention, the modern state would lack any counterbalance to its own power, particularly if its resources came to be controlled by a military-bureaucratic elite with imperial designs. Weber therefore argued for the protection of a competitive economic sphere (the capitalist market) as well as the strengthening of a competitive political sphere (the legislative branch of government). Without these checks and balances, the modern state would most likely end up serving the interests of ambitious politicians, whose legitimacy would be based less on legality and reason, and more on personal appeal or "charisma."

Weber's concern here was with the establishment of accountable government. As we have noted, Enlightenment thinking gave intellectual justification to new demands emerging throughout Europe for equal individual rights, now known as "civil rights." These rights include the right to one's life, physical integrity, and personal property. Today they include the rights to a fair trial and the legal prohibition of arbitrary arrest, torture, and forced disappearance. In other words, the individual became a subject of rights through the establishment of limits on governmental power. This transformation was associated in Europe with the political ideology known as liberalism. As we saw in chapter 1, liberal ideas were imported into Latin America during the nineteenth century, although by the end of that century they tended to be subordinated to a more conservative preoccupation with internal order and governability.

Civil rights marked a first check on the arbitrary power of rulers and were therefore important for the establishment of accountability, that is, the ability of citizens to demand that rulers act according to a universal set of norms enshrined in the rule of law and a national constitution. We can distinguish at least two main forms of accountability in modern states. The first is often termed "vertical accountability" and refers to the relationship between citizens and government as mediated by publicly elected officials. In a representative democracy, vertical accountability is achieved through regular elections and the responsiveness of government to the demands of the citizenry. The second form is known as "horizontal accountability" and refers to the checks and balances that exist between the different branches of government (the executive, legislature, and judiciary). The development of modern nation-states has been marked by a constant concern with the extent to which politicians can be held accountable to the citizens, as well as with the shifting balance of power within the government apparatus itself.

Accountable government does not necessarily imply inclusiveness. Although the newly emerging capitalist classes in Europe successfully established a new model of democracy that differed from the old order, early, or "classical," liberalism soon created its own inequalities. This was especially damaging for a doctrine that legitimized itself by appeals to the equality of all individuals. In the face of economic and social exploitation, liberal intellectuals and popular movements fought for the extension of "civil rights" to "political rights." These included the right to participate in public decision-making, which was most clearly manifested in the extension of the right to vote beyond the property-owning classes, in order to enfranchise the mass of the population – at first restricted to adult males, but finally incorporating women in the early twentieth century. The introduction of universal suffrage would have profound implications for governments in Europe and North America. Among these would be the creation of more broadly representative party systems and the organization of mass constituencies for competing projects of economic and social modernization. Political participation was therefore linked to the election of representatives in competitive party systems.

State formation in Europe rested on the kinds of struggles, negotiations, and concessions that resulted from social conflict during the late nineteenth and early twentieth centuries. Government–citizen relations reflected a class compromise in which liberal capitalism continued to operate as the dominant economic model, while the working class gained political representation through the extension of the vote, the rights of free assembly and association, and freedom of the press (Rueschemeyer, Stephens and Stephen 1992). With this increase in political participation, modern politics became mass politics as broad-based parties sought to capture votes among a newly enfranchised population.

Samuel Barnes describes three patterns of partisan mobilization in Europe and North America during the twentieth century (Barnes 1997). The first was characterized by the mobilization of relatively strong social identities, for example, industrial labor's support for socialist parties. After 1945, and with the gradual decline of class-based identities, voters were mobilized by political identification with particular parties and candidates. In the postwar era, mass parties could no longer rely on a guaranteed social base of support and became "catch-all" parties, whose success depended on their appeal to a broader and more complex electorate. Parties became machines for winning elections, rather than expressions of a unified class identity. Since the 1970s, and with the growing influence of the mass media, partisan mobilization has become increasingly focused on appeals to the individual desires of voters. Ideological distinctions between the main parties have become blurred, and neither voters nor parties are likely to uphold the kind of social or partisan identities that were common in the past. As a result, there are more and more independent voters whose temporary allegiances the political parties must compete for. The ideal vehicle to do so is television and mass advertising, which uses increasingly sophisticated techniques to "sell" the image of rival candidates. In this context, many citizens may feel that their participation in elections has become dependent on the public relations skills of party bureaucracies, while campaigns are marked by excessive spending and the virtual disappearance of policy alternatives. One result has been the high abstention rates recorded at national elections in the oldest democracies, such as Great Britain and the United States.

Participation is not restricted to elections and parties. The expansion of civil and political rights allowed more and more citizens to participate in labor unions and other interest groups that sought to influence public policy. In order to plan the complex economies of postwar Europe, some governments actively encouraged the participation of national associations of business and labor in the design of economic and social policy. This form of interest-group representation is known as "societal corporatism" and has been strongest in Germany and the Scandinavian countries. Another model of interest-group representation is known as "pluralism," which refers to the competition between numerous groups that seek governmental support for their particular goals. An example of this model is the United States, where interest groups are not formally integrated into the government's decision-making apparatus as in societal corporatism. Instead, they mobilize their unequal economic and political resources in an effort to shape policies and legislation that reflect their members' interests.

As discussed on page 67, in Latin America political participation appears to share many of the same features that we have noted for Europe and North America. The extension of the right to vote came after a period of social conflict and formed part of a new class compromise, political parties have been a key mechanism for linking citizens and the government since the early twentieth century, interest groups have participated in decision-making on important matters of public policy, while the emergence of a broad range of civil associations has added a greater degree of pluralism to traditionally exclusionary political systems. However, there are some crucial differences that demand our attention. Participation has traditionally been conditioned by the dominance of patrimonial forms of political control in which powerful leaders or bureaucrats act to further their own interests without regard for the rule of law. Political parties often lack firm roots in society and are frequently seen as vehicles for the enhancement of personalistic ambitions rather than a meaningful vehicle for the representation of popular demands. In general, politicians and parties are seen as corrupt and self-serving, although they are also often the only channel to gain access to state resources. This gap between the mass of the citizenry and the actions of the political parties poses serious dilemmas for achieving greater levels of participation, with generally negative effects on vertical accountability and regime legitimacy.

Legitimacy, accountability, and participation in Latin America

How have legitimacy, accountability, and participation evolved in Latin America? The first point to note is that the form in which civil and political rights were extended in the region tended to coexist with (and were often fomented by) patrimonial forms of social control. The most pervasive (and enduring) of these is known as "clientelism," which can be defined as the political domination of individuals ("clients") by political leaders ("patrons") who provide protection and services in exchange for loyalty and guaranteed votes. Clientelism, which also existed in early modern Europe, was based on a form of legitimacy rooted in tradition or "what has always existed." People were not free individuals who could appeal to the impersonal application of a universally accepted law, but clients who were expected to act out pre-ascribed social roles, accepting the legitimacy of their patrons as long as they were provided with security against competing claims of rival elites. Participation was limited to supporting the same traditions, while accountability rested less on the satisfaction of individual goals and more on the capacity of traditional patrons to continue to protect "their" constituencies from the predations of other patrons. This meant that when civil and political rights were formally extended in Latin America in the early twentieth century, the mechanisms by which they were practiced still tended to be shaped by personalistic ties between patrons and clients. Participation included the right to vote in elections, but the results tended to reflect the interests of patrons rather than those of free individuals. In fact, clientelism did not disappear with the consolidation of modern state structures. Instead, it became the basis for integrating the newly enfranchised masses through the clientelistic manipulation of their civil and political rights.

In Europe, clientelism continued to influence modern electoral politics well into the twentieth century. However, the legitimacy of the modern state came to be identified less and less with loyalty to personalistic rulers and traditional practices, and more and more with the political authority of bureaucracy and the rule of law. As noted earlier, state formation in Latin America was marked by patrimonial forms of rule which gave elites the flexibility to selectively support some groups and individuals over others, rather than having to submit to an impersonal bureaucracy and the universal application of the rule of law.

In chapter 1, we saw how the consolidation of "conservative liberalism" in Latin America in the late nineteenth century was also marked by the monopolization of the capitalist market by the export-oriented oligarchy. We also noted how the belief in elitist rule in this period limited the effective political participation of important sectors of the newly emerging middle classes, labor, and peasantry. The basis of governmental legitimacy in Latin America would evolve in the twentieth century, but it is noteworthy that "charisma" would continue to play a central role, even in today's new democracies. In the period of conservative liberalism, governments effectively insulated themselves from demands for accountability and sought to restrict citizen participation to largely symbolic institutions such as the legislature. Decision-making remained the prerogative of those factions of the social, economic, and military elites that allied most closely with the personalistic leadership of the president of the republic.[2]

In Latin America, the political crises of the 1930s gave way to a variety of forms of charismatic leadership which have often been referred to collectively as "populism." As we saw with Weber, all forms of government must seek to legitimize their rule. If the emerging modern state would increasingly turn to legality to satisfy this requirement, the weak legitimacy of national government in Latin America was manifested in the failures of liberal constitutionalism, the ravages of civil war, and the consolidation of regimes for whom the concept of the "rule of law" was heavily conditioned by particularistic interests (see chapter 4). Under these conditions, legitimacy, accountability, and participation were likely to take on some very different forms than those prescribed by European thinkers, although they were not so alien as to be totally unrecognizable to outside observers.

Populism fitted into this contradictory picture precisely because it combined the expansion of a bureaucratic, centralized state apparatus, with earlier forms of domination based on tradition and charisma. In fact, these diverse sources of legitimacy came together in an all-encompassing appeal to a nationalist political identity that sought to transcend ethnic and social differences by identifying the sources of conflict as originating *outside* the nation. Legitimacy was based less on procedural norms than on a mythical founding moment of the new nation. The old oligarchy was seen as having sold out the national interest to foreign governments and corporations, leading to an unacceptable degree of dependency on external markets and imperialist ambitions. The adoption of import-substitution industrialization (ISI) policies in the 1930s was not simply a matter of economic adjustment to the great depression. It was also linked to a cultural and political project to establish new bases of legitimacy for Latin American governments. In Argentina, the rise to power of Juan Domingo Perón in 1945 expressed such a founding moment for the construction of a new myth that cast the old export-oriented oligarchy as the enemy of national progress. Perón effectively included popular demands for social justice into his government's program, linking the fate of the working class to that of his own political project. The Peronists even called their party the Partido Justicialista (Justice Party) and established one of the most enduring ideological traditions in Latin American politics.

A similar "nationalist myth" was that of the Mexican revolution of 1910–17. The dominant-party regime which emerged from this revolution made effective use of the main social demands of workers and peasants. Claiming to represent the will of the nation, the ruling PRI was able to base its legitimacy on the distribution of material resources to the poorest sectors of society. As in Argentina, the PRI combined the modern form of state, particularly the bureaucratic and centralized power of the executive branch and the dominance of one single party, with the more traditional forms of political domination such as clientelism and charisma. In Mexico and Argentina, the development of the modern state did not replace earlier forms of control and legitimacy. It simply institutionalized them. Patrons now became key players in the flow of resources and political power from the central authorities of the charismatic leaders and inner circles of the ruling party.

Participation in modern states has been achieved not solely through the expansion of civil and political rights, but also as a result of social reforms that provide the majority of citizens with access to basic economic resources and public services. In this way social upheavals and revolutions have been averted or delayed as a result of compromises between the main social classes. For example, in post-1945 Europe, class compromises were achieved in which capitalism was retained as the dominant economic system, but was also regulated by the state in ways that allowed the mass of the population to gain access to public education, health, and housing, provided by an expanding welfare state. T. H. Marshall (1964) viewed this establishment of the welfare state in terms of the inevitable extension of citizenship rights in modern societies, passing from civil to political and, finally, "social rights." However, this process was by no means inevitable and can be better understood as the result of social change and political struggle that culminated in various types of class compromise.[3]

In postwar Latin America, "social rights" remained subject to institutionalized clientelism and its daily manifestations in corruption, nepotism, favoritism, and violence. In short, populism was based not on the legitimacy of citizenship rights, but on the combination of charisma, clientelism, and nationalist myths, now promoted through the institutional form of the modern state.

In this scenario accountability also became synonymous with economic performance rather than responsive politicians or checks and balances between the branches of government. If populism provided an adequate flow of material goods to an ever-increasing number of "clients," few cared to quibble about the mechanisms of decision-making or service delivery. The style of populist government was deliberately vague on procedural issues, preferring to test its accountability through shows of mass support, such as the frequent rallies of official labor unions outside the national palaces in Buenos Aires and Mexico City. Similarly, participation was carefully controlled so as to reaffirm mass approval of governmental decisions. The activities of independent unions and parties were severely curtailed. Anti-foreigner sentiments were easily mobilized against imperialist powers such as Great Britain or the United States. However, they were also used against communist and socialist leaders who were seen as guilty of importing foreign ideologies and destabilizing the national unity of the working class. The populist state sought to establish its own monopoly over interest representation, particularly in relation to industrial labor and domestic capital – the key pillars of ISI policies. This led to the creation of "state corporatism," in which the leadership of social organizations (trade unions, business associations, peasant groups, etc.) was either imposed or tightly regulated by the state, in contrast to the democratic forms of "societal corporatism" noted above (p. 64) for Europe or the dominant "pluralist" model in the United States. Participation of citizens was therefore restricted to those forms deemed useful for the goals of the state. Other forms of participation were marginalized or outlawed through violent repression. Elections continued to be held, but politicians and parties gained their legitimacy from how well they could access government largesse in an ever-expanding network of institutionalized clientelism. Rarely did parties present alternative programs to deal with the problems of poverty and development. Instead, parties were simply vehicles for the ambitions of political intermediaries, creating ample opportunities for corruption and personal enrichment for cliques of party bosses, labor leaders, and other "popular representatives."

Elsewhere in the region, the success of revolutionary movements tended to reproduce similar forms of legitimacy, limited accountability, and tightly controlled forms of participation. The Cuban revolution in 1959 and the Nicaraguan revolution of 1979 both sought to legitimize themselves by reference to the long nationalist struggle against US imperialism and oligarchic rule. The constant threat of US intervention drove the Cuban government into the arms of the Soviet Union, which gladly supplied financial and military support until its collapse in 1991. Accountability was restricted to the internal channels of the Communist Party of Cuba and, as with other regimes in Latin America, tended to be based more on results than procedures. In the case of Cuba, as well as Nicaragua under the Sandinistas in 1979–90, such results were measured by improvements in literacy, education, healthcare, land reform, and income distribution. Participation in both revolutions also tended to be shaped heavily by the goals of their respective leaderships. Citizens were able to express demands and concerns through the mass organizations affiliated to the Communist Party of Cuba or the Sandinista Front of National Liberation. In the face of external aggression, independent dissent was closely monitored and censored, although less so in Nicaragua. In both cases, legitimacy derived from a combination of charismatic leadership (especially in the case of Cuba), nationalist myths of anti-imperialist revolution and international support, combined with familiar Western models of state centralization, Marxist-Leninist theories of socialism, and rational, scientific administration. In the case of Nicaragua, this latter form of state power led to conflict between the Miskitu Indians on the Atlantic Coast and the Sandinista government, which was eventually resolved through the granting of a measure of regional autonomy.

Although the Cuban revolution survived US hostility (including the attempted overthrow of the government with the Bay of Pigs invasion in 1961, covert actions by the CIA, and the general policy of isolation and trade sanctions), most of the populist experiments succumbed to military coups in the 1960s and 1970s. Contrary to the expectations of US government, the new middle classes of Latin America did not adopt democratic values but instead feared for their property as populist governments not only failed to meet rising expectations among increasingly mobilized popular sectors, but also were unable to control rampant inflation and public deficits.[4]

In Brazil (1964) and Chile (1973), important segments of the middle classes responded to political instability and ideological polarization by turning to the armed forces as the only national institution capable of restoring order. Military rule would see a renewed attempt to establish legitimacy, while simultaneously restricting accountability and participation. For the generals, the legitimacy of their rule was derived from the need for intervention itself. They argued that national integrity of their countries was threatened by deep social polarization and the threat of external political ideologies. The armed forces believed they had a mandate to purge their nations of social ills and alien ideas. In the name of national security and economic progress, legitimacy would have to be based on goals that went beyond mere party politics. Pointing to the corruption of parliamentary structures of representation, coup leaders argued for a new national program of unity behind the armed forces. The immediate repression of thousands of political activists opposed to military rule sent an unmistakable message to the rest of the population.

Legitimacy once again became grounded on economic performance rather than popular support. It would be the most privileged sectors of society who provided internal legitimacy to military regimes, while the US government provided important external

legitimacy to what it saw as important Cold War allies against communism and the influence of the Cuban revolution. Transnational corporations and pro-business economists also lent legitimacy to military
rule, believing that it would provide a secure environment for large-
scale investment and capitalist modernization. During this period, it
was not only the number of actors providing legitimacy that was
limited. Vertical and horizontal accountability were reduced even
further than in the populist regimes as decision-making was deliberately placed outside the view of elected representatives and political
parties. Technocratic modes of decision-making were less accountable
to domestic actors and more accountable to external actors, particularly the representatives of transnational corporations and the US
government. Citizen participation was more restricted than ever, due
to the extensive use of state terror, surveillance, and censorship. Participation took on a clandestine form, first in shape of largely unsuccessful guerrilla movements, and later as the embryos of grassroots
movements in defense of human rights and economic survival.

Domestic support for continued military rule began to wane in the
late 1970s. In part, this was due to the mixed results of economic stabilization. Although the Chilean military was able to establish a stable
pattern of economic management, the benefits were skewed in favor
of the wealthiest sectors and came at the cost of the dismantling of
social services for the poor. During 1981–2 Chile also suffered the
effects of economic recession in the rest of the world and protest
movements reemerged in 1983, demanding an end to the dictatorship
and alleviation from poverty and unemployment. In Brazil, the military was also able to achieve high rates of economic growth during
the 1970s, although its income distribution remained one of the most
unequal in the world. The government also became dependent on the
inflow of loans from foreign banks, which undermined the ability to
maintain growth into the 1980s as debt service began to take up a
larger share of national revenue. By 1982, important segments of the
middle classes began to withdraw their support for the prolongation
of military rule. When it became clear that the military could no
longer rule effectively, its allies (including the US government) began
to promote a negotiated return to civilian government. Significantly,
international actors, particularly the International Monetary Fund
(IMF) and the World Bank, appeared to be in a stronger position
than most internal actors when it came to demanding accountability,
although their primary concern was with financial stability rather
than human rights violations.

In the above discussion of legitimacy, accountability, and participation, we have not been able to include every country, nor pay

sufficient attention to nuance and difference within and between countries. However, we can identify not only the relative absence of democratic forms of government–citizen relations, but also some significant historical trends. These include the dominance of patrimonial forms of political control that have conditioned the form and scope of popular participation, a strong tendency to base governmental legitimacy on short-term results rather than long-term procedures, and an emerging gap between transnational and domestic actors in terms of demanding governmental accountability. Each of these patterns are of course debatable and vary in their intensity between different countries. Nevertheless, as we shall see, they do raise important questions regarding the future consolidation of specifically *democratic* forms of legitimacy, accountability, and participation.

The recent wave of democratization thus came after a particularly repressive phase in Latin America's political history. It also occurred amid global economic restructuring which placed new constraints on national governments. In short, the new democracies could not return to the populist form of state that preceded military rule, when the linkages between government and citizens were based on ideological appeals to social justice and nationalist paths to development. Both of these appeals had been undermined by the hierarchical and arbitrary nature of populist rule itself. However, they were more fully purged from the political scene by the military governments of the 1960s and 1970s. In an insightful analysis, O'Donnell (1979) argued that the return to democracy in Latin America would require the creation of new linkages (or "mediations") between government and citizens. The political coalitions that were associated with the populist promise of social justice were weak and, after 1982, national decision-makers were constrained by economic realities and conditionality requirements attached to the extension of aid and the implementation of structural adjustment programs (SAPs). Similarly, how could new civilian elites appeal to populist forms of mass mobilization if the military had brutally suppressed civic participation, producing a decline in traditional forms of organizing in labor unions and leftist parties? Although labor and the left continued to be important political actors, they lacked the form or force that they possessed in previous decades. In the short term, the only possible mediation could be that of democratic citizenship, which, as we have seen, was the historically weakest of all possible mediations in Latin America's modern history. Nevertheless, if democracy were to survive, it would have to build a stronger form of citizenship, overcoming the legacies of patrimonialism, clientelism, populism, and military rule. This would involve the democratization of governmental institutions and their relations to the citizenry, the focus of the following chapters of this book.

Neoliberalism, governments, and citizens

In the above sections we have discussed the evolution of government–citizen relations by referring to the domestic politics of Latin American countries. In this section we turn our attention to the current global context and its impact on government–citizen relations in the region. An understanding of democracy and citizenship today requires some reference to transnational processes of economic, cultural, and political integration, or "globalization." Previous "democratic waves" were also shaped by international relations. Samuel Huntington (1991) referred to the relatively slow adoption of democracy in the West between 1828 and 1926. This wave was reversed by the rise of totalitarian forms of government in Germany, Italy, Japan, and the Soviet Union. A second wave followed the end of the Second World War, with the defeat of fascism and the international legitimacy of liberal democracy. This wave was reversed in the early 1960s and lasted until the current "third wave" began with the democratic transition in Portugal in 1974. As noted in chapter 2, the collapse of military regimes and the return to democratic government in Latin America is very much part of this "third wave."

Although domestic factors played the most important part in bringing an end to military rule in Latin America, the emergence of new regimes occurred at a moment when transnational bodies were exercising unprecedented levels of influence in the affairs of sovereign states. Latin America had certainly experienced foreign intervention before, particularly in the form of US military and economic domination. However, the 1980s saw a qualitative shift towards global sources of power that transcended the policy preferences of all but a few powerful states (of which the US is the most influential). This new power was both centralized and dispersed, creating a web of institutional constraints for the newly democratizing countries of Latin America. Centralization occurred in the form of the financial might of mainly Western banks and intergovernmental institutions that were able to use the debt crisis to gain leverage over national fiscal and monetary policies. By the early 1990s, Latin American governments were discovering that their legitimacy rested as much on controlling inflation and public spending as on the consolidation of the rule of law. New democracies were constrained in their policy

choices as they sought to establish new forms of legitimacy, accountability, and participation. Globalization was therefore both a curse
and a blessing. On the one hand, macroeconomic policy was tied
closely to the US-led efforts in favor of privatization and free
trade (known as the "Washington Consensus"). On the other, democracy enjoyed a level of legitimacy that provided fragile regimes
with enough breathing space to avoid any immediate authoritarian
reversals. Nevertheless, the simultaneous emergence of the new
global political economy and the "third wave" created some very
specific conditions under which democracy and citizenship would
develop.

In this regard, comparative studies of democratic transitions
tended to warn of the dangers represented by overloading new governments with too many popular demands. Haggard and Kaufman
(1995), for example, concluded that new democracies needed to insti-
tutionalize demand-making through stable and unified party systems.
Economic reforms could only succeed if democratic contestation was,
to some degree, limited and contained by legitimate forms of governance. Civil society was both welcomed and feared, as the polarization of social demands could undermine the ability of governments
to govern. As noted earlier, the new democracies were not committed to the kinds of policies associated with populism and, given
that a key objective of political and economic reform was the reduction in the size and role of the state, the link between political legitimacy and social welfare policies was transformed to one
emphasizing limited and targeted spending for the poorest, combined
with support for market-based solutions for the rest of society. In
sum, "third wave" democracies were to avoid the specter of
ungovernability by institutionalizing a unified party system, a man-
ageable civil society and a fiscally responsible executive.

This preference for governable democracies was no doubt shaped
by the memory of populism and the concern with the lingering threats
posed by hardliners of outgoing authoritarian regimes. Despite the
widespread disapproval of dictatorship, few could afford the luxury
of assuming that democracy was safe from internal threats. Many
political scientists appeared to accept the inevitability of economic
austerity and restructuring, while stressing the urgent need for political institutionalization of democracy. As a result, institution-building
came to occupy a central place in both governmental and scholarly
debate. Civil society would be seen less as a site of social conflicts,
and more as a necessary supplement to political parties and state
institutions (Diamond 1999).

The neoliberal model has been highly contested in Latin America, not only because of its impact on social conditions, but also because of its implications for legitimacy, accountability, and participation. Rather than include neoliberal reform as a matter for negotiation and compromise, newly installed elites (some more accountable to the electorate than others) moved quickly to depoliticize civil society, to strengthen the executive over the legislature and tightly control economic decision-making. The result was a conspicuous gap between the ideal of liberal democracy and competitive capitalism on the one hand, and the reality of illiberal democracy and monopolistic capitalism on the other. National governments in Latin America in the 1990s claimed the legitimacy provided by multiparty elections and the constitutional order, but the range of political choices was systematically restricted to those that could guarantee legitimacy in transnational arenas. All Latin American governments have become more accountable to the terms established by regional trade agreements and economic integration, such as those stipulated by the North American Free Trade Agreement (NAFTA, comprised of Mexico, the United States, and Canada). The proposed Free Trade Area of the Americas (FTAA), which is scheduled to come into effect in 2005, will create not only one single market from Alaska to Tierra del Fuego, but also a set of rules and expectations to which national governments can be held accountable.

Today many people are concerned that globalization is occurring without sufficient mechanisms for demanding accountability from transnational corporations and multilateral institutions. Latin America is no exception and the efforts to consolidate national democratic institutions must take into account this global context.

4 | CONSTITUTIONALISM AND THE RULE OF LAW

Political order

Constitutionalism and the rule of law have been seen as the primary mechanisms through which modern states maintain public order. At the same time, however, they have been seen as institutions that have an ambivalent relationship with the principle of democracy. On the one hand, constitutionalism was deemed to provide orderly and just government (Blondel 1998: 72), while the rule of law protected the so-called "negative" rights of liberty by curbing the worst excesses of state encroachment in the lives of citizens (Sejersted 1993: 131; Foweraker and Landman 1997: 10–11). On the other hand, democracy was seen as having the potential for "mob rule" and disorderly behavior from members of the undesirable social classes who threatened the interests of the "enlightened" middle classes (Blondel 1998: 72). Thus, there is certain natural tension between constitutionalism and democracy.

Following the Second World War, constitutionalism came into disrepute as many countries in the developing world saw it as an obstacle on the road to democracy and as a Western invention to maintain imperialism (Blondel 1998: 72). Many newly independent states resulting from the process of decolonization sought nationalist routes to modernity and did not want to be hindered by an adherence to abstract principles and procedures developed during different historical periods in different political contexts. More recently, however, constitutionalism has emerged as a "critical dimension" of political democracy (see chapter 2 this volume; Hartlyn and Valenzuela 1994: 100–1), while the rule of law is argued to be a "key arena" of consolidated democracies (Linz and Stepan 1996: 7). Moreover, the emergence of a universal doctrine of human rights as embodied in international, regional, and national legal instruments has brought the rule of law and its importance for democracy to the forefront of contemporary political debate (Davidson 1993).

This chapter considers the evolution of constitutionalism and the rule of law in the context of Latin America in two important ways. First, it demonstrates that the tension between constitutionalism as a source for order and as the backbone of modern democracy permeates the politics of the region from the period of independence to the present day. Second, it examines the ways in which Latin America is party to the post-Second World War expansion of international human rights law and how the Inter-American System for the protection of human rights has reiterated the importance of constitutionalism and the rule of law in the region. These two considerations reveal that now, during an era of democratization and at the dawn of a new age of rights, constitutionalism and the rule of law have increasingly become seen as vital factors to maintaining political stability, democratic viability, and individual and collective well-being in the region.

Constitutionalism and the rule of law

Constitutions provide the authority and basic framework for modern governance. They establish the structure of government (presidential, parliamentary, mixed system), the powers of its various branches (executive, legislature, judiciary), the basic rights and freedoms of citizens, and the rules for mediating conflicts in society, as well as the mechanisms for making and breaking governments themselves. They are thus the skeletal structures around which governments are organized and carry out their functions, and the legal protections to which citizens can make appeals. The *principle* of constitutionalism, on the other hand, suggests that constitutions ought to transcend the political passions and events of history and provide the necessary continuity for successful and stable rule. They thus provide the legal framework for the functioning of government and a structure for continuity throughout the history of the nation.

In contrast to this abstract and somewhat idealistic view, history has shown that on many occasions constitutions have been the product of particular historical periods and the legal vehicles for individual political leaders or regimes. At the same time, constitutions create a certain institutional "path dependency" that constrains the political choices of future generations.[1] For example, the Constitution of the United States reflects radical ideas of the late eighteenth century forged during the tumultuous years of the American Revolution and Founding. While many ideas in the US Constitution have successfully transcended history and empowered groups and movements, other features have constrained US politics in ways that were never envisaged by the Framers. On the one hand, the struggles for civil rights by African-Americans and equal rights by women were articulated through demands for justice couched in the original terms of the Constitution. On the other hand, the second amendment guaranteeing the right to bear arms, which was designed to raise local militias in defence against foreign incursions during the early years of the new nation, has polarized American society on policies to control the proliferation of guns. In addition, the propensity for postwar periods of divided government in the United States[2] is a direct result of the model of separation of powers, which can produce elected branches of the government that represent competing political constituencies.

Europe also provides examples of constitutional continuity and constraint. The French Fifth Republic is a response to constitutional weaknesses of the Fourth Republic, as well as a reflection of the personal interests of Charles de Gaulle. The legacy of this constitutional moment is the creation of a strong quasi-presidential system, where the institutional arrangements provide for both a president and a prime minister. The president is elected through a popular vote, while the prime minister is the leader of the political party with a plurality of seats in the French General Assembly. These institutional arrangements have at times produced periods of "cohabitation" similar to divided government in the United States, where the president is of one political party, and the prime minister is from an opposition party. Germany's constitution, the Basic Law, contains many features designed to compensate for the weaknesses of the Weimar Republic and prevent the development of extremist political parties. The electoral system establishes a minimum threshold to exclude fringe parties from competing for seats in the Bundestag and Bundesrat, while the constitutional court has the power to ban extreme political groups and propaganda.

The experience in Latin America is no different. Like the United States, the first constitutions in Latin America were born of an era of struggle against the Iberian colonial authority of Spain and Portugal, as well as a product of the interests of liberal elites at the time. Independence leaders in Latin America were inspired by the liberal ideas of the American and French Revolutions. Both the ideas behind these revolutions and the institutions set up shortly thereafter served as important models for the new Latin states. Indeed, between 1811 and 1830, seventeen Latin American countries established republican constitutions that were inspired in large part by the US model founded in Philadelphia in 1787.

Like the US Constitution, these new constitutions established three branches of government, comprising the president, a bicameral legislature, and a judiciary, each with separate and shared powers. In addition, important French, Spanish, and Roman constitutional principles, legal doctrines, institutions, and practices had a strong influence on the governance of the new states. These influences include such institutions as "Councils of State, administrative courts, interior ministries, local and provincial administrative structures, and ministerial countersignatures to authenticate presidential decrees" (Hartlyn and Valenzuela 1994: 108). Thus, a combination of continental legal doctrine and North American constitutional design permeated the founding legal documents of the newly independent Latin American nation-states. Moreover, the basic governmental form of presidential institutional design has remained unchanged in Latin America since this period and is therefore unlikely to change in the future (see Jones 1995; Foweraker 1998a and chapter 6 this volume).[3]

The constitutional and historical record of the period immediately following independence reveals three striking features. First, these constitutions often established Catholicism as the official state religion, and even where the Church was formally and legally separated from the State, it maintained a significant role in determining social policy. In this sense, the new constitutions were not complete secular and "legal-rational" instruments (see chapter 1), but reflected in part the historical and cultural legacies of the colonial period that extended from 1492. Second, the new constitutions contained many exceptions to the protection of individual rights, which hollowed out any notion of a "liberal" and "democratic" constitution, making the resulting governments "regimes of exception" (Loveman 1993). Third, and probably most striking, is that across seventeen countries from the region in the nineteenth century there were a total of 105 constitutions, which means each country had numerous and different constitutions across a relatively short period of time (Loveman 1993; Hartlyn and Valenzuela 1994). Such frequent constitutional engineering is not limited to the late nineteenth century, as during the 1990s seventeen Latin American countries have undergone processes of constitutional reforms (van Cott 2000b: 11).

The abundance of constitutions during this period in part reflects a certain faith among political elites that the rule of law could serve as the basis for order and progress. This faith or belief in the doctrine of legal positivism suggests that the law provides a technical fix for the social, political, and economic ills that face any given country. Thus, political leaders who wished to mold or change the particular political reality with which they were confronted sought to do so through amendments to existing constitutions or through writing new constitutions (Hartlyn and Valenzuela 1994: 109). Subsequent constitutional developments in the region saw legal mechanisms put in place to legitimize authoritarian practices in the populist regimes of the 1930s and 1940s and, more recently, in the authoritarian regimes of the 1970s and 1980s.

For example, the *Estado Nôvo* (New State) in Brazil, established by President Getúlio Vargas, was founded on the Constitution of 1937. Vargas had come to power through a military coup in 1930 and sustained his rule through another coup in 1935, but increasingly sought legitimacy through constitutional means. In an effort to eliminate armed insurrection from the left and the right, he instituted the new 1937 Constitution that replaced the 1891 Constitution of the First Republic.[4] The 1937 Constitution greatly expanded the power of the federal executive over the state governments and thereby created a "truly national government" for Brazil; a process of centralization that the founders of the original 1891 Constitution sought to avoid (Skidmore 1988: 33–5). The new Constitution thus gave the federal executive increased capacity to oversee economic restructuring and a national plan of industrialization that had a profound impact on the country's development.

More recently, the authoritarian periods in Brazil (1964–85) and Chile (1973–90) demonstrate how constitutions provide the framework and legitimacy for military leaders that seize power from civilian elites. In both countries, the military intervened as protectors of the Constitution, ostensibly rescuing the system from the "extra-constitutional" behavior of Presidents João Goulart in Brazil and Salvador Allende in Chile. Shortly after the overthrow of democracy in both countries, the military juntas sought a legal basis for their rule. In Brazil, the military passed new Constitutions in 1967 and 1969, which gave increasing power to the executive, while maintaining a functioning two-party system housed in a national legislature (see chapter 7). Throughout the authoritarian period, the military used a series of Institutional Acts that empowered the government to repress civil society, impose governors on strategically important states, and manipulate the electorate. In Chile, Augusto Pinochet soon emerged as the President of the Republic, and consolidated his authority through a series of Constitutional Acts in 1976, decree laws, and a new Constitution in 1980. The 1980 Constitution, currently in place in democratic Chile, contained a series of "transitory articles" that allowed the government to repress civil society, control labor organizations, and ban political party activity (see Foweraker and Landman 1997: pp. 244–7).

These cases of populist and military authoritarian rule illustrate the ways in which the principle of constitutionalism has legitimized non-democratic forms of governance, while enforcing a particular system of law and order. The constitutional and legal terrain over which the military regimes tread often changed, providing possible routes of exit for authoritarian leaders. In the case of Brazil in 1985, the military established an electoral college and sought to control the choice of the first civilian president in 1985. Its preferred candidate was unsuccessful in securing enough electoral college votes thus leading to an opposition president overseeing the final phase of the democratic transition (Skidmore 1989: 30–1). During this final phase, the Brazilians opted to write a new Constitution in 1988. Perhaps the most comprehensive constitution ever written, it contains articles comprising not only the structures and functions of government, but protections for a broad range of political, civil, social, economic, cultural, and solidarity rights (see below, pp. 83–5, for a discussion of these rights). In Chile, Augusto Pinochet gambled and lost on a national plebiscite for continued military rule in 1988, and oversaw a rapid democratic transition. Unlike Brazil, however, the Chileans kept the 1980 Constitution, which ensures a disproportionate amount of political authority to forces on the right, and protects the interests of the military. Even though center and center-left coalitions have been victorious in the elections following the transition, the protections for the political right make it difficult to secure enough votes to amend the Constitution (see Siavelis 2000).

Like the cases of Brazil and Chile, processes of democratic transition in the region (see chapter 2) are often accompanied by a critical moment in which the country decides the terms of extraction from the military period and the substance of the new democratic constitutional order. In some cases, such as Peru in 1978 and Brazil in 1988, representatives of the dominant political groups and parties form a "constituent assembly" and draft a new constitution, which is then ratified through popular consent. In other cases, such as Argentina and Uruguay, constitutions from earlier periods are resurrected to serve as the basis for the new democratic era. In each instance, either the resurrected constitution or the newly drafted one provides the legal framework for the new democratic period. Yet, both forms of constitution tend to replicate the basic models of government established during earlier periods.

Even those countries that did not experience the military authoritarian regimes found in Brazil, Chile, Uruguay, Peru, and Ecuador have undergone some constitutional reform in an effort to reequilibrate the political system after long periods of constricted democratic governance. The democratic systems of Colombia and Venezuela were forged after long periods of domestic political violence, where new constitutions served to codify elite-negotiated settlements. In 1958, the National Front Pact in Colombia and the Pact of Punto Fijo in Venezuela established new systems for sharing power between two blocs of dominant elites: the Liberals and Conservatives in Colombia and the Democratic Action Party (AD) and the Committee for Political Organization and Independent Election (COPEI) in Venezuela. By the end of the 1980s, however, both countries experienced increased citizen dissatisfaction with these elite settlements and pressed for constitutional reform. Carried out in 1991, the reformed constitutions of Colombia and Venezuela expanded political contestation to a larger set of political party organizations and modified the political system to achieve a fairer representation of interests. The subsequent political crises in both countries, characterized by political unrest and economic instability, suggest that such institutional "fixes" may be too little too late. Despite such crises, similar reforms were carried out three years later in Bolivia in an attempt to extend real citizenship to its large indigenous population (van Cott 2000b: 1), and President Hugo Chávez oversaw another period of constitutional reform in Venezuela.

Finally, as argued in chapter 1, constitutions during the contemporary democratic period have also been amended to promote the personal political ambitions of individual leaders. In Argentina, former President Carlos Menem negotiated a deal with opposition leaders to amend the 1853 Constitution to enable him to compete for a second term of office. In Brazil, President Fernando Henrique Cardoso amended the 1988 Constitution to compete for a second term. In both cases, the amendments were ratified and both incumbents were successfully returned to office. The principle of nonreelection and term limitation extends deep into the political culture of Latin America. The original Constitutions sought to provide term limits so as to prevent personalistic regimes. Indeed, the Mexican system prides itself on the six-year term limit with no reelection, and the United States had to pass an amendment to its constitution to limit the presidential term after Franklin Roosevelt won an unprecedented fourth term to office. The Brazilian and Argentine examples highlight that even during democratic periods of governance, popular political leaders can mobilize the necessary support to change the basic legal framework of a country, and alter significantly future political events through such actions.[5]

The constitutional record of Latin America thus demonstrates the classic tension between the need for law and order and the principle of legitimate and democratic government. Rather than representing some exotic variant on the world history of constitutionalism, the region's experience mirrors much of the experience in other parts of the globe. Constitutions have justified democratic and non-democratic regimes alike; however, as the next part of the chapter will demonstrate, the world system now seeks to preclude such arbitrary uses of constitutionalism. The principles of constitutionalism, the rule of law, and democracy have gained new importance with the development of international, regional, and national human rights systems based on a universal understanding of individual and collective rights. It is to these systems and the ways in which Latin America fits into them that the discussion now turns.

Human rights and Latin American governance

The defeat of fascism in Europe ushered in a new period of international concern and awareness that a global system of legal guarantees and mechanisms had to be established to promote and protect individual and collective rights, as well as to ensure that the Holocaust would never be repeated. These desires found expression in the creation of the United Nations system and its key documents for the promotion and protection of human rights: the 1945 UN Charter and the 1948 Universal Declaration of Human Rights. These two founding documents were soon followed by a series of other more legally binding human rights instruments, most notably the International Covenant on Civil and Political Rights and the International Covenant on Economic, Social, and Cultural Rights, both of which were enacted in 1966.[6] Together, these instruments and those that followed them have created an international legal system for the promotion and protection of human rights, which comprise three sets, categories, or generations of human rights.

The first set of rights includes civil and political rights, which uphold the sanctity of the individual before the law and guarantee his or her ability to participate freely in the political system. Civil rights include such rights as the right to life, liberty, and personal security; the right to equality before the law; the right of protection from arbitrary arrest; the right to the due process of law; the right to a fair trial; and the right to religious freedom and worship. When protected, civil rights guarantee one's "personhood" and freedom from state-sanctioned interference or violence. Political rights include such rights as the right to speech and expression; the rights to assembly and association; and the right to vote and political participation. Political rights thus guarantee individual rights to involvement in public affairs and the affairs of state. In many ways, both historically and theoretically, civil and political rights are considered fundamental human rights which all nation-states have a duty and responsibility to uphold (see Davidson 1993: 39–45).

The second set of rights includes social, economic, and cultural rights. Social and economic rights include such rights as the right to a family; the right to education; the right to health and well-being; the right to work and fair remuneration; the right to leisure time; and the right to social security. When protected, these rights help promote individual development, social and economic development, and self-esteem. Cultural rights, on the other hand, include such rights as the right to the benefits of culture; the right to indigenous land, rituals, and shared cultural practices; and the right to speak one's own language and bilingual education. Cultural rights are meant to maintain and promote sub-national cultural affiliations and collective identities, and protect minority communities against the incursions of national assimilationist and nation-building projects. In contrast to the first set of rights, these social, economic, and cultural rights are often seen as aspirations and programatic rights that national governments ought to strive to achieve through progressive implementation. They are thus considered less fundamental than the first set of rights (Davidson 1993; Harris 1998: 9).

The third set of rights comprises what are usually called solidarity rights, which include rights to public goods such as development and the environment. This collection of rights seeks to guarantee that all individuals and groups have the right to share in the benefits of the earth's natural resources, as well as those goods and products that are made through processes of economic growth, expansion, and innovation. Many of these rights are transnational in that they make claims against rich nations to redistribute wealth to poor nations, cancel or reduce international debt obligations, reduce environmental degradation, and help promote policies of sustainable development. Of the three sets of rights, this final set is the newest and most progressive, and reflects a certain reaction against the worst effects of globalization, as well as the relative effectiveness of "green" political ideology and social mobilization around concerns for the health of the planet.

In light of these important developments, the world at the turn of the twenty-first century has an international legal system in place that seeks to promote and protect a very broad range of individual and collective rights. Within the context of this global system for the promotion and protection of human rights, a set of regional systems has also evolved in Europe, Africa, and Latin America. The European system is based on its own Convention (1950), has its own Court of Human Rights, and other institutions that promote and protect human rights in the member states of the European Union, as well as those members of the Council of Europe. The African system is based on the 1981 African Charter supported and enforced by the African Commission for Human Rights. The African Charter does not have provisions for a court of human rights and, of the two systems, the European system is more developed institutionally, while the African Charter is considered to be the most comprehensive since it aspires to promote and protect solidarity rights alongside political, civil, social, economic, and cultural rights (Davidson 1993: 19).

Like the European and African systems, the countries of Latin America along with the United States are part of the Inter-American System of Human Rights. Initially formed in 1948 with the ratification of the Charter of the Organization of American States (OAS), and expressed explicitly in the American Declaration of the Rights and Duties of Man (1948) and the American Convention on Human Rights (1969), the Inter-American System shares many of the same features of the global and other regional systems. Like the European system, it has both a Commission and Court for human rights; however, these institutions have different powers than their international or regional counterparts. The Inter-American Commission for Human Rights has the power to conduct *in loco* country reports on human rights violations as well as respond to individual petitions concerning human rights abuses. Over the years, the power to conduct the country reports has allowed the Commission to shame those countries in the region with the most egregious violations of human rights, while the capacity to accept individual petitions provides an institutional mechanism of legal redress for such violations. The Inter-American Court, on the other hand, is a judicial body that interprets the American Convention or any other treaties that are binding on member states (see Harris 1998). To date, the majority of the human rights work in the region tends to be carried out by the Commission, but there has been increasing pressure within the system to refer more cases to the Court.

The official documents that provide the foundation for the international and regional systems, whether they be conventions, instruments, covenants, or protocols, are generally known as treaties, which are agreements between one or two states that establish legally binding rules in a particular area (Davidson 1993: 53). In other words, states that sign and ratify such treaties are legally bound to uphold the obligations, rights, and duties contained within them, unless they declare certain reservations at the time of signature or apply for derogations from certain provisions during times of national emergency. To avoid nullifying the effectiveness of legal protection of human rights, the various systems have specified certain rights, such as freedom from torture, as non-derogable. More importantly for this chapter, however, is the fact that participation in such treaties means that the obligations contained within them must become part of the domestic legal system, a process that occurs automatically in countries with "monist" constitutions or through national legislation in countries with "dualist" constitutions. Some countries like Brazil have a mixed system for incorporation, while others such as Argentina are monist. This basic obligation of states is spelled out in Article 1 (1) of the American Convention of Human Rights:

> The states parties to this Convention undertake to respect the rights and freedoms recognised herein and to ensure to all persons subject to their jurisdiction the free and full exercise of those rights and freedoms, without any discrimination for reasons of race, color, sex, language, religion, political or other opinion, national or social origin, economic status, birth or any other social condition.

This rather long exegesis on the basis of the international and regional systems for the promotion and protection of human rights is necessary to demonstrate how by the turn of the twenty-first century, Latin American countries have become increasingly embedded within these systems and legally obliged to promote and protect human rights through their own constitutions and rule of law. Even though, as we have seen, past constitutions have delimited similar sets of rights, the evolution of the international and regional systems has added a further external legal dimension to the promotion and protection of human rights. Moreover, these various legal systems have empowered new social actors, such as social movements, non-governmental organizations (NGOs), and "transnational advocacy networks" (Keck and Sikkink 1998) to apply pressure on national governments to improve their record on human rights (see chapter 7).

Table 4.1   Status of selected international human rights instruments in Latin America, 1999

Country[a]	International instruments[b]								
	I	II	III	IV	V	VI	VII	VIII	Total[c]
Argentina	2	2	2	2	2	2	2	2	16
Bolivia	2	2	2	1	2	2	1	2	14
Brazil	2	2	2	2	2	2	2	2	16
Chile	2	2	2	2	2	2	2	2	16
Colombia	2	2	2	2	2	2	2	2	16
Costa Rica	2	2	2	2	2	2	2	2	16
Dom. Rep	2	2	2	1	2	2	1	2	14
Ecuador	2	2	2	2	2	2	2	2	16
El Salvador	2	2	2	2	2	2	2	2	16
Guatemala	2	2	2	2	2	2	2	2	16
Haiti	0	2	2	2	2	2	0	2	12
Honduras	2	2	0	2	2	2	2	2	14
Mexico	2	2	2	2	2	2	2	0	14
Nicaragua	2	2	2	2	2	2	1	2	15
Panama	2	2	2	2	2	2	2	2	16
Paraguay	2	2	0	1	2	2	2	2	13
Peru	2	2	2	2	2	2	2	2	16
Uruguay	2	2	2	2	2	2	2	2	16
Venezuela	2	2	2	2	2	2	2	0	14
United States	1	2	0	0	2	1	2	1	9
Total[d]	37	40	34	35	40	39	35	35	

[a] 0 = no signature; 1 = signature; 2 = signature and ratification.
[b] Key to human rights instruments: I = International Covenant on Economic, Social, and Cultural Rights (1966); II = International Covenant on Civil and Political Rights (1966); III = International Convention on the Elimination of all Forms of Racial Discrimination (1966); IV = International Convention on the Prevention and Punishment of the Crime of Genocide (1948); V = Convention on the Rights of the Child (1989); VI = Convention on the Elimination of All Forms of Discrimination against Women (1979); VII = Convention against Torture and other Cruel, Inhuman, or Degrading Treatment or Punishment (1984); VIII = Convention Relating to the Status of Refugees (1951).
[c] Maximum row total = 16.
[d] Maximum column total = 40.
Source: UNDP (1999) Human Development Report, pp. 242–5

Table 4.1 summarizes the comparative status of eight selected international human rights instruments in Latin America and the US. The table assigns a value of 0 to those countries that have not yet signed the instrument, 1 to those that have signed but not ratified, and 2 to those that have signed and ratified. A country signing and ratifying all eight instruments yields a row total of 16, while nineteen countries signing and ratifying yields a column total of 40. It is clear from the table that Haiti and Paraguay have signed and ratified the least number of instruments, and that the Convention on Racial Discrimination has the least number of state signatories, followed by the Convention on Torture, the Convention on Refugees, and the Covenant on Economic, Social and Cultural Rights. On balance, however, the table illustrates a remarkable participation of Latin American countries in the international system for the promotion and protection of human rights, while the US shows the lowest participation.

Table 4.2 summarizes the comparative status of Inter-American human rights instruments for a selected number of countries in the region. Again, the table assigns values to non-participation (0), signatures without ratification (1), and signatures with ratification (2). Since there are six relevant instruments in the Inter-American System, the maximum row total is now 12, while the maximum column total is 40. The table reveals that only Panama and Uruguay have signed and ratified all six instruments, while Haiti and Colombia have signed and ratified the least, followed by Bolivia, Chile, Honduras, and Mexico. Of the six instruments, the Protocol on the Death Penalty has been signed and ratified by the fewest countries, while the American Convention itself and the Convention on Torture has been signed by the most countries. Again, it is telling that the United States has only signed but not ratified the American Convention on Human Rights.

There is thus a significant gap between Latin America's participation in the International System for Human Rights and the Inter-American System for Human Rights. Interestingly, the Inter-American System provides for a series of powers that allow external visits and arbitration over internal matters of state, which are more likely to be used since fewer states are governed by the system. But the full development of the Inter-American System is still a recent phenomenon. Indeed, the Inter-American Court of Human Rights started to hear cases only in 1985. In addition to the gap of formal participation in the Inter-American System, the historical record of Latin America in the postwar period demonstrates patterns of systematic and gross violations of human rights well-documented by organizations such as America's Watch, Human Rights Watch, Amnesty International, the US State Department, and domestically based human rights NGOs. These violations include such practices as forced disappearances, execution, torture, political imprisonment, political exile, as well as restrictions on freedom of the press, expression, assembly, and association.

Table 4.2 Status of Inter-American human rights instruments, 1998

Country[a]	Inter-American instruments[b]						
	I	II	III	IV	V	VI	Total[c]
Argentina	2	1	0	2	2	1	8
Bolivia	2	1	0	1	1	2	7
Brazil	2	2	2	2	1	2	11
Chile	2	0	0	2	1	1	6
Colombia	2	0	0	1	1	0	4
Costa Rica	2	1	1	1	2	2	9
Dom. Rep	2	1	0	2	0	2	7
Ecuador	2	2	1	2	0	2	9
El Salvador	2	2	0	2	0	2	8
Guatemala	2	1	0	2	1	2	8
Haiti	2	1	0	1	0	0	4
Honduras	2	0	0	1	1	2	6
Mexico	2	2	0	2	0	1	7
Nicaragua	2	1	1	2	1	2	9
Panama	2	2	2	2	2	2	12
Paraguay	2	1	0	2	1	2	8
Peru	2	2	0	2	0	2	8
Uruguay	2	2	2	2	2	2	12
Venezuela	2	1	2	2	1	2	10
United States	1	0	0	0	0	0	1
Total[d]	39	23	11	33	17	31	

[a] 0 = no signature; 1 = signature; 2 = signature and ratification.
[b] Key to human rights instruments: I = American Convention on Human Rights (1969); II = Additional Protocol to the American Convention on Human Rights in the Area of Economic, Social, and Cultural Rights (1988); III = Protocol to the American Convention on Human Rights to Abolish the Death Penalty (1990); IV = Inter-American Convention to Prevent and Punish Torture (1985); V = Inter-American Convention on the Forced Disappearances of Persons (1994); VI = Inter-American Convention on the Prevention, Punishment and Eradication of Violence Against Women.
[c] Maximum row total = 12.
[d] Maximum column total = 39.
Source: Harris and Livingstone (1998), Appendix VIII, pp. 562–75

While these violations tend to occur during periods of authoritarian rule, the region has seen the persistence of urban and rural violence carried out by state and non-state actors against predominately subordinate and underprivileged groups throughout the recent periods of democratic transition and consolidation (Harris 1998; Méndez et al 1999; Payne 2000). Police forces in need of quick convictions and with latent public support may use illegal means of

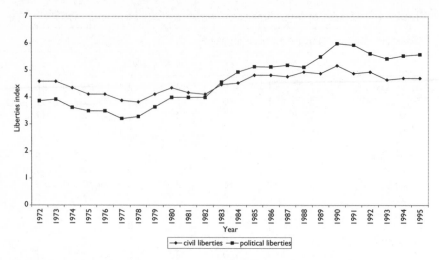

Figure 4.1   Political and civil liberties in Latin America
Source: Freedom House (www. freedomhouse. org); see also Landman (1999)

obtaining confessions from suspects, such as torture and other forms of coercion. Middle-class residents and entrepreneurs threatened by theft and burglaries may enlist the vigilante services of private security personnel. Countries with large sectors of their population of African descent, such as Brazil, have not yet begun to recognize patterns of racial discrimination. Moreover, while political rights have largely been protected during this period (apart from Cuba), social and economic rights such as income distribution, adequate housing, infrastructure, and educational facilities have not seen substantial improvement (see chapter 7). This difference between political and social and economic rights effectively constrains political participation of subordinate groups, as well as limiting their access to justice significantly (O'Donnell 1999b), and the most excluded group tends to be poor women (see chapter 7).

Figure 4.1 illustrates the growing disparity between the protection of political liberties on the one hand, and civil liberties on the other. The figure uses a popular measure of these liberties compiled by Freedom House, which ranges from 1 to 7, where a higher score means a greater protection of the two sets of liberties (see Freedom House 1990, 1997, 2002). The figure averages the liberty indices across seventeen Latin American countries and demonstrates that between 1982 and 1995 the protection of political liberties has increased dramatically, while the protection of civil liberties has lagged far behind, even decreasing towards the end of the period. The overall rise in the protection of political liberties reflects the increasing number of countries that underwent a process of democratic transition from 1980 onwards, including among others Peru (1980), Ecuador (1980), Argentina (1983), Uruguay (1984), Brazil (1985), and Chile (1990). During this period of democratic transition, constitutions and governments increasingly protected rights to assembly, speech, association, and participation, while the decline in the protection of civil liberties reflects the continued failure to protect rights to personal security and integrity.

Forms and practices

These observations suggest that there remains a significant gap between the constitutional forms and political practices in the region that may jeopardize the maintenance of democracy and the full protection of individual rights (Foweraker and Landman 1997: xvii). The presence of this gap has led some commentators to claim that there now is an "(un) rule of law in Latin America" (Méndez, O'Donnell, Pinheiro 1999), which can only be transcended through significant legal, judicial, and political reform. These persistent problems of violence, social exclusion, and discrimination require governments in Latin America to take several important steps. First, they need to strengthen historically weak judiciaries through proper training, recruitment, and appointment procedures. Second, they need to reform the police system through enhanced human rights training programs and increased levels of education. Third, serious reform of these political systems can only take place by lowering the socioeconomic barriers to entry through development strategies that begin to redistribute national resources and income, and raise basic standards of living. Finally, and perhaps most challenging of all, Latin American governments need to inculcate a new culture of rights that upholds the values and norms of constitutionalism, the rule of law, and democracy.

PART III
REPRESENTATION, POLITICAL, AND SOCIAL RIGHTS

5 | POLITICAL PARTIES

Alphabet soup

Political parties in Latin America have a long history, and in some cases can trace their roots to the struggles for independence at the beginning of the nineteenth century. This is simply to say that they have not emerged freshly minted from recent transitions to democracy in the continent. But in the new democratic era they have multiplied and changed, and they continue to change. The changes involve their leaderships, organizations, goals, platforms, styles, and not least their names. Consequently, it is no easy task to present a coherent account of the panorama of political parties across the twenty democratic republics of Latin America. On the one hand, the many changes do not necessarily occur all in the same direction, and so may not compose a clear pattern. On the other, the plethora of party labels and acronyms can soon lead to confusion, and leave us swimming in an alphabet soup (see table 5.1).

One way to respond to this challenge is to look beyond the intricate and varied world of party politics in particular republics towards the general characteristics of political parties across the continent. This itself is easier said than done. There may be no general agreement about such general characteristics, and the character of the political parties may not be fixed but in flux. For these reasons, this chapter presents seven "theses" or propositions about the nature and activity of political parties in Latin America, on the understanding that each thesis is open to debate, amendment – and even eventual refutation. The presentation of theses as a way of clarifying complex realities has a good pedigree in studies of Latin America

Table 5.1   Examples of political parties in the Americas

Name	Acronym	Country
American Popular Revolutionary Alliance	APRA	Peru
Christian Democrat Party	PDC	Chile
Concertation		Chile
Conservative party	PC	Colombia
Democratic Action	AD	Venezuela
Democratic party		United States
Institutional Revolutionary Party	PRI	Mexico
Liberal party	PL	Colombia
National Action Party	PAN	Mexico
National Democratic Union	UDN	Brazil
National Renovating Alliance	ARENA	Brazil
Nationalist Republican Alliance	ARENA	El Salvador
Nationalist Revolutionary Movement	MNR	Bolivia
Party of the Democratic Revolution	PRD	Mexico
Peronist party		Argentina
Radical Civic Union	UCR	Argentina
Radical party		Chile
Republican party		United States
Sandinista Front for National Liberation	FSLN	Nicaragua
Social Democratic Party	PSD	Brazil
Socialist party	PS	Chile
Workers' Party	PT	Brazil

These parties are used throughout chapter 5 and do not represent an exhaustive list.

(Stavenhagen 1968; Fuentes and Frank 1989; Foweraker 1998b), and should help us see the wood as well as some of the trees.

The seven theses can be simply stated. One, political parties in Latin America are not well rooted in the political soil of their societies. They are parties unattached to political publics. Two, they are patronage parties. They do not express the preferences of mass publics but serve as political vehicles for individual leaders or elite factions. Three, they are undisciplined. They are not bound together by ideology but stretched by particular and disparate interests. Four, they cannot now, if they ever could, be easily situated on a traditional left–right political spectrum. Not only do left and right mean different things in different republics, but the spectrum itself no longer serves to define party positions. Five, they are populist. Their fortunes rise and fall on a shifting sea of political promises rather than reflecting real political achievements. Six, they are short-lived. Either they rapidly appear and disappear, or they change their political color from one political moment to the next. Seven, they nonetheless make a positive contribution to the political stability of the new democratic era. In this sense, their democratic role adds up to much more than the sum of their political characteristics.

Political parties are not well rooted in their societies

In theory, political parties serve a dual purpose. They aggregate the interests, opinions, or preferences of political publics, and then translate them into government policy. They therefore play a key democratic role in allowing elected governments to respond to the wishes of the electorate. The degree of their responsiveness can be taken as an effective measure of the quality of democratic government (Huber and Powell 1994). In the context of the parliamentary democracies of Western Europe it has been shown that political party platforms – the promises that parties make to electorates before and during election campaigns – are in fact a sound guide to the policies they eventually pursue if elected to govern (Klingemann, Hofferbert, and Budge 1994). But if parties are not well rooted in their societies, if they have no effective political presence at the grassroots level, then they cannot easily fulfill this democratic role.

It is alleged that in Latin America the presence of well-rooted parties is the exception rather than the rule (Mainwaring and Scully 1995). In a few republics like Chile and Uruguay political publics both recognize and identify with political parties, and this is both consequence and cause of the continuity of these parties over the years, through political crises including military intervention and periods of authoritarian rule. But in the majority of countries like Peru, Ecuador, and Brazil, parties do not have a mass presence in this sense, and so can only achieve a very partial and tenuous representation of mass interests or preferences. Both party identity and party organization is unstable, and parties cannot easily mobilize political publics around political platforms or projects. The principal consequence is a combination of high rates of electoral abstention and high degrees of electoral volatility – with party fortunes fluctuating wildly from one election to the next (see chapter 6).

A long view of the traditional pattern of political party activity in Latin America seems to suggest that the allegation is overstated. Parties had a continuous and mass presence not only in Chile and Uruguay, but also in Mexico (the PRI or Institutional Revolutionary Party and PAN or National Action Party), Argentina (the Peronist and Radical parties), Colombia (the Liberal and Conservative parties), and Venezuela after 1958 (especially AD, the Democratic Action party). Brazil also enjoyed a relatively stable political party regime during the democratic years between the end of the Estado Nôvo in 1945 and the beginning of military rule in 1964. There have even been instances of the recent birth of mass parties that found firm social roots, such as the Sandinista party in Nicaragua. During the 1980s, the Sandinistas were successful in mobilizing Nicaraguan society against armed insurrection, while maintaining effective government and adhering to the electoral timetable (see chapter 1).

Yet the thesis may be closer to the current democratic reality of Latin America, where even the political parties that were traditionally well rooted are now becoming increasingly detached from their political publics. The closed elites and narrow political agendas of the traditional parties in Colombia have provoked, first, recurrent attempts to forge an electoral third force, and, latterly, popular insurrection and armed struggles. The elitist organization of the traditional parties in Venezuela, and the corporate management of the legislative assembly, led to widespread popular disenchantment and the "non-party" electoral insurgency of Hugo Chávez. The sclerosis of the upper echelons of the PRI in Mexico, and its refusal to recognize changing popular sentiment, led to a gradual but inexorable erosion of its electoral support and the election in 2000 of an opposition party president for the first time in over seventy years (see chapter 1).

New parties are not immune to these pressures. The Party of the Democratic Revolution (PRD) in Mexico was forged from the mobilization of social movements and unions at the end of the 1980s, but has become similarly bureaucratized and detached, with internal debates raging over the reasons for and solutions to its dilemma. Some older parties, on the other hand, have successfully bucked the trend, especially the so-called Concertation of the Christian Democratic and Socialists in Chile, which has pursued a coherent program of government with steady and widespread popular support. The most genuinely "rooted" of the newcomers is the Workers' Party (PT) in Brazil, which carefully nurtures its internal democracy and strives to maintain close contact and consultation with its grassroots (see chapter 2).

The failure or success of the political parties in retaining or achieving social roots is owing, at least in part, to their variable response to new interests, new movements, new constituencies, and new agenda (see chapter 8). Once in government, this capacity of response will closely affect the quality of the new democracies of Latin America. But responsiveness is not the only democratic virtue. Political party elites in Venezuela attempted to come to terms with public disenchantment with the hermetic politics of smoke-filled rooms, and sought a solution in new electoral rules. The result was the collapse of the traditional party system and a looming threat to the survival of Venezuelan democracy. In Bolivia, on the other hand, the electoral rules for choosing the president make the parties in the legislative assembly the final arbiters of the popular vote, so promoting a pattern of elite negotiation and horse-trading that makes the parties themselves much less responsive to their publics, but succeeds in stabilizing Bolivian democracy. Here we see a clear *trade-off* between the "rootedness" and responsiveness of the *parties* and the stability and resilience of the *party and democratic systems*. It follows that any assessment of party "rootedness" must remain sensitive to the broader constitutional and political contexts.

Political parties are patronage parties

Patronage parties are parties that dispense favors and other tangible resources, often in exchange for votes. They are therefore constructed piecemeal from complex networks of favor and exchange between "patrons" and their clients, and this form of political organization and activity is usually referred to as clientelism. Clientelism is present in greater or lesser degree in most political activity in most places, but is thought to be omnipresent and pervasive in Latin American politics, and in political party activity in particular (see chapter 3). The patrons are simply political bosses who expect loyalty from their clients in return for favors and protection. The clients, for their part, provide work, services, loyalty, and votes in order to survive, and possibly prosper. Political careers depend on advancement through patronage networks controlled by the bigger political bosses. In the Latin American vernacular these networks are known as *camarillas*.

This style of politics is not peculiar to Latin America. The strength of the Democrat vote in the Southern states of the United States was sustained over decades by strong clientelist networks, organized around electoral ward bosses who composed the registers and got out the vote. The political bossism and exchange of favors and protection so typical of clientelism characterized the Democrat dominance in Chicago during the time of the first Mayor Daley (1955–76). As these US comparisons illustrate, clientelism can flourish in conditions of electoral politics, and the return of many Latin American republics to electoral and democratic politics over the past two decades has revived and expanded the operation of clientelism, not diminished it.

Patronage parties may be constructed from networks of individual exchanges, but this does not mean that they cannot be mass parties. Examples of traditional clientelist parties with a mass presence are the Radical party in Chile in the 1940s and 1950s, which operated much like the Democratic party in Chicago in the same era, and the Institutional Revolutionary Party (PRI) in Mexico from the 1950s through the 1970s. The Peronist party in Argentina was also a mass party, but its clientelist networks were more institutionalized, and the political exchanges that maintained the party were organized along corporatist lines. Nor are patronage parties necessarily devoid of political beliefs and ideology, although these do not define their character. The Conservative and Liberal parties in Colombia have always been clientelist, but their partisans killed and maimed hundreds of thousands of Colombians during the "violence" of the early 1950s. But in the party politics of Latin America today, clientelism tends to be more diffuse, more neutral, more subtle, and more chameleon in style. It is not a form of organization so much as a *modus operandi*.

Whether with a mass presence or not, patronage parties are political vehicles for political bosses and elite factions. They therefore fit the mainstream accounts of democratic transition in Latin America as depending on the "short-term manoeuvring" and negotiation of elite actors (Levine 1988: 385). In this perspective the patronage parties are agile enough to take the decisions that establish the terms of the pacts and settlements that will found the new democratic regime (e.g. Higley and Gunther 1992; Hagopian 1990). Competitive electoral politics are central to the institutional arrangements that will underpin the pacts and set the boundary conditions for procedural consensus among the elite actors. But the pacts between party elites nonetheless tend to exclude any popular input, and popular participation continues to be controlled in greater or lesser degree by clientelist mechanisms. The pacts may therefore succeed in establishing democracy by "institutionalising uncertainty" (Przeworski 1986, 58–9), but only at the cost of excluding the *demos* (see chapter 3). This is one component of the trade-off between responsiveness and political stability.[1]

Yet the successful operation of clientelist politics, and clientelist controls in particular, always implies a measure of material distribution. Material favors have to be dispensed to retain loyalties, maintain networks, and win votes. In other words, clientelism operates as a form of restricted or "individualized" social welfare. But in recent years the accumulating effects of the debt crisis and debt repayment, combined with the fiscal constraints imposed by International Monetary Fund (IMF) stabilization packages, have radically reduced the state resources available for clientelist forms of material distribution (see chapter 3). Inevitably this has had a strong impact on the operational effectiveness of patronage parties, and will have contributed to further "detach" them from their social bases (see p. 98; Cavarozzi and Garretón 1989). Patronage parties across the continent have responded by developing targeted social spending programs designed, in part, to shore up their core vote. But where fiscal constraints are compounded by financial crisis the political effects can be dramatic. There is little doubt that the peso crisis of 1994 in Mexico rapidly eroded the legitimacy of the Institutional Revolutionary Party and contributed directly to terminate its uninterrupted seventy years in power in the presidential elections of 2000.

Political parties are undisciplined

The notion of an undisciplined party relates, first, to a lack of political coherence and purpose in party organization, and, second, to a lack of coordinated policy positions and voting behavior by party representatives in legislative assemblies. This lack of discipline, if it exists, is explained by an absence of the kind of ideology that acts as political cement, building a party and binding it to itself. Ideology in this context refers to a coherent set of ideas and values that can underpin party organization and ensure the loyalty of party members. In this way the party can develop consistent political objectives and achieve some continuity of interest and identity. In other words, ideology can ensure that the party acts as a party and not as a collection of diverse and disparate actors and interests.

Where ideology is absent, individual ambitions and factional interests tend to assert themselves, and party behavior in legislative assemblies tends to be driven by the direct relationships of favor and exchange between individual representatives and their constituencies. In these conditions "all politics is local politics," as Tip O'Neill, former Democratic speaker of the US House of Representatives once said, and local politics becomes the politics of the pork barrel. In other words, the alleged indiscipline of political parties in Latin America is an alleged predominance of pork over ideology. The consequences for the legislative process is that voting does not necessarily occur along party lines, and, more dramatically, that there are often high rates of defection by individual representatives from one party to another during the lifetime of an assembly. Some argue that this makes it more difficult for the executive to put through a coherent legislative program (e.g. Stepan and Skach 1994). Others argue the opposite, since the lack of discipline allows for logrolling and clientelistic alliances around particular legislative initiatives (e.g. Linz 1994).

It is alleged that pork barrel politics is prevalent in countries like Ecuador, Bolivia, Brazil, and Mexico. Indeed, as the Mexican legislature has emerged from executive dominance and control in recent years, so the incidence of such politics has increased. But it is easy to overdraw the distinction between pork barrel- and constituency-based politics, on the one hand, and a political party system characterized by clearly defined and ideologically based policy positions on the other. After all, in the United States the close relationship between legislators and constituency interests is notorious, yet the Republican and Democrat parties are easily identifiable on ideological grounds. Similarly in Brazil, pork barrel politics characterize the political careers of nearly all legislators, yet the great majority of assembly votes follow clear party lines (Figueiredo and Limongi 2000). Moreover, there are a number of parties in Latin America, including the Socialist and Christian Democrat parties in Chile, the Workers' Party in Brazil, the Sandinista party in Nicaragua, and possibly the Party of the Democratic Revolution in Mexico that do maintain an organizational discipline based on ideologically coherent policy positions.

In theory, it was argued above, political parties act to aggregate interests and preferences across a national territory. Insofar as they do so they can be said to represent the political public of that territory. Yet in Latin America the representative role is impaired as parties become increasingly detached from their publics. But votes still have to be won in elections, and these votes are often cast for the individual representative not the party program. Interests are therefore not aggregated nationally but differentiated across distinct sectors, regions, communities, and projects. In some degree this tendency reflects the fact of pork barrel politics. But in equal degree it reflects the real process of the multiplication, differentiation, and assertion of interests and identities within increasingly heterogeneous state territories (see chapter 8).[2] Stated as such, an increasing diversity of interests and identities within legislative assemblies may be no bad thing: from their origins parliaments were conceived as places where such diversity might be reconciled and composed through debate and deliberation. But the tendency also raises the question of the possible corruption of the representative and legislative process by disloyal or noxious interests that pursue their ends despite the claims of the republic or the common good. In Latin

America there are fears that the concentrated financial powers of the drug cartels are corrupting democratic politics in this way – although this is a problem not just for Latin America but for democracies everywhere.

Political parties cannot be placed on a left–right continuum

Since the time of the French Revolution, when delegates of the "third estate" began to define "where they stood by where they sat," it has been common practice to define political party positions along a left–right spectrum. This way of defining party positions has worked reasonably well in Latin America during most of its modern history. In the nineteenth century the spectrum was mainly composed of conservative parties on the right and liberal parties on the left. In the early decades of the twentieth century this picture was complicated, and the spectrum stretched, by communist and socialist parties on the left and fascist or "integralist" parties on the right. Political party positions became further differentiated as industrialization and especially urbanization created new political publics with greater political awareness. Some parties, like the Radical party in Chile, sought to occupy the "center" ground by emphasizing patronage not policy.

The spectrum continued to define party positions following the Second World War, at least in some countries of the continent like Chile, Argentina, Brazil (in some degree), and Venezuela. But it could not be so easily applied either to Mexico, where the dominant Institutional Revolutionary Party occupied a massive center, or Colombia, where party differences had become purely traditional. There were also successful patronage parties like the Social Democratic Party (PSD) in Brazil that included both left and right in its sprawling organization, and self-consciously centrist parties like the Christian Democrat Party (PDC) in Chile. Yet, whereas in the Western Europe of the time left and right had a common content, the meaning of left and right in Latin America had begun to vary across countries. In Europe it was generally a question of social democracy, state intervention, and equality of outcomes (on the left) versus traditional values, market outcomes, and equality of opportunity (on the right). In Latin America the "left" clearly meant different things for the Peronist party in Argentina, the American Revolutionary Popular Alliance (APRA) in Peru, and the Socialist party in Chile – and the "right" was also differentiated according to national context.

Contemporarily it is suggested that the spectrum is no longer effective in locating political party positions. In one respect this is just a particular application of a larger thesis about the "end of ideology" (Bell 1960) and later, the "end of history" (Fukuyama 1992). According to this thesis, ideology has ended because market capitalism and liberal values are everywhere triumphant. On a more objective view, one particular ideology is now predominant, and political party positions must all cluster in the policy space constructed by neoliberal philosophy and policy prescriptions. In other words, the spectrum has not dissolved but it has contracted, and it has contracted much more from the left than from the right. At a global level the contraction occurred, as Fukuyama suggested, because of the demise of the Soviet empire and the collapse of "really existing socialism." Within Latin America the pressures on the left increased because of the elite pacts underpinning democratic transitions that remained closely conditional on the protection of private property and the permanent exclusion of political projects seeking economic redistribution and social justice. The political "solutions" promoted by the left were no longer either permissible or relevant (Castañeda 1994).

There is little doubt that the left of the political spectrum in Latin America has been squeezed. The parties of the right, in contrast, have only had to move a small way towards the center, as well as modifying both language and style. So openly authoritarian parties like the Nationalist Republican Alliance (ARENA) in El Salvador or the National Democratic Union (UDN) in Brazil have adopted a language of party competition, individual rights, and democratic solutions, while rejecting radical changes in their political platforms. The result is a narrower ideological spectrum with a political center of gravity that has moved to the right. In Chile, the "concertation" of Christian Democrat and Socialist parties sits squarely in the center, not on the center-left. In Argentina, the Peronist party moved dramatically from the left to right of the spectrum in the early 1990s. In Mexico the long-awaited democratic transition of 2000 took place towards the right not the left. Indeed, since the election to the Peruvian presidency of the APRA candidate Alán García in 1985, there has been no government elected in Latin America on a political platform at odds with the prevailing neoliberalism of the "Washington Consensus" (see chapter 1 and chapter 3).

There are parties that are exceptions to the rule and sit outside the confines of neoliberal policy prescriptions. But, since their political agendas are defined in opposition to these prescriptions, they make strange bedfellows. On the one hand, there is the Workers' Party (PT) in Brazil and the Party of the Democratic Revolution (PRD) in

Mexico. On the other is the "patriotic pole" of Hugo Chávez in Venezuela. It may also be conjectured that the squeezing of the left has left many sectors, groups, and constituencies without political representation, and this may explain in part the rise of armed opposition movements in Peru and Colombia. At the same time, party positions may still be differentiated according to distinct policies towards the distribution of costs and benefits of closer integration into the global economy. In other words, the question of social democracy has not disappeared, and cannot disappear, entirely – although it is now couched in terms of the kind of "good governance" (World Bank 1992) that seeks poverty alleviation rather than a broader social justice.

Political parties are populist

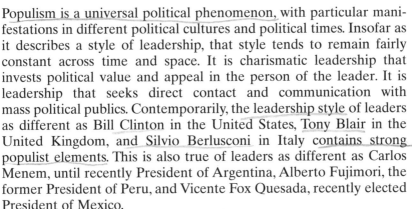

Populism is a universal political phenomenon, with particular manifestations in different political cultures and political times. Insofar as it describes a style of leadership, that style tends to remain fairly constant across time and space. It is charismatic leadership that invests political value and appeal in the person of the leader. It is leadership that seeks direct contact and communication with mass political publics. Contemporarily, the leadership style of leaders as different as Bill Clinton in the United States, Tony Blair in the United Kingdom, and Silvio Berlusconi in Italy contains strong populist elements. This is also true of leaders as different as Carlos Menem, until recently President of Argentina, Alberto Fujimori, the former President of Peru, and Vicente Fox Quesada, recently elected President of Mexico.

Yet populism in Latin America has involved much more than a style of leadership. Since populism appeals to the "people," populist leadership strategies have tended to promote national development, social welfare, and fiscal redistribution. During the early decades of the twentieth century, populism in Latin America grew in tandem with the creation of mass publics in the major cities of the region as a result of immigration, industrialization and rural–urban migration. Populist leaders both responded to and nurtured this new public through policies of import-substituting industrialization and social welfare (see chapter 1). It was an era of mass politics, with leaders who could make direct appeals to the people through mass media in newspapers and especially radio.

The broad appeal of populism in this first era of mass politics depended on a popular perception of real social benefits and material redistribution. But the benefits themselves were delivered through traditional clientelistic mechanisms that secured political support for the populist leaders. These traditional forms of patronage were extended and transformed, with benefits often channelled through major labor corporations. Organized labor became the preferred institutional context for clientelist exchange and control. Although the appeal of populism was broad and general by its very nature, its real benefits were delivered to particular publics organized in specific ways.

not true of neo-pop.

Populism in Latin America today also seeks to appeal to a mass public, although the appeals are now mainly made on the television not the radio. But the fiscal constraints that have followed the debt crisis and externally imposed stabilization packages in the 1980s have further restricted the delivery of real benefits. Populist appeals have therefore to be couched in the language of the "Washington Consensus" and stated as promises of economic dynamism through market mechanisms, and of the creation of economic and social opportunities. Traditionally, populist leaders strove to portray themselves as "fathers of the poor" or protectors of the unprotected. Today, they invoke criteria of technical efficiency and cost-effectiveness, and promise better targeted poverty alleviation programs.

I disagree

In this regard, it can be argued that it is not the political parties that are populist, but the political leaders. Indeed, in Latin America today populist leaders often appear and prosper almost without party organization or support. In the electoral context they are "outsider" candidates who seek to break the mold of the political party system (Mainwaring and Scully 1995). This is true of Fernando Collor de Mello in Brazil, Alberto Fujimori in Peru, and Hugo Chávez in Venezuela. The political messages they send – the nature of their appeal – are different one from the other. Collor de Mello promised to run Brazilian government with the same efficiency as private business. Fujimori promised both administrative efficiency and social peace. Chávez promised to eliminate the corruption associated with the old political elites of the traditional party system. But, in these cases at least, the appeals all have a pronounced authoritarian streak. Whatever the message, it tends to imply more law and order and the firm smack of government.

Other populist leaders emerge within established parties, but maintain a distant relationship with the party, especially insofar as they seek to use the party organization as a vehicle for their personal ambitions. Thus, Carlos Menem was elected on a Peronist party platform, but immediately set out to impose an entirely different – and in most ways "anti-Peronist" – set of policies that emphasized market disciplines not social benefits. Vicente Fox was elected leader of the National Action Party (PAN) in Mexico, but chose to mobilize a personal network of support through the "friends of Fox" when campaigning for the presidency of the country. Neither Menem nor Fox felt bound by the limits of party platforms, but sought to craft policy in a pragmatic manner, constrained only by market criteria. Both leaders chose ideologically diverse cabinets that ignored the traditional location of their parties on the left–right spectrum.

Thus, populism in Latin America today has an ambiguous relationship with political parties. The role of parties – in theory once again – is to aggregate the *political* interests and preferences of the public. Populism, in contrast, appeals to the generic values and aspirations of market consumerism. Vicente Fox promised "*bocho, changarro y tele*" (a car, a small business and a TV) for everyone. Collor, Chávez, and Menem all made similar promises. They are not promising social welfare or an increased social wage (clinics, schools, and subsidized urban transport). They are promising a certain consumer lifestyle that is intimately familiar to their publics through television advertising and television soap operas. The promise is that the excluded will now be included not through education or housing or health, but through their new identity as consumers. This new consumer populism is even evident among the "indianist" or *cholo* parties of Bolivia and Ecuador.

Political parties are short-lived

The image of evanescent political parties corresponds in large part to particular processes of democratic transition that have spawned numerous political parties in the initial stage of open political competition, only to see the great majority disappear within a few months or a year. In Spain over thirty parties emerged following the death of Franco, while in Poland over 150 parties set out to contest the first democratic elections at the end of the 1980s. The majority of these parties were nothing more than the clienteles of political "notables," or the political expression of rather narrow regional or sectoral interests. The rigors of electoral competition rapidly reduced their numbers until something like a stable political party system was achieved.

At first glance the political party picture in Latin America is different. The great majority of the democratic transitions of recent decades did not achieve democracy for the first time, and political party organizations and traditions had often been forged during previous democratic experiences. Moreover, in several countries political parties had developed tradition and stability by early in the twentieth century (Colombia, Uruguay, Chile, Costa Rica), or by its mid-point (Argentina, Mexico). Consequently, the democratic transitions in Colombia in the 1950s and in Argentina, Uruguay, and Chile in the 1980s saw the reemergence of well-known political parties. But, although the political landscape was easily recognizable, the rules might have changed. The main parties agreed to share power in Colombia. The Peronist party was no longer subject to an informal military veto in Argentina. The Pinochet constitution favored the parties of the right in Chile. In Mexico, in contrast, it was the changes in the electoral rules to achieve a free and fair competition after decades of electoral fraud that enabled the democratic transition of 2000 to take place.

However, there are as many countries where the political party regime had not been well established, and in these cases there is often a rapid turnover of parties at the time of democratic transition, or afterwards. In Brazil, the military government of 1964–85 dismantled the political party system and set up a new one. Elections were maintained under rules imposed by the military. The new parties underwent rapid changes once liberalization began in the late 1970s, and these changes continued throughout the democratic transition of the 1980s. Elsewhere well-established parties like APRA in Peru and the Nationalist Revolutionary Movement (MNR) in Bolivia reemerged intact and sometimes with increased electoral strength, but the presence of new parties changed the dynamics of electoral competition. In Central America new parties were born of the armed opposition to military and oligarchic regimes in Nicaragua and El Salvador, and came to play a key part in constructing new party systems. In Venezuela, in contrast, the successful political party system of the post-1958 period declined and finally collapsed in the 1990s.

Thus the picture in Latin America is a highly variegated one, including cases of stable party systems, of party systems that take a long time to settle (Brazil), and of party competition without any sense of settled party system (Ecuador). The failure to achieve a relatively stable party system is sometimes associated with the arrival and success of "outsider" candidates in presidential elections (see above, p. 106), usually with unwelcome consequences. Such a combination of circumstances led to the impeachment of Collor de Mello in Brazil, the suppression of democracy by *autogolpe* in Peru, the impeachment of the president and severe social unrest in Venezuela, and mass social protest and the forced resignation of the president in Ecuador. The stability of the political party system is clearly important to the stability of the democratic system overall.

Political parties contribute to political stability

In the light of what has gone before, it may seem odd to assert that political parties contribute to political stability. It may be more accurate to assert that it is a stable or "institutionalized" party *system* that contributes to political stability (Mainwaring and Scully 1995). But this assertion is tautological, by a narrow definition of political stability, simply recognizing that some countries have stable party systems while others do not. Thus, Bolivia's political parties are elitist, clientelist, undisciplined, and detached from the political public, but the party system is stable; and the constitutional inducements to coalition-making provides a firm legislative platform for pushing through difficult policies like economic stabilization packages. In contrast, the breakdown of the established party systems in Peru in the early 1990s, and Venezuela during the same decade, led to pronounced political instability.

But there are general senses in which political parties contribute to the political stability of Latin America's new democracies. First and foremost, they are the main means of political competition in the electoral arena where the composition of government is decided "by a universalistic process of fairly counting each vote as one" (O'Donnell 1997: 49). Recurrent elections conducted in a relatively free and fair fashion are the principal measure of democratic viability in democracies where the rule of law is otherwise patchy and ineffective (see chapter 4). The electoral arena remains "ring-fenced" from the imperfections in the rule of law, not least because of the kind of horizontal accountability achieved through political party competition. At the same time, the parties are the principal vehicles for political participation, even if they fail to reflect the full diversity of interest and opinion in the political public at large.

In this regard, political party competition in the electoral arena is a signal that the citizens of Latin America's democracies may enjoy the basic political rights of freedom of opinion, movement, and association – even if their civil rights of personal integrity and equality before the law are infringed or ignored (see chapter 2 and chapter 7). This also contributes to political stability insofar as it usually proves sufficient to garner international legitimacy, and the kind of international aid and loan arrangements that today depend on recognized criteria of "good governance." Membership of the democratic club brings privileges and serves to assuage sanctions, and governments can only claim membership so long as elections proceed regularly and without let or hindrance. It is then less important that the military may enjoy "reserve domains of power" (see chapter 2), the police may be unaccountable for its actions, and oligarchies may oppress the poor with impunity.

Political parties have also contributed to political stability by forging the political pacts that have underpinned the social peace following periods of civil war or guerrilla insurgency in countries like El Salvador, Guatemala, and Mexico. Right-wing parties in particular have often played a salient role in negotiating either social peace or democratic transition (or both), and have changed (ARENA in El Salvador) or disappeared (ARENA in Brazil) as a consequence. Yet the elitist nature of many political parties and most democratic transitions may leave substantial publics disenfranchised, so inviting a return to uncivil movements or even armed insurgencies like those that have multiplied in Colombia.

The average lifespan of a Latin American democracy following the democratic transitions of recent decades is now about fifteen years. On balance, political parties have played a positive role in achieving the degree of political stability that is measured by this lifespan. It may be objected that political parties compete in a rather limited, or "electoral," democracy that lacks the civil liberties and protections characteristic of liberal democracy (see chapter 2 and Diamond 1999), that they contribute to legitimate a rather unrepresentative form of representative democracy, and that they are sometimes overshadowed by media-smart populist leaders. But they have proved resilient and representative enough to maintain the rhythm of competitive party politics across the continent, and have thus defended the key institutional attributes of democratic government. So far, with only one or two exceptions, they have succeeded in keeping both military interventions and radical anti-democratic populists at bay.

6 | PRESIDENTS, LEGISLATURES, AND ELECTIONS

Government and governability

As noted in chapter 2, the general elections in Chile and Brazil in 1989 marked "the first time that all the Ibero-American nations, excepting Cuba, enjoyed the benefits of elected constitutional governments at the same time" (Valenzuela 1993: 3).[1] This achievement was not as dramatic or visible as the collapse of Communism and the transitions to democracy in Eastern and Central Europe, which began in the same year, but it did mark an historical watershed. As discussed in chapter 2, after almost two centuries as independent states, the countries of Latin America had now joined the democratic universe.

Yet Latin America's presence in this universe is marked and constrained by strong institutional traditions that are rooted in its history and culture (described in chapter 1). Specifically, the strength of the presidential tradition means that Latin American democracy is presidential, and will almost certainly remain so. In contrast to Eastern Europe, where the democratic transitions were "about institutions," leading to a search for the most effective form of government, the transitions in Latin America took place "through institutions," with little or no institutional innovation (Mainwaring 1990: 171). This may mean that the authoritarian legacy remains important, as in Chile, or that the rules and procedures of a prior democratic period are revived (Geddes 1996: 30).

Not everyone believes that this presidential tradition is a good thing. Some have even argued that a parliamentary system would be far preferable (e.g. Linz 1994). But it remains true that "no existing presidential system has ever changed to a parliamentary system" (Shugart and Carey 1992: 3), and attempts to change to a parliamentary form of government in Argentina, Bolivia, and Brazil – following their transitions to democracy – were all comprehensively rejected by their electorates. But the fact that all Latin American governments are presidential does not mean that they all have equal success (or lack of success) in governing. On the contrary, they vary considerably in their degrees of political stability and legislative capacity. In particular, some are much better at avoiding "gridlock" – the institutional impasse between executive and legislature – than others. In other words, the same institutional type of *government* can encompass a wide variation in degrees of *governability*.

Presidentialism and governability in Latin America

In the broad compass of democratic political systems, the countries of Latin America comprise a distinctive category, defined by a combination of presidentialism and legislative assemblies elected on the basis of proportional representation (Lijphart 1993: 150).[2] The continent mainly conforms to a model of pure presidentialism, where the chief executive is popularly elected and holds a separate mandate from representatives in the legislature. The terms of both executive and legislature are fixed and do not depend on mutual confidence. In other words, each branch has democratic authority, and the legislature can only remove the executive through the process of impeachment, in contrast to parliamentary systems, where the prime minister can be removed after a vote of no confidence. The government, or cabinet, is named and directed by the executive, and the president enjoys at least some constitutionally granted law-making authority.[3] But its combination with proportional representation (PR) is alleged to create fundamental problems of political instability and poor economic performance. The conclusion is that "the Latin American model remains a particularly unattractive option" (Lijphart 1993: 151).

The fact that all presidential systems embody two separate elected authorities means that they contain the potential for legislative stalemate (gridlock) and political instability. Since the legislative assembly is elected by proportional representation, the executive is unlikely to have a working majority in the assembly. The result may produce the "double minority" (Valenzuela 1993: 7) of a president elected by plurality who has no majority support in the assembly. In these circumstances the assembly can always block executive initiatives, even if it cannot directly control the president, while the president remains incapable of forcing a majority in the assembly through threat of dissolution of the assembly as in parliamentary systems (Mainwaring 1993).

In Latin America, presidents tend to be seen as strong, while legislatures are seen as weak and subservient, with the oft-cited exceptions of Chile, Costa Rica, and Uruguay. The main dangers to democracy are said to derive from the legislative and emergency powers of the president, or from the tendency of the legislature to delegate powers to the presidency in order to overcome gridlock. It is true that presidents have extensive formal powers.[4] But this should not imply that assemblies are weak in consequence, still less that they willingly delegate their power to the executive. On the contrary, the evidence shows that assemblies are powerful bodies with a proven ability to check the executive in countries as different as Brazil, Ecuador, Uruguay, and Venezuela. The real problem is that the executive often has great difficulty in pursuing its legislative agenda, since it lacks the means to lever a recalcitrant assembly.

This executive incapacity can tempt presidents to seek new powers through constitutional reforms (e.g. Hugo Chávez in Venezuela) – or to rule largely by issuing decrees. In this way gridlock can lead to *decretismo* (rule by decree), and eventually to the phenomenon of "delegative democracy" (O'Donnell 1992) that describes rule by a president who ignores the "checks and balances" of the democratic system, and exercises power as if it were directly delegated by popular mandate (see chapter 1).[5] Alternatively executive–legislative stalemate can lead to military *golpes* (Brazil 1964, Peru 1968, Chile 1973) or *autogolpes*[6] (Uruguay 1973, Peru 1992, and the attempt in Guatemala 1993), and the breakdown of democracy (see Stepan and Skach 1994; Cohen 1994).

Explaining variations in governability in Latin America

Even if all the presidential systems of Latin America suffer problems of governability, it is apparent that some suffer more than others. Moreover, with an average post-transition democratic longevity of some fifteen years, it is clear that these systems are proving more stable and resilient than the "theory" predicts. What explains this difference between theory and practice, or this variation in governability across similar presidential systems? The variation in governability is best explained by focusing on five main factors, namely: (1) the size of the presidential party support in the legislative assembly; (2) the number of effective parties in the party system; (3) the electoral rules (especially for the election of the executive); (4) the process of legislative coalition-formation; and (5) the degree of ideological polarization in the legislature. This chapter shows that these five factors are separate but closely interrelated, and that, together, they contribute to explain why the democratic governments of Latin America are proving "more stable than expected."

Presidential party support in the legislative assembly

It is self-evident that the larger the presidential party support in the legislative assembly, the less likely it is that the system will experience legislative gridlock. This is the key variable, with most observers agreeing that effective presidential government requires a working majority in the assembly, or, at the very least, a large congressional delegation from the president's party (Mainwaring and Scully 1995, 33).[7] It is a fact that the few long-lived presidential democracies (Colombia, Costa Rica, United States, Venezuela, and Uruguay prior to 1973) have provided their presidents with majorities or near-majorities, with the average share of assembly seats controlled by the presidential party in the lower or only chamber of the legislature as follows: Colombia 1974–86: 52.2 percent; Costa Rica 1974–86: 50.9 percent; United States 1968–86: 45.8 percent; Venezuela 1973–88: 49.9 percent; and Uruguay 1942–73: 49.3 percent. The exception was Chile 1946–73 with 30.2 percent, which constitutes the only historical case of a presidential democracy surviving for over a generation without such a majority.[8]

Presidential success in maintaining party support in the assembly will depend in large degree on party discipline. It is argued that individual deputies are potentially less loyal than parliamentary regimes, since there is no direct incentive of forming or defending a government. Indeed, there may be a hemorrhage of support with impending elections, as deputies seek to bolster their chances of reelection. But even without "natural" incentives, party discipline may be fostered by electoral laws, such as closed and "blocked" lists which give the parties greater control over their candidates. Such discipline is considered to be relatively strong in Argentina, Chile, and Venezuela, and relatively weak in Ecuador and Brazil. There is relatively little evidence to support the view that party discipline may actually accentuate gridlock where the executive has to construct a working majority through coalitions (Linz 1994: 35), although it is plausible that in some circumstances governability may be enhanced by the "pork", logrolling, and local clientelistic alliances associated with weak, undisciplined, and catch-all parties (see chapter 5).

The number of effective parties in the party system

The strength of presidential party support in the assembly is directly related to the number of parties in the party system,[9] with the likelihood of a "presidential" majority or near-majority diminishing as the number of political parties increases. For this reason political scientists have argued that "the combination of presidentialism and a fractionalised multiparty system" is "especially inimical to stable democracy" (Mainwaring 1990: 168). In effect, no stable democracy is currently multiparty presidential, and Chile 1933–73, once again, is the only historical exception. In this view it is only two-party systems that have a fair chance of providing the required degree of presidential support (Mainwaring 1993), since interparty coalition-building is assumed to be so difficult. But there are salient exceptions that place this assumption in doubt. In Bolivia, since the executive is ultimately elected by congress from the frontrunners in the popular vote, the (prospective) president must seek to compromise with political competitors and build viable coalitions from the outset. In Chile, a multiparty left-center coalition divided up the cabinet and maintained discipline in the assembly, partly as a legacy of the anti-Pinochet coalition, and partly out of fear of an authoritarian reversal.

Nonetheless, a recent inquiry into the relationship between party systems and presidential support in the assemblies of sixteen contemporary democratic systems in Latin America demonstrates a close association between low levels of multipartism and presidential majorities or near majorities (Foweraker 1998a). In contrast, the presidential party presence is especially low in the four cases where the effective number of parties rises above 3.5, namely Bolivia, Brazil, Ecuador, and Guatemala. A quite different approach to party systems by Mainwaring and Scully (1995) divides them into institutionalized and non-institutionalized or "inchoate" systems, but reaches remarkably similar results. Consistently institutionalized are Chile, Colombia, Costa Rica, Uruguay, Venezuela, and, to a lesser degree, Argentina. Consistently inchoate are Bolivia, Brazil, Ecuador, and Peru. The consistency in the two sets of results suggests that it is the institutionalization of the party system that increases the likelihood of effective presidential support in the assembly.

It is not just the number of effective parties that is important to governability, therefore, but also their character. Party organization was weak in Bolivia, Brazil, and Ecuador during the 1980s, while party organization and identification declined dramatically in Peru over the same decade. The personalization of parties, often associated with high rates of party "switching," meant that the executive could not even count on its own party for support, leading to the usual symptoms of stalemate and *decretismo*. Peru and Ecuador continued to suffer these symptoms in subsequent years, while the party systems of Bolivia and Brazil began to stabilize. The character of the highly factional but nonetheless disciplined parties of Colombia and Uruguay is distinctive, with party factions presenting their own electoral lists according to established conventions.

Electoral rules for executive elections

Just as multipartism affects the degree of presidential support in the legislative assembly, so electoral rules influence the number of parties in the system. In this way multipartism tends to act as an *intervening variable* between electoral laws and governability, since the electoral rules have an impact on the number of parties, and the number of parties, in turn, has an impact on governability (Jones 1995, ch. 1). In parliamentary systems it is the choice between plurality (or first past the post as in the United Kingdom) and PR systems, as well as the type of PR and the "effective magnitude" of the constituencies that have most impact on the composition of the assembly (Lijphart 1994). On the one hand, plurality systems usually generate two dominant political parties, such as the Conservative and Labour parties in the United Kingdom, while PR systems tend to generate more than two dominant political parties as in the German and French systems. On the other hand, larger constituencies, with the possibility of multiple representatives, increase the electoral opportunities for smaller political parties and therefore may fill the legislative assembly with more parties.

In contrast, the rules governing the election of the *executive* in presidential systems most influence the degree of presidential support in the assembly. This influence occurs both directly (in concurrent elections only) and indirectly (through their impact on multipartism). In particular, it is executive election by plurality and concurrent elections for executive and assembly that promote presidential majorities or near-majorities. Election by majority run-off, or *ballotage* in the French usage, leads to higher levels of multipartism and decreased linkage between executive and legislative elections in concurrent systems, while non-concurrent elections have the same dual effect, in both instances leading to a reduced presidential support in the assembly. In other words, presidents that are elected through a "first past the post" system at the same time as the members of the legislative assembly have a greater chance of achieving majority support in the legislative assembly, thereby reducing problems of governability.

It is interesting to note that all the countries identified as having high degrees of multipartism and low degrees of presidential support also elect their executives by majority runoff, including Bolivia, Brazil, Ecuador, Peru, and Guatemala.[10] Brazil and Ecuador also run non-concurrent elections, while the "open" party lists operating in both Brazil and Peru tend to encourage party indiscipline. Taking these additional effects into account, it is safe to conclude that the democratic systems of Latin America can be divided between those which run plurality-concurrent executive elections, have low levels of multipartism, and habitually generate presidential majorities or near-majorities in their assemblies, and those which do not.

Legislative coalition-formation

The problem with this conclusion is that it ignores the prevalence of coalition-formation and coalition government – as do most of the political science studies on governability in Latin America. Yet, even on a restrictive definition that requires both party participation in the cabinet and party cooperation in the assembly, coalition governments have recurred in Bolivia, Brazil, Chile, Ecuador, and Peru, and even in the mainly two-party systems of Colombia and Uruguay. The only cases of uniformly single-party government have been Argentina, Costa Rica, and Venezuela (after 1968). Contrary to the evidence, most commentary tends to refer to coalition-formation as exceptional and confined to cases of extreme party fractionalization, or difficult and beset by party indiscipline and factionalism. In part this may be a consequence of focusing exclusively on *pre-electoral* coalitions (Mainwaring and Shugart 1997: 400) rather than looking more broadly at all *governing* coalitions.

Recent evidence suggests that well over a half of all governments in Latin America are coalition governments, while some two-thirds of all majority governments secure their majority through coalition-formation (Dehesa 1997). Moreover, there are as many post-electoral coalitions as pre-electoral coalitions, with one-third of all presidents lacking an initial majority forming coalitions to overcome their minority status. The real conditions of governability in Latin America would therefore appear to depend closely on coalition-formation. But if these coalitions are fragile, as is often asserted for presidential systems (Lijphart 1984), they can be prevalent without being significant. In Latin America this assertion turns, once again, on the question of party indiscipline, and the doubtful loyalty of individual deputies. If such indiscipline makes coalitions ineffective then they cannot work to repair the imperfections of multiparty presidentialism, and the usual strictures on governability still apply.

However, here as elsewhere, the dangers of party indiscipline can be overstated, since discipline can be applied not only through control of candidate selection and the list system but also through assembly rules and procedures, and, in particular, by party leaders' control over key procedural resources. Take the case of Brazil that is sometimes seen as the best example of a fragmented party system with highly undisciplined parties that create coalitional fragility and cabinet instability – making it almost impossible to pursue an effective legislative agenda. In fact, the evidence reveals a high degree of party discipline and legislative predictability achieved by party leaderships in the assembly's College of Leaders (Limongi and Figueiredo 1995), and the formation of firm and stable coalitions that are bound by ideology. Indeed, the presence of the coalitions tends to reinforce internal party cohesion and legislative discipline, and the rate of executive–legislative success is similar to that found in parliamentary regimes.

Attempts have been made to explain why these presidential systems work better than the traditional emphasis on fragmented party systems and party indiscipline can possibly predict by recourse to the presidential powers of legislation, decree and veto (Mainwaring and Shugart 1997, ch. 1). But the balance of evidence suggests that presidential powers are less important that the prevalence of coalition-formation (pre- and post-electoral) in mitigating gridlock. Thus, it seems the case that governability is enhanced wherever coalition-formation has created a presidential majority or near-majority. For example, the Bolivian government succeeded in implementing a difficult economic stabilization package, while the Cardoso government in Brazil (from January 1995) put through a series of radical reform measures, including a constitutional reform to allow reelection of the president himself. Instability has ensued, in contrast, wherever the failure to form coalitions has created minority governments: the suppression of democracy by Fujimori's *autogolpe* in Peru; the impeachment of the president and severe social unrest in Venezuela (despite the much vaunted discipline of its political parties); mass social protest and the forced resignation of the president in Ecuador.

The degree of ideological polarization

It is agreed that in parliamentary systems there is a strong association between the number of parties and the degree of ideological polarization (Sartori 1976). Systems with a broader ideological span can accommodate a greater number of parties.[11] No such relationship can be established for the presidential systems of Latin America, partly because the available measures of polarization are less reliable. But two-party (or two-party plus) systems are understood to reduce polarization by promoting patterns of competition that bring parties closer to the center of the ideological spectrum. Conversely, it appears certain that increasing polarization had some part to play in the breakdown of two-party systems in Colombia (1947–53) and Uruguay (1970–3), and of multiparty systems in Brazil (1961–4) and Peru (1962–8). This has led some commentators to argue that it is the *combination* of multipartism with a high degree of polarization that spawns inchoate party systems and creates "acute problems of governability" (Mainwaring and Scully 1995: 32).

Yet conclusions of this kind must remain incomplete if coalition-formation is not taken into account. It is not simply that a lower degree of polarization can make coalitions more likely and so "facilitate governability" (Mainwaring and Scully 1995: 32). (This is demonstrably true of parliamentary regimes, and probable of presidential regimes.) More importantly, successful coalitions can dampen the dangers of polarization, whatever its degree, just as their absence can increase them. Furthermore, the likelihood of coalition-formation depends not only on the degree of polarization, but also on presidential powers, including powers of patronage, and the quality of political leadership in both executive and congress.

Take the "difficult" case of Chile from 1933 to 1973, which recurs time and again in the literature as the only case of enduring multi-party presidentialism. In Sartori's terms, the Chile of this period was a multipolar system with a wide ideological span and centrifugal competition. The system had parties that represented the far left, the center, and the far right, where competition between them had the potential to split apart the political system as finally happened in 1973. In principle, these conditions should have made coalition-formation difficult or impossible. In fact, the system followed the logic of "moderated pluralism," with a consistent pattern of coalitions built between the center and either one of the poles, which only broke down when the polar parties became anti-system (Mainwaring and Scully 1995: 24). By analogy with Chile's center party, it can be argued that in multiparty presidential systems the president is able to play a mediating role, and move along the ideological spectrum in order to build coalitions and achieve a working majority. If this is true, then successful coalition-formation will depend on a combination of the degree of polarization and the quality of political leadership.

Classifying the democratic governments of Latin America

It is clear that the Latin American democratic governments do have significant institutional features in common, if only because they are all presidential-PR systems. But it is equally clear that there are salient legal and party systemic differences between them. In particular, they can be distinguished according, severally, to the executive electoral formula, the institutionalization of the party system, the degree of multipartism and party discipline, and by the presence or absence of presidential majorities or near-majorities in the legislative assembly. They also vary according to the degree and direction (centripetal or centrifugal) of polarization within the party system, and in their capacity for coalition-formation.

Some of their distinguishing features are not well known or understood, in part because they have been thought to be typical of, and integral to the parliamentary-PR systems of Western Europe, and hence "unimportant" to presidential regimes. Thus, there is no adequate comparative account of the conditions of coalition-formation, and no proper measures of ideological polarization. In sum, although much is known about the formal and legal differences between these governments, a fuller understanding of key elements of their comparative performance like coalition-formation must await further investigation of their *informal* institutions, and especially the committee structure, procedural rules and norms, and operational constraints of their assemblies.

Yet the present state of our knowledge does demonstrate, beyond reasonable doubt, that the legal and institutional variation across these regimes has significant implications for governability, understood as government stability, legislative capacity, and the avoidance of gridlock. Furthermore, the five key variables in this respect all have to do, more or less directly, with electoral rules and the party system. Thus, these regimes will be more or less governable according to variations in executive electoral rules, the effective number of parties in the party system, the degree of presidential support in the assembly, the degree of ideological polarization, and the conditions of coalition-formation. This can be illustrated in a synoptic and simplified fashion,

Table 6.1   Varieties of Latin American presidential democracies

Presidential support	Effective parties	Executive elections	Polarization	Coalition
>45%	*<2.5*	*Plural-concurrent*	*Low*	*Yes*
Argentina	Chile	Uruguay*	Argentina	Bolivia
Chile	Colombia	Venezuela	Colombia	Brazil
Colombia				Chile
Uruguay				Colombia
				Uruguay
<45%	*>2.5*	*Mixed*	*High*	*No*
Bolivia	Argentina	Argentina	Bolivia	Argentina
Brazil	Bolivia	Bolivia	Brazil	Ecuador
Ecuador	Brazil	Brazil	Chile	Peru
Peru	Ecuador	Colombia	Ecuador	Venezuela
Venezuela	Uruguay	Chile	Peru	
	Venezuela	Peru	Uruguay	
			Venezuela	
		Majority non-concurrent		
		Ecuador		

*Uruguay majority runoff and concurrent from next election.

by dividing these variables into two dichotomous categories, and distributing the nine South American countries discussed in this chapter, namely Argentina, Bolivia, Brazil, Chile, Colombia, Ecuador, Peru, Uruguay, and Venezuela – as shown in table 6.1.

The calculations that underpin the categories of the first two columns of the table are based on averages taken over all the years of the current democratic government. The first column divides presidential support in the assembly into two categories of up to 45 percent and 45 percent and above – the critical threshold for a "near-majority." The second column divides the effective number of parties in the system (calculated according to Laakso and Taagepera's criteria) into two categories of fewer than 2.5 parties and 2.5 parties or more – the notional threshold for passing from a two-party or two-party plus system to a multiparty system. The third column characterizes the executive electoral rules as plurality-concurrent, mixed or majority runoff non-concurrent. The fourth column divides ideological polarization into low and high (according to Mainwaring and Scully 1995). The final column divides the countries into those with or without a legislative coalition producing a working majority for the government in the year 1993.

On the basis of these distributions it can be suggested that the initial key to governability is a degree of presidential support in the assembly exceeding the critical threshold of 45 percent. This is determined in large degree by the effective number of parties in the system, that itself is closely conditioned by the profile of executive electoral rules. But it also appears that a high degree of polarization may promote multipartism (although the direction of causality cannot be clear), and therefore damage governability both by reducing presidential support in the assembly and by making it more difficult to overcome minority status through coalition-formation. Finally, favorable conditions of coalition-formation can clearly compensate for the difficulties of multipartism and polarization. If this still highly hypothetical line of argument is correct, then it is possible to distinguish South America's most governable countries (Argentina, Chile, Colombia, Uruguay) from its least governable countries (Ecuador, Peru, and contemporary Venezuela), with the current governability of Bolivia and Brazil remaining closely contingent on (very different) processes of coalition-formation.

7 | POLITICAL AND SOCIAL RIGHTS

In chapter 2 we presented two broad definitions of democracy. On the one hand, procedural democracy is concerned with a narrow set of rules, guarantees, and rights that make inclusive political participation possible. On the other, social democracy relies on the existence of such rules, but is also concerned with the substantive outcomes of democracy that promote political and social equality. A procedural definition of democracy thus focuses on the political rights necessary for effective political contestation and participation in government and other public affairs. In contrast, the core concern of social democracy is social rights, which establish important basic thresholds for the maximum realization of human potential within a political system. As the discussion of human rights in chapter 4 demonstrated, some see these two categories of rights as mutually exclusive and of an inherently different status. Others argue that both normatively and empirically, it is possible to demonstrate that these different sets of rights are of equal status and are highly interrelated.

To elaborate on this debate within the context of Latin America, this chapter presents a fuller account of each category of rights and shows that regardless of their inherent status, the region has made dramatic improvements in the protection of political rights over the last twenty years and variable improvements in different aspects of social rights. Indeed, despite the advance in political rights, there are vast pockets in the region suffering from income maldistribution, low investment in healthcare, the prevalence of under-nourishment, and problems of hunger. These contrasting trends are illustrated through comparative evidence from Latin America on both sets of rights, while the discussion draws larger inferences about how the variable

Table 7.1 Political rights and social rights

Political rights (contestation and participation)	Social rights (equality and realizing human potential)
The right to assembly	Social security
The right to association (civic associations and political parties)	Social welfare services
The right to free speech and expression	Work and choice of work
Participation in government and public affairs	Just, favorable, and healthy conditions of work
Access to public service	Vocational guidance and training
Right to democracy	Food
Right to vote	Health
	Education
	Protection of employed women
	Protection of migrant workers
	Collective bargaining
	Formation of trade unions

Source: Davidson (1993: 193–6); Jones (1995: 172–89); Foweraker and Landman (1997: 12–17; 51–62)

performance in the provision of social welfare may affect the protection of political rights, and, more importantly, the quality and stability of democracy itself.

Defining political and social rights

Table 7.1 outlines the key political and social rights that emerge from normative political theory on rights and democracy, as well as dominant international human rights instruments (see chapter 4 this volume). Broadly speaking, political rights include those freedoms necessary to contest public authority fairly and to have the opportunity to participate fully in the political system. Participation has best been realized through some form of democratic governance in which leaders and representatives are chosen through free and fair electoral procedures that are extended to all eligible citizens without restriction on the basis of property, literacy, race, ethnicity, gender, or attributes other than age (Jones 1995; Donnelly 1999; Beetham 1999). Social rights, on the other hand, are substantive rights that seek to guarantee the best socioeconomic conditions for the betterment and protection of human existence. They therefore include rights to broad categories of health, education, and welfare, as well as those rights that set standards for conditions of work. Taken together, a society with broad protections of both kinds of rights means that individuals have the opportunity to participate fully in the political system, and have the basic economic means and protections that provide for a meaningful existence.

In normative political theory and in the practical world of politics, it has been argued that these two categories of rights are inherently different. On the one hand, political rights represent universal claims that are "amenable to formal expression in the rule of law and in the equality of political opportunity" (Foweraker and Landman 1997: 15). In this view, political rights can be written into national constitutions and international legal instruments, and are therefore justiciable.[1] On the other hand, realizing social rights depends on the relative wealth, resources, and fiscal capacity of states to distribute the benefits of socioeconomic development. Rather than representing equal and universal rights, this view sees social rights as nothing more than "conditional opportunities" (Barbalet 1988: 67), that are realized through programatic policy agendas pursued by governments through substantive legislation. This division between the two sets of rights suggests that political rights are more enforceable than social rights; however, the argument has recently been made that such rights can be made justiciable (see Hunt 1996: 24–31), and that political rights may also be more expensive to protect than first imagined.

In this view, countries party to the International Covenant on Economic, Social, and Cultural Rights (ICESCR), for example, have international legal obligations to achieve particular benchmarks in the provision of social welfare, and can be mandated to achieve them within specified periods of time. Failure to do so can result in a legal judgment being passed stipulating that the country has violated the protection of social rights. The UN Committee on Economic, Social, and Cultural Rights at present monitors country performance on social rights, but is moving in the direction of increased justiciability. With respect to the cost of protecting political rights, the US presidential elections of 2000 showed that even the richest country in the world has some difficulty guaranteeing the right to vote (at least in the state of Florida). Electoral registration, observation, and administration necessary to hold free and fair elections is costly, particularly in large countries with large populations.

Regardless of the division between these different categories of rights, persistent violation of either set means that individuals are being deprived of full participation and potential in any given society. As argued in chapter 2, legally equal individuals (e.g. those with the full enjoyment of political rights) may not be socially equal (e.g. those who are denied access to basic goods and resources), where a denial of access to basic resources may limit an individual's ability to participate politically. It is possible for a country to have free and fair elections, but economic obstacles for the poorer sectors of society may preclude them from taking part. For example, registering to vote may require literacy and writing skills, competency in the national language as opposed to an indigenous language, long distances to travel, and a reasonable level of political knowledge to make a meaningful choice. Low levels of education and lack of access to registration and voting centers may therefore result in political disenfranchisement, and limit full political participation. Moreover, poor conditions of health, nutrition, and access to food may create different sets of political preferences for those who are most vulnerable in society, and, as we shall see, increasing disillusionment with democracy.

Mapping political and social rights

The history of Latin America has shown that the guarantee and protection of political rights have been restricted during the nineteenth century and expanded during the twentieth century, although such expansion was conditioned by frequent military interventions during which political rights (and other rights) were severely compromised (see chapter 1). The oligarchic democracies of the late nineteenth century and early twentieth century limited political rights through restrictions on suffrage based on property ownership, gender, and literacy. Such restrictions guaranteed that those individuals eligible to vote would be wealthy, landowning, well-educated, white (or *mestizo*) males. Suffrage was extended to women during the period between 1932 and 1967 (see table 7.2), while property and literacy restrictions on suffrage were maintained in such countries as Brazil, Chile, and Peru until the late 1970s and early 1980s (Hartlyn and Valenzuela 1994: 132). Ironically, much of the suffrage extended to women came during military rule since military officers saw women as natural forces for conservatism that would support a strong leader (Bunster 1988). Today, however, there is universal suffrage throughout Latin America, with the only remaining restrictions based on age.

The frequent swings towards authoritarianism throughout the twentieth century meant that political rights were often curtailed by military rule, whereby the rights to assembly, association, speech, expression, and vote were suspended. Some of the longest periods of

Table 7.2 Women's suffrage in Latin America

Country	With some restrictions	With no restrictions
Argentina		1947
Bolivia	1938	1952
Brazil		1934
Chile	1931	1949
Colombia		1954
Costa Rica		1949
Ecuador	1929	1967
El Salvador	1939	1961
Guatemala		1946
Honduras		1955
Mexico	1947	1953
Nicaragua		1955
Panama	1941	1946
Paraguay		1961
Peru		1955
Uruguay		1932
Venezuela		1946
USA		1920

Source: Inter-Parliamentary Union (1997) *Men and Women in Politics: Democracy in the Making.* Geneva: SRO-KUNDIG

authoritarian rule took place in the 1970s and 1980s, when military leaders saw it necessary to limit political participation through closing legislative assemblies, suspending elections, censoring newspapers and other publications, and banning independent associations. Only the Brazilian military regime (1964–85) allowed elections for the Senate and the Chamber of Deputies, but, from 1966 to 1979, only two political parties were eligible to contest the elections: the National Renovation Alliance (ARENA) for the regime and the Brazilian Democratic Movement (MDB) for the opposition. Moreover, the regime extended and retracted suffrage to illiterates in an attempt to manipulate electoral outcomes for these two chambers, and banned direct elections for governors and mayors of strategically important states and cities (Skidmore 1988).

Apart from the Brazilian case, the proliferation of democratic transitions in the region that started with the 1978 Peruvian transition (see chapter 2 this volume) saw a dramatic improvement in the protection of political rights. Figure 7.1 shows a measure of political rights[2] averaged across seventeen Latin American countries from 1972 to 1995 punctuated by the various democratic transitions.

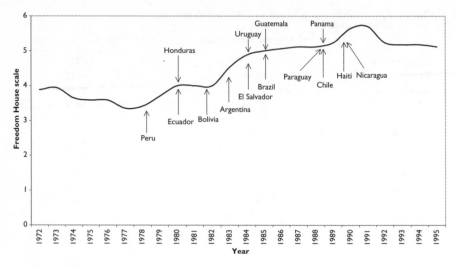

Figure 7.1 Political rights and democratic transitions in Latin America, 1972–1995
Source: Freedom House (www.freedomhouse.org); authors

Indeed, the moment of democratic transition involves the establishment of a constituent assembly and a call for new elections. Both of these steps require an increased protection of political rights, since freedoms of assembly, association, speech, and expression allow different groups in society to organize and take part in the representative process. The figure shows a clear upward trend in the protection of political rights that accompanies the wave of democratic transitions, illustrating the growth in "electoral democracy" in the region (see chapter 2 this volume and Diamond 1999).

Another important indicator that shows the exercise of political rights is voter turnout in national elections. Turnout is a measure of how many of the eligible voters actually cast a valid vote in a given election. Compared to Western Europe, Oceania, Eastern Europe, the Middle East, Asia, North America, and Africa, Latin America has the lowest voter turnout for the period 1945–98, with an average of 54 percent. However, it has the second largest number of elections (223) for the same period after Western Europe (312), and, between 1950 and 1990, a larger proportion of stable democracies than other parts of the developing world (Przeworski et al. 2000: 13–77). Figures 7.2 and 7.3 show voter turnout in Latin America by year and by country, respectively. Figure 7.2 shows that the region has seen a dra-

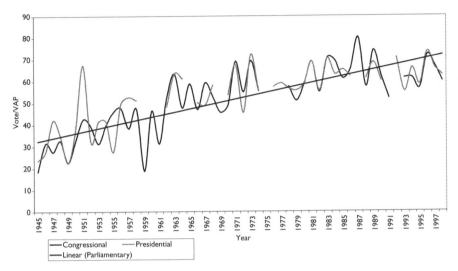

Figure 7.2   Voter turnout in Latin America by year, 1945–1997
Source: Center for Voting and Democracy (www.fairvote.org)

matic rise in formal political participation in the electoral process since 1945, where the "best fit" line in Figure 7.2 increases from just over 32 percent in 1945 to just over 70 percent in 1998. That the average turnout in the latter part of the period is so high suggests that there is a considerable commitment among Latin American publics to the electoral process in the era of the "third wave" (see chapter 2). In comparison, turnout rates in the United States have fallen over the years to levels below 50 percent. Figure 7.3 shows that Argentina, Costa Rica, Uruguay, and Venezuela have the highest turnout for the period, while Brazil, Colombia, and Guatemala have the lowest turnout. Thus, despite average increases in turnout, there is still great variation across the region.

These two figures plot a particular measure of voter turnout that divides the number of people who voted by the total voting-age population. Low turnout rates in the early years in figure 7.2 are partly due to people not voting, but also partly due to poor efforts at registering voters. If a state is to guarantee the right to vote, it has a certain obligation to make registration procedures open, free, and accessible. In the United States, voter registration drives within poor and ethnic minority communities are common, and a popular legislative solution has been the passage of "motor-voter" bills, which automatically register all people who apply for drivers' licences. In the context of

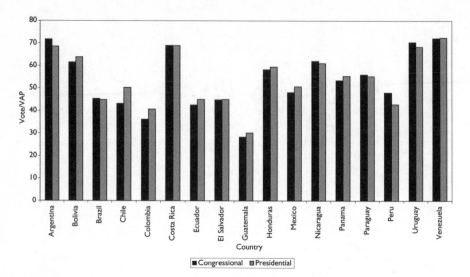

Figure 7.3   Voter turnout in Latin America by country, 1945–1997
Source: Center for Voting and Democracy (www.fairvote.org)

Latin America, however, efforts to register voters are made more difficult for reasons of geographical remoteness, poor funding at the
local level, and intimidation. A US-style "motor-voter" policy solution for Latin America is simply absurd since the vast majority of
Latin Americans does not own or have access to automobiles. Despite
these difficulties, the dramatic rise in voter turnout over the period
depicted in figure 7.2 shows that some of these obstacles have been
overcome.

    In sum, the various indicators show that the region has seen a
general improvement in the protection of political rights that accompanied the third wave of democratization and increasing levels of
formal political participation in the electoral process. As noted in
chapter 2, since 1989, all leaders in Latin America, with the exception
of Cuba, have been elected and, with the exception of Peru and
Ecuador, there have been repeated peaceful transfers of power
between governments. This is indeed a remarkable and laudable
achievement for a region that had so recently experienced prolonged
periods of authoritarian rule. The (re) establishment of national Constitutions in the new democracies has enshrined political rights in law,
and the recent historical record demonstrates that, with minor exceptions, these rights are now protected and are being observed throughout the region.

In contrast to political rights, social rights are less easy to measure and map. Popular development indicators such as per capita GDP, government expenditure on health, education, and welfare, and measures of access to food and other essentials are *outcomes* of economic development and government policy but not rights indicators *per se*. They give us a sense of the results of government policy but not of government behavior. Establishing standard measures of social rights that are comparable across different political contexts is problematic since, as we noted above, the provision of economic and social resources that comprise the best proxy indicators of social rights depend on the overall fiscal resources of the state. It is difficult to measure specific violations of social rights, but it is possible to demonstrate whether a state has failed to meet a stated programatic social objective. Using extant measures of socioeconomic development can begin to demonstrate the degree to which different governments in the region have sought to achieve developmental goals and improve overall levels of welfare. Thus, this section of the chapter considers the comparative socioeconomic performance of Latin American governments to provide a preliminary portrait of social development in the region, including income and income distribution, human development, healthcare, education, nutrition, and hunger.

Income and income distribution

Annual income represents the general wealth of a country and its overall set of resources for possible expenditure on health, education, and welfare. For some, income is "simply the best overall indicator of the choices people enjoy in their lives" (Przeworski et al. 2000: 5) since enhanced resources increase the number of choices available to individuals in society. Income is usually measured by considering either overall gross domestic product (GDP), or by dividing GDP by population, which yields the per capita gross domestic product. Figure 7.4 shows per capita GDP between 1960 and 2000 for Latin America and the Caribbean region as compared to Latin America. Measured in constant 1995 US dollars (i.e. adjusted for inflation), the average per capita income for the region rose from between just over $1,500 in 1960 to just under $2,000 in 1980. It then stagnated and even declined for much of the 1980s, leading many to brand this period of no growth in income as Latin America's "lost decade." Growth in income only rose above the 1980 levels by the mid-1990s, and, by 1999, Latin America ranked third in income growth next to the Arab oil states, and East Asia (UNDP 1999: 154). A second, and perhaps

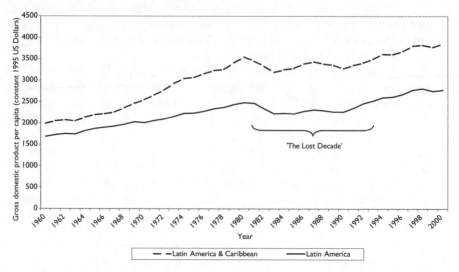

Figure 7.4   Gross domestic product per capita in Latin America, 1975–1996
Source: World Bank 1999

more interesting measure, is income distribution, which takes into account how the wealth of a country is distributed throughout the population. In contrast to per capita GDP, which simply divides GDP by population, income distribution is a more accurate measure of the degree to which the population enjoys the fruits of development. For example, Brazil has a very large per capita GDP, but income is highly concentrated in the hands of the few, suggesting that the fruits of development and economic progress have not been shared across a broad cross-section of the population.

The most popular measure of income distribution is the Gini coefficient, which estimates the cumulative percentage of national income distributed to the cumulative percentage of households that make up the overall population.[3] The Gini coefficient ranges from 0 to 1, where 0 represents perfectly equal income distribution and 1 represents perfectly unequal income distribution. While both values are theoretically possible, the coefficient for all countries in the world lies somewhere between these two extremes. Figure 7.5 shows the Gini coefficient for sixteen Latin American countries from 1989 to 1998, where it is clear that despite the general increase in income over the long term as shown in the previous figure, there is much variation in income distribution across the region. Indeed, despite its general

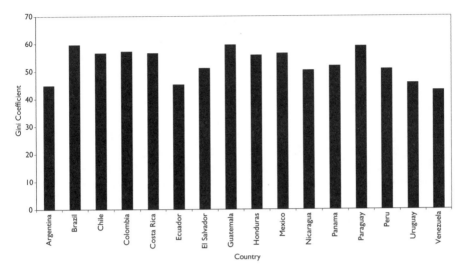

Figure 7.5   Income distribution in Latin America, 1989–1998
Source: World Bank 1999

levels of economic success in terms of income growth, Brazil shares
the worst income distribution along with Guatemala and Paraguay.
On the other hand, Argentina, Ecuador, and Venezuela show the
most equal income distribution for the sixteen countries.

These differences in the distribution of income observed across the
region can be explained by a multitude of factors, including initial
factor endowments and long-term patterns of economic development, the presence of patrimonial elites and "rent-seeking" agents
within the state apparatus who enjoy privileged access to the fruits
of development, and long-term problems of inequality owing to land
tenure patterns and the rise of powerful industrial elites. In Central
America, it was typical for countries like El Salvador and Nicaragua
to have vast concentrations of wealth and power in the hands of the
few. Indeed, before the 1979 Nicaraguan revolution, the Somoza
family owned land, factories, shipping companies, and even airports,
while in El Salvador, it was a group of twelve large families
who owned such assets. In South America, the rural sector is dominated by the existence of *latifundios*, or large landed estates, whose
ownership is guaranteed through a system of inheritance and the protection of the right to property. It is not uncommon for a Brazilian
landowner to have 4 million hectares, 20 percent of which lies fallow.
In urban South America, especially in those countries that underwent

large processes of industrial development (Argentina, Brazil, Chile), bourgeois elites who benefited under state-led development and import substitution industrialization (ISI) retain their hold on national capital as well as political influence to curb efforts at redistribution.

Human development

Beyond considerations of income and income distribution, there are important aspects of social development in Latin America, which reflect income as well as education and health. The United Nations Development Program (UNDP) has compiled a "Human Development Index" (HDI), which combines measures of per capita GDP, life expectancy, and literacy. Taken together, these three indicators reflect "achievements in the most basic human capabilities – leading a long life, being knowledgeable and enjoying a decent standard of living" (UNDP 1999: 127). It is plausible to assume that government policy in the areas of health, education, and welfare would contribute to these indicators of human development and provide us with another proxy measure of the degree to which governments seek to realize social rights. The index ranges from 0 to 1, where the higher the value, the higher the overall level of human development. Figure 7.6 shows the Human Development Index (HDI) for sixteen Latin American countries from 1975 to 1999, where Argentina shows the highest score and Guatemala the lowest. Comparatively, in 1999 Latin America's human development score was second highest in the developing world next to East Asia (UNDP 1999: 137) and, as figure 7.7 shows, the region has improved its level of human development by over 15 percent from 1975 (HDI = .64) to 1999 (HDI = .74).

It is encouraging to see that the region has enjoyed an overall improvement in human development over the years, but increased longevity without family planning and a population policy can lead to continued population growth and therefore lower per capita GDP, as well as the persistence of poverty. According to Vilas (1997), Latin America saw 80 million "new" poor in 1980, 48 million of whom live in cities, while in the 1990s, there are 190 million people living in poverty, which represents 46 percent of the total population of the region. As argued in chapter 3, Latin American governments faced new international constraints during the last twenty years under the aegis of neoliberalism, which reduced their ability to spend on social programs and created increasing levels of poverty and societal polarization (see also Brohman 1996: 173–97).

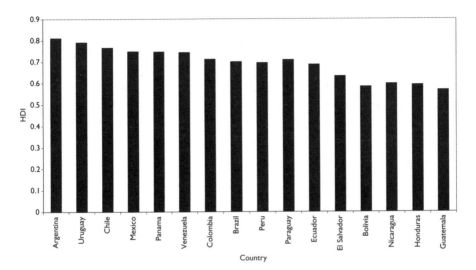

Figure 7.6 Comparative human development for Latin America, 1975–1999
Source: UNDP 1999

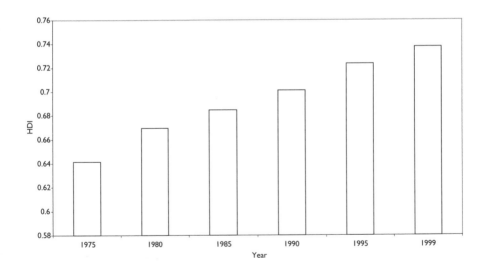

Figure 7.7 Human development over time in Latin America, 1975–1999
Source: UNDP 1999

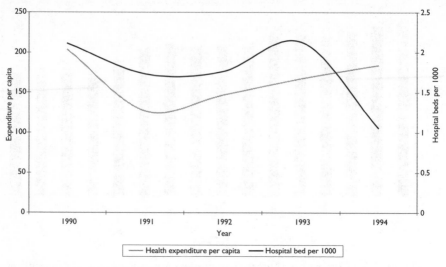

Figure 7.8 Healthcare expenditure in Latin America, 1990–1994
Source: World Bank 1999; ECLA 2000

Health and education

As part of their national budgets, governments spend revenues on healthcare, which seek to improve the overall quality of people's lives. The Human Development Index in figure 7.7 shows a general rise in life expectancy, but spending on healthcare provides another measure of government commitment to achieving better welfare and, by extension, social rights. Figure 7.8 shows two indicators of health-care in Latin America in the early 1990s, expenditure per capita and the number of hospital beds per 1,000 people. Both indicators show a dramatic decline in 1991 with gains through 1993, but it is clear that the number of hospital beds has declined relative to health expendi-ture, reflecting a possible change in priorities in the healthcare system. Figure 7.9 shows illiteracy rates for the region from 1970 to 1995, where the level of illiteracy has dropped from 25 percent to just over 15 percent, suggesting an overall improvement in basic educa-tional levels. Figures 7.10 and 7.11 show overall levels of expenditure on education by country and by year, where it is evident that, while average levels of spending have increased across the region, there is great variation across all the countries. Belize, Costa Rica, and Nicaragua have the highest levels of expenditure. As part of the 1949 elite pact in Costa Rica, the military was eliminated and the decision

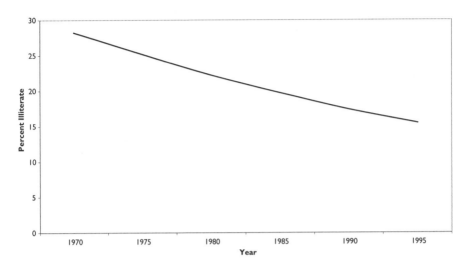

Figure 7.9 Illiteracy rates in Latin America, 1970–1995
Source: World Bank 1999

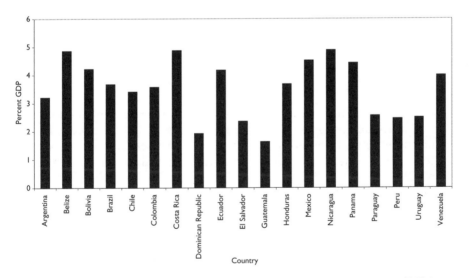

Figure 7.10 Expenditure on education in Latin America by country (ECLA 2000)
Source: ECLA 2000

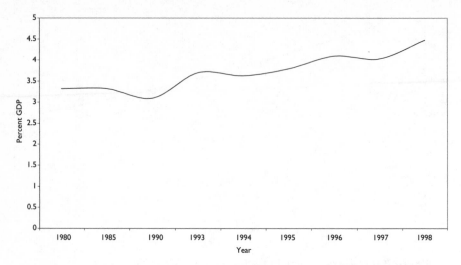

Figure 7.11   Expenditure on education in Latin America, 1980–1998
Source: ECLA 2000

was taken in subsequent years to invest heavily in the education system. In Nicaragua, the levels of expenditure on education reflect the commitment of the Sandinistas to invest, like the Cubans, in their educational system (see chapter 1).

Food and nutrition

The final area of provision considered here concerns food and nutrition in the region, again reflecting the general state of social welfare and well-being without directly measuring protection of the right to food *per se*. The Food and Agriculture Organization of the United Nations (FAO) compiles data on "food security" in the world, and two popular measures that it uses are the prevalence of undernourishment and depth of hunger. The first measure is the percent of the total population considered by the FAO to be undernourished, while the second measure is the number of calories (kcal) per person per day that fall short of the FAO's minimum benchmark level. In both cases, a large number means that a country has problems with food security. Figures 7.12 and 7.13 show both these measures for Latin America. The figures show that the prevalence of undernourishment is highest in Peru, Honduras, and Nicaragua, while lowest in Mexico, Costa Rica, Uruguay, and Chile. In most cases, the prevalence of undernourishment has declined across the three time periods;

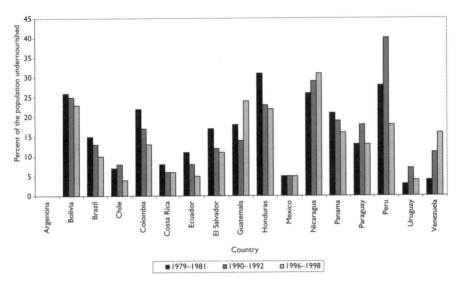

Figure 7.12 Prevalence of undernourishment in Latin America, 1979–1998
Source: FAO 2000: 27–30

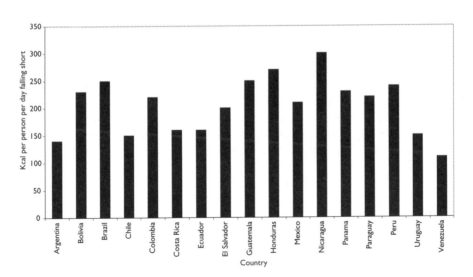

Figure 7.13 Depth of hunger in Latin America
Source: FAO 2000: 27–30

however, it is clear from figure 7.12 that in Guatemala, Nicaragua, and Venezuela, levels of undernourishment have actually increased over time. Figure 7.13 shows that the depth of hunger is highest in Nicaragua, Honduras, Guatemala, Brazil, and Peru, and lowest in Venezuela, Argentina, and Chile. These figures suggest that across the region, there are general patterns of undernourishment and hunger that are not necessarily related to the overall wealth of a country. For instance, using aggregate measures of GDP, Brazil is a wealthy Latin American country, yet it features as one of those countries in the region with a high degree of hunger. Lack of access to food and adequate nutrition stems from problems with climate and other exogenous shocks to the economy, problems with the infrastructure and distributional networks, and at the individual level, poor choices of foodstuffs within the family home, or sets of preferences that place less value on quality food. At the governmental level, lack of access to food may reflect an emphasis on production for export at the expense of meeting domestic demand for food.

Political rights, social rights, and democracy

What sense can we make of these tables and figures? This chapter has defined and mapped political and social rights in the region, and the comparative evidence presented here suggests that despite advances in the protection of political rights over the last twenty years, the region has great variation in its economic performance and the provision of social welfare. Bringing political and social rights together suggests that the advance of procedural democracy (i.e. an increased protection of political rights) has not necessarily brought about an advance in substantive democracy (i.e. increased provision of social welfare and protection of social rights). In chapter 2 we saw a remaining gap between "electoral democracy" (i.e. procedural aspects are in place) and "liberal" democracy (i.e. full protection of political and civil rights), while highlighting remaining threats to democracy in the region. In this chapter, we again observe a gap between two aspects of democracy, as expressed through an examination of rights protection, which may threaten the stability of democracy in the region.

This gap that may threaten democracy is manifested in three important and interrelated ways. First, as Vilas (1997: 11) notes, the emphasis on rules and procedures in place to guarantee the protection of political rights ignore power relations and power resources which are distributed unequally throughout the region. Chapters 1 and 3 showed that such power relations are embodied in long-term practices, such as patrimonialism, clientelism, populism, and corporatism, where unequal mediating structures between citizens and the state disproportionately favor some groups over others. Within the state apparatus itself, political actors can establish fiefdoms of loyalty and engage in "rent-seeking" behavior in which they gain favored access to state resources. The persistence of such power imbalances in the region affect not only how the fruits of socioeconomic development are distributed, but undermine any notion of equal political participation, despite such equality being formally guaranteed through the rule of law.

Second, our mapping of social welfare indicators showed that improvements over time have been made in variegated fashion across the region, and that wealthy countries may not be achieving high levels of social welfare provision and continue to exhibit patterns of inequality. These different patterns of provision and problems of distribution suggest that certain individuals and groups within Latin American society are undernourished, hungry, illiterate, have limited access to hospital care, low life expectancy, and low levels of income relative to others within their own societies. Prolonged patterns of poverty, social exclusion, and lack of access to basic welfare services limit political participation and hollow out broader conceptions of substantive democracy. Such patterns of inequality and impoverishment "shape political environments and outcomes in the search for alternative forms of social and political participation" (Vilas 1997: 4), since those that are socially excluded may see no point in taking part in conventional forms of political activity, such as joining political parties and voting in elections.

Third, it has been a common trend to associate democracy with economic development, but as the tables and figures show here, the process of democratization in the region, however minimal, has not necessarily brought about an improvement in people's daily lives in terms of the provision of goods and services. Indeed, it is a popular view among Latin Americans to expect the delivery of tangible goods from democratic government, and yet it is precisely under democracy, with the protection of political rights in place, that aggrieved groups in society can organize and mobilize for change. Social movement activity emerges from the "multiple manifestations of poverty" (Vilas 1997: 5), but in the new era of democracy and globalization (see chapter 3), no mass-based large and sustained mobilizations have taken place (Chalmers, Martin, and Piester 1997: 543). There have been riots and short-term protests over economic stabilization plans, for example, in Venezuela in 1992 and Argentina during the Menem

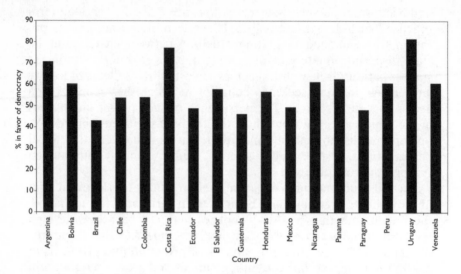

Figure 7.14 Support for democracy by country in Latin America, 1995–2001
Source: Latinobarometro, *The Economist*, July 28, 2001, p.37

and de la Rúa administrations. But, the protests in Venezuela were largely led by the middle classes, and the protests in Argentina were not noticed until joined by members of the middle class.

These three observations about power relations, social exclusion, and the possibility for social mobilization suggest that Latin America may face increasing popular dissatisfaction with democracy. Our final considerations for this chapter thus focus on popular attitudes toward democracy in Latin America. Since 1995, the *Latinobarometro* surveys (modeled after the *Eurobarometer*) have probed citizen attitudes toward democracy. Across all seventeen Latin American countries, the surveys have asked random samples of the public if democracy is preferable to any other form of government. Figure 7.14 shows average levels of support for democracy across the countries for the period 1995–2001, where it is evident that such support ranges from a low of 45 percent in Brazil to a high of 80 percent in Costa Rica and Uruguay. Figure 7.15 shows the average level of support for democracy over time, where it is clear that the start of the new century sees a decline in average support.

Finally, figure 7.16 links our concerns with social rights to the support for democracy in an effort to show how performance on social rights may have an impact on the exercise of political rights.

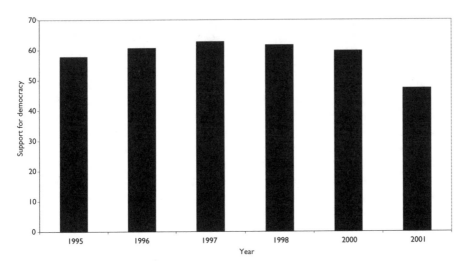

Figure 7.15 Support for democracy by year in Latin America, 1995–2001
Source: Latinobarometro, *The Economist*, July 28, 2001, p.37

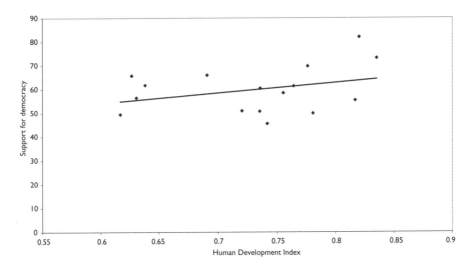

Figure 7.16 Human development and support for democracy in Latin America, 1998–2000
Source: Latinobarometro, *The Economist*, July 28, 2001, p.37

The figure is a scatterplot between the average human development index and the average support for democracy for 1995–2000. The figure shows that higher levels of human development are associated with high support for democracy, while low levels of human development are associated with low support for democracy. While establishing a causal relationship between the two is beyond the scope of this book, the figure is suggestive in showing a positive relationship between levels of human development and the support for democracy. The further inference that can be drawn from the figure is that continued patterns of poor performance in terms of human development may erode the popular support for democracy. Students of Latin American politics should be aware of the degree to which economic vulnerability and dissatisfaction as illustrated in this chapter can affect political stability and faith in democracy.

PART IV
PARTICIPATION, CONTESTATION, AND CIVIL RIGHTS

8 | NEW POLITICAL ACTORS

Social movements and civil society

In previous chapters we have discussed the historical, institutional, and economic factors that have shaped current forms of democracy in Latin America. We have noted the advances, but also the limits, of political contestation, the rule of law, and participation in the region. Patrimonialism, clientelism, and state corporatism were seen as obstacles inhibiting the emergence and development of democratic forms of legitimacy, accountability, and participation. This chapter examines how this situation is affected by the political mobilization of previously marginalized groups, such as women, indigenous peoples, and the urban poor. We see such groups as significant new political actors in Latin America, represented by a variety of social movements, social movement organizations (SMOs), and non-governmental organizations (NGOs) that have worked independently of the party system and traditional corporatist organizations. They seek to open up new channels for political representation and to put new issues on the political agenda.

Who are these "new political actors"? We can point to a vast array of popular movements that emerged in the context of the struggles against authoritarianism and social exclusion, became a significant component in the process of democratization, and remain vigilant of government policy during the new democratic period. They are a large and varied group of actors that defy easy categorization. Consider the following list of some of the most commonly found movements in the region today: human rights advocates, feminist and women's movements, indigenous peoples' organizations, urban social movements, gay and lesbian organizations, environmentalist movements, independent labor unions, peasant organizations, artistic and cultural collectives, alternative media, church groups, student movements, and non-governmental organizations (NGOs). It is common to refer to such movements and organizations as inhabiting "civil society," which includes that dense network of voluntary associations, guilds, clubs, groups, and other collectivities that do not occupy positions of power in politics, economy, or the state. The essence of civil society is its voluntary nature and its capacity to promote levels of "civic" behavior, social capital, and social mobilization.

But it is important to recognize two other points about movements and civil society. First, most commentators argue that civil society is inherently "good" since the groups that comprise it are voluntary, democratic, contribute to the social fabric of society, and help develop the political culture supportive of democracy. Yet, civil society is also host to "uncivil movements", which draw on resentments, grievances, and anti-democratic forces that seek to destabilize democracy and present often violent challenges to both the state and other groups in civil society.[1] Second, most studies of social movements explain them in terms of civil society and confine them to civil society alone. But social movements have developed in continual and intimate interaction with the state. Since the state is the main source of scarce resources and tends to monopolize power and decision-making, it becomes a prime focus of protest and demand-making (Foweraker 1995). This chapter recognizes the diversity of "civil" and "uncivil" movements. But since the threat such "uncivil" groups pose to democracy has already been examined (see chapter 2), the discussion in this chapter centers on the "civil" groups in civil society and examines how their emergence, activities, and interaction with the state have shaped politics in the region.

Beyond the material demands for better distribution of scarce resources, movement activities also include the making of political and cultural demands that challenge established ways of doing politics in Latin America. Concrete examples include the weekly demonstrations in the Plaza de Mayo of Buenos Aires, Argentina, by the mothers of the victims of military repression; the frequent occupation of Mexico City's central square, the Zócalo, by independent unions and popular movements; the 1992 Indian march on the Bolivian capital of La Paz to protest the quincentenary of the European conquest; and the armed uprising in 1994 by the Zapatistas, a movement made up primarily of impoverished Mayan Indians in the southern Mexican state of Chiapas. In each case, people were mobilizing not only for material demands but also for the right to participate as full citizens. Such demand-making using the language of rights included calls for land rights, employment rights, educational rights, and human rights (see chapter 10).

The proliferation of political actors presents us with a more complex picture of popular participation. In the "third wave" democracies there has been a relative decline in the role of hierarchical forms of mass organization that were linked to the state through corporatist organizations. Today we find greater diversity in patterns of citizen participation. This shift has been understood in very different ways. Some have tended to stress the weakness of this new "civil society" in the face of authoritarian legacies and neoliberal economic policies. This approach notes the extreme level of fragmentation of the popular sectors, produced by poverty, violence, and the co-optation of leaders into purely symbolic positions within the state apparatus. Others are more optimistic that we are witnessing the formation of an increasingly active citizenry that refuses to be subordinated to political parties and mass organizations. In this account, the creation of new political identities is a sign of the vitality of civil society in Latin America, rather than its weakness. As this chapter demonstrates, most social movements combine their desire for autonomy with the need for representation through pragmatic alliances with parties, institutions, and other movements, while simultaneously seeking to maintain grassroots mobilization and the affirmation of distinctive political and cultural identities. In part, this is owing to the fact that the transitions from authoritarian rule saw a general decline in social movement activity as political parties reemerged as the central actors of the new democracies. The new political actors cannot avoid dealing with the existing institutions and party systems, although relations between them are often fraught with difficulties.

This chapter explores the political significance of new political actors in Latin America by examining three concerns: (1) what is "new" about these new political actors, (2) what impact they have had on government and politics, and (3) how they have evolved to include increased levels of formal organization and linkages with a new global network of important political actors.

The novelty of new political actors

In earlier chapters we have noted the historical dominance of patrimonial forms of political control in Latin America and how they have shaped and constrained popular participation in the region. Given this context, how do new political actors differ from earlier forms of political organization, and what do they mean for the process of democratization?

There are at least four novel aspects of contemporary popular mobilization. First, there has been an *explosion in the sheer number of groups and organizations who present demands toward the state.* Demand-making in Latin America is tied most often to material or "bread-and-butter" issues such as access to land, jobs, food, housing, or healthcare. Given the grave inequalities in the region, it is not surprising that such concerns are at the top of the agenda for many grassroots organizations, such as those found in urban shanty-towns and impoverished rural areas. Like their counterparts in Africa and Asia, Latin American popular movements must deal with the daily hardships caused by poverty and material need. In this regard, they must also deal with government institutions, political parties, and other agents capable of providing tangible solutions to their problems. Nevertheless, unlike the period of populist corporatism, when material demands were channeled through a restricted number of state-sanctioned mass organizations, since the 1970s more and more actors have competed for access to government institutions and have sought to influence the distribution of economic resources. The relative decline of the corporatist system of interest representation, first as a result of dictatorship, then as a consequence of neoliberal restructuring, has created a new context for the proliferation of alternative associations that claim to be more representative of societal demands.

The early efforts of the 1960s focused on popular organization and education. The grassroots groups of the 1970s were more fully engaged in the struggle against poverty and the fight for citizenship rights. Those of the 1980s were more concerned with gender issues, survival strategies, and human rights. In very recent years the priority agenda is the environment and "micro-financing," such as communal banks, rural cooperatives and credit unions (ALOP 1999), as well as local development projects and technical assistance (Valderrama 1998: 11). These diverse initiatives have accumulated over the years, and are all present in greater or lesser degrees in Latin American civil societies today, so that the panorama of grassroots organizations has become ever more plural (Patrón 1998: 194). There is thus novelty in the proliferation of sites in which demands are now made.

A good example of this novelty can be found in the green movement in Latin America, which for many observers holds the greatest potential for activism, since unbridled destruction of the natural environment is taking place, while the majority of the population relies on the environment for its basic subsistence (García-Guadilla and Blauert 1992: 12). Although enlightened middle-class activists seek redress to environmental degradation in Latin America (Collinson 1996: 3), there is potentially more resonance of green issues among the poor and indigenous classes, who combine their demands for land and territorial rights with demands for access to their environmental means of production (Leff 1992: 48; Martínez 1992: 114). But despite the natural affinity between being poor and fighting for the environment, the green movement in Latin America relies on a collaboration between the affluent and marginalized sectors of society (Redclift 1987; Collinson 1996: 2–3).

Overall, Latin American green groups criticize the developmentalist logic that dominates the region, and issue specific demands such as protection of wildlife and vegetation; opposition to agrochemicals and the use of insecticides, fungicides, and herbicides; and stricter controls on water pollution and the destruction of the landscape, including vast tracts of the Amazon forest (Viola 1988: 214). This demand for protection is linked to human survival and social justice (for example by the rubber-tappers of Acre, Brazil), and even extended to a demand for political liberalization, in the case of Mexico, and democratic transition, in the case of Brazil and Chile. Once democratic transitions occurred in Brazil (1985) and Chile (1989), green groups pushed for a more participatory form of democracy and new forms of political articulation (Galbadón 1992: 31–2; Kaimowitz 1996: 28).[2]

A second novel feature of new political actors is that they have *mobilized around identity and cultural difference rather than limiting themselves to purely material or economic demands.* For example, women's struggles for access to basic urban services have also involved identification as women, rather than simply as the urban poor. As a result, women have presented gender-specific demands and challenged traditional patterns of male domination in government, as well as within their own social organizations (Molyneux 1985; Conger Lind 1992; Stephen 1996). Similarly, indigenous people have formed powerful new movements to demand respect for cultural traditions and the opening up of new channels of political representation. These movements have been particularly strong in Ecuador and Bolivia, where they have negotiated significant degrees of local autonomy over issues pertaining to development, justice, and education. In Guatemala, a broad network of organizations has formed a Pan-Mayan alliance that seeks to transform deep cultural biases in a country with a long history of suppression of indigenous people (Warren 1998).

Gays and lesbians have also mobilized to protest against discrimination, creating new independent movements in defence of gay rights in the face of traditional morality and codes of conduct, such as *machismo* and the extensive presence of Catholicism in Latin culture (Trevisan 1986: 15–16; MacRae 1992; Crapotta 1994). Although these actors have engaged in struggles over material resources, their goals and identities cannot be reduced to class position. In fact, in many cases, new movements have criticized class-based organizations for ignoring their needs and aspirations, prompting them to pursue their own independent paths. For example, feminist and women's organizations have had to overcome opposition from the predominantly male leadership of leftist parties for whom gender was a secondary consideration to class struggle (Sternbach et al. 1992).

A third area of novelty concerns the *distinctive forms of organization created by new political actors*. In this regard, it is important to consider the context of their emergence. In those countries that experienced military rule during the 1970s, traditional forms of popular participation were systematically repressed. In this situation, the Catholic Church acted as an umbrella institution that not only protected, but also promoted, local community groups that were negatively affected by military rule and economic hardship. In several countries, Ecclesiastical Base Communities (or CEBs for their Spanish and Portuguese names) provided a new arena for grassroots participation that drew on religious traditions and radical critiques of unjust social structures. A Christian–Marxist dialogue combined elements of both sets of beliefs in a powerful and practical model for radical social change, known as Liberation Theology. In 1968 the Latin American Council of Bishops adopted the "preferential option for the poor" and instructed the clergy to work for material as well as spiritual liberation. Unlike traditional actors, including the Church itself, liberation theologians and the new CEBs promoted broader and more self-aware forms of participation. Through a deliberate strategy of consciousness-raising, they sought to help people identify the structural causes of their poverty and marginalization in ways that went beyond former understandings (Gutiérrez 1973; Mainwaring and Wilde 1989). Bible readings conducted by lay preachers in Spanish and Portuguese rather than Latin became a key tool in the development of radical social analysis and oppositional consciousness. Furthermore, in many cases the CEBs became experiments in new, less hierarchical forms of organization, which contrasts sharply with the exclusionary nature of traditional Church structures.

Although Liberation Theology did create a powerful movement against authoritarian rule and economic inequality, it also reproduced some of the features of traditional political behavior, including restrictive and exclusionary organizations at the grassroots level. For example, Burdick (1992) has argued that in urban Brazil, CEBs tended to lose potential supporters to rival religious associations because of a series of biases and limitations. The emphasis on bible reading, full-time commitment, broader macro-analyses and ethnic stereotypes tended to exclude those community members who were less literate, those who had demanding work schedules or other obligations, the victims of domestic violence (seen by some CEB leaders as a "private" matter), and blacks who were suspected of practicing Afro-Brazilian religions. In addition, the meaning and purpose of the CEBs cannot be deduced simply from the publications and statements of the most visible representatives, since individual members often have their own, distinct reasons for participating in such a movement. These points serve as a necessary reminder of the complexity of political participation. An exclusive concern with numerical evidence of participation may conceal more ambiguous and contradictory processes of decision-making by groups and individuals. In fact, the meaning of participation may also be seen as yet another area of contention rather than one of easy consensus.[3]

A fourth area of novelty is the *adoption of democratic political discourses by new political actors*. In the context of authoritarian rule, social demands often became expressed in a new discourse of rights. We have noted how the expansion of civil and political rights in Latin America has been constrained by clientelism and non-democratic forms of government. However, the end of military rule and the impossibility of a return to populism meant that new actors would deploy the language of democracy and citizenship as they sought to shape the regime transitions of the 1980s and 1990s. This was not restricted to those groups most concerned with the juridical and electoral arenas (such as human rights organizations and civic associations), but also found its way into the discourse of popular movements for whom access to land, work, housing, and education became couched in the language of rights. Moreover, using the language of citizenship rights, which have a universal content (insofar as the rights must apply equally and across the board to be rights at all) meant that groups necessarily challenge the particularism of the clientelistic power relations that are so pervasive throughout the continent.

Lehmann has argued that rural movements in Brazil have tended to turn more on questions of citizenship and fair treatment than on the seizure of state power and the subsequent transformation of class relations. Land reform is valued not because it undermines the capitalist mode of production (in fact the opposite is often the case), but because it embodies a political struggle against the systematic violation of the agrarian, labor, and human rights of the rural poor (Lehmann 1990:155–60). Comparative research on rural social movements in Latin America and the Philippines has similarly emphasized the problems facing the establishment of channels for effective representation in electoral and sectoral arenas, accountability of state institutions, and protection of civil and political rights (Fox 1990).

One of the best-known movements that uses democratic discourse while drawing on local traditions is the Zapatista Army of National Liberation (EZLN) in the state of Chiapas, Mexico (Harvey 1998; Womack 1999). The EZLN, whose members are mostly poor Mayan Indians, erupted onto the political scene on January 1, 1994, briefly occupying seven towns and issuing a list of demands for land, jobs, housing, food, healthcare, education, independence, freedom, democracy, justice, and peace. Note that these demands were not restricted to local material problems, but also included the need for structural change in Mexico's economic model and political system. The Zapatistas have sought to insert their proposals in the broader struggle for democracy in Mexico, in which the objective is not to gain power but to democratize power by challenging authoritarianism in every arena of social life. Unlike earlier guerrilla movements, the EZLN does not aim at seizing the state or winning positions of power, but in demanding that those who govern, govern by obeying the citizens (*mandar obedeciendo*), a principle which is drawn from traditional forms of indigenous community governance in Chiapas. Concretely, this has led the EZLN to organize several national and international forums on the future of indigenous peoples, the struggle for democracy, and resistance to neoliberalism. The Zapatistas' faith in the potential of the non-partisan associations of civil society, that is, Mexico's "new political actors," was clearly expressed in 1995 in the following statement:

> Today, and in the spirit of Emiliano Zapata, and having heard the voices of all our brothers and sisters, we call upon the people of Mexico to participate in a new stage of the struggle for national liberation and the construction of a new nation, through this Fourth Declaration of the Lacandon forest, in which we call upon all honest men and women to participate in the new political force born today, the Zapatista Front of National Liberation, a Mexican civil and non-violent organization, independent and democratic, which struggles for democracy, liberty

and justice in Mexico. The Zapatista Front of National Liberation is born today and we extend an invitation to

The factory workers of the Republic,
The laborers of the countryside and the cities,
The indigenous peoples,
The urban dwellers,
The teachers and students,
The Mexican women,
The young people across the country,
The honest artists and intellectuals,
The responsible priests and nuns,
And all the Mexican people who do not seek power,
But rather democracy, liberty and justice for all of us
And for all our children.

We invite civil society, those without a party, the citizens and social movements, all Mexicans, to help build this new political force.
A new political dynamic which will be national.
A new political dynamic based in the EZLN.
A new political dynamic which forms part of a broad opposition movement, the National Liberation Movement, as a space for citizens' political action where there may be a confluence with other political movements of the independent opposition, a space where popular wills meet and coordinate united actions with one another.
A political dynamic that does not aspire to take political power.
A force that is not a political party.
A political force that can organize the demands and proposals of those citizens and is willing to govern by obeying . . .
A political dynamic not interested in taking political power but in building a democracy where those who govern, govern by obeying.'
(EZLN 1996)

From this brief summary of the novelty of new political actors, we can establish some basic distinguishing features. In contrast to previous patterns of government–citizen relations (see chapter 3), we are now faced with a broader array of political actors that cannot be subsumed under the corporatist system of social control. Issues of cultural identity have become more salient, leading to new and sometimes conflictive relations with political parties. Many of these new actors have also sought alternative means of participation in less hierarchical and more inclusionary forms of organization. Finally, new political actors have tended to adopt an explicitly democratic discourse, demanding respect for rights within a broad critique of authoritarian institutions and practices. While each of these aspects can be found in different cases, we should also be aware of the tensions and ambiguities that mark the political practices of new actors.

Impact of new political actors

From the above description of new political actors, we can note their dual nature. In most cases they must deal with the government while attempting to retain their autonomy. Leaders walk a fine line between representation and co-optation. These new actors do not seek to over-throw the regime, but to make it more legitimate and accountable, or, in the Zapatistas' words, to "govern by obeying the citizens." However, they are not simply seeking acceptance into the existing rules of the game. In sum, the new political actors are at the same time institutionalist and non-conformist, combining instrumental, strategic action with efforts to promote changes in the political culture. They struggle for material resources as well as political and cultural recognition. This dual nature is also reflected by the impact of popular mobilization.

The impact of movements may occur at three different levels. First, they have an impact on their own constituencies and movement members, raising levels of consciousness, learning new forms of organization and dialog, and developing alternative modes of politi-cal activity. Second, they have a legal-institutional impact through new government legislation and judicial decisions, an impact on polit-ical party agendas, and even on the formation of new political parties, such as green parties or the Workers' Party (PT) in Brazil. Third, they have a broader impact on values and political behavior, which may lead to changes in the views and practices of social movement participants themselves, the "diffusion of movement ideas" to other movements (McAdam and Rucht 1993; Tarrow 1994), as well as changes in public opinion and popular attitudes towards the issues around which they originally mobilized. Taken together, the activities and organizations of the new political actors represent a significant challenge to the way in which politics is conducted in the region. Thirty years after their appearance during periods of authoritarian rule, they have contributed to the process of democratic transition by organizing under conditions where the protection of civil and politi-cal rights was still precarious and contributed to the "resurrection of civil society" (O'Donnell and Schmitter 1986: 26). However, once the moment of democratic transition passed, the new political actors have had an uneven impact on politics in the new democratic era. Indeed, their activities have led to relatively little policy change or innovation, where "modest reforms are the most likely outcome of struggle" (Tarrow 1994: 170).

One useful way to illustrate these different aspects of the impact of the new political actors is by examining the evolution of the various strands of the women's movement in Latin America. Much of the research on women's movements since the 1970s has focused on three main types of women's activism: economic survival strategies, human rights advocacy, and struggles against all forms of male domination, or "patriarchy" (Jaquette 1994; Fisher 1993; Radcliffe and Westwood 1993; Stephen 1997). As noted in earlier chapters, the military dictatorships in Brazil, Argentina, Uruguay, and Chile were comprised of alliances between the armed forces, technocratic policy-making elites, and multinational corporations. Their economic policies were designed to benefit the wealthier sectors at the expense of wages and social welfare provision. In Chile, for example, the Pinochet regime (1973–90) had a devastating impact on employment and real wages. The privatization of state-owned corporations led to massive layoffs, while the rapid opening to foreign investment forced thousands of bankruptcies among domestic firms unable to compete in the global market. The loss of traditional manufacturing jobs and the expansion of the service sector led to the incorporation of larger numbers of women into the workforce, although they tended to be concentrated in low-paying jobs with few protections or benefits. If temporary employment in government work schemes is excluded from official calculations, the jobless rate in poor urban areas reached as much as 80 percent by 1987.[4]

It was in this context that poor women organized communal kitchens and self-help cooperatives. In Chile, women set up "popular economic organizations" (*organizaciones económicas populares*, or OEPs). By 1982 there were almost 500 OEPs in the metropolitan Santiago area. By 1985 this figure had more than doubled. Women made tapestries together, prepared food for neighborhood residents, and bought basic foods at lower prices through their own shopping collectives (*comprando juntas*). Elsewhere in Latin America, women organized similar grassroots organizations that could provide a minimal degree of security against hunger and poverty. Many of these organizations developed related demands for urban services such as waste disposal and drinking water as well as daycare centers, clinics, and schools. In sum, what began as a necessary response to urgent problems snowballed into a more deliberate and self-conscious effort to create broad-based popular organizations. In the process, many women became politically active in new ways by projecting their daily experiences into the formerly male-dominated arenas of public protest and negotiation. As a result, the study of participation in Latin American politics has had to take account of the daily life of citizens in local contexts. Although participation in parties and elections remains a key concern for political scientists, there is increasing recognition of the importance of other arenas that are perhaps more closely tied to the day-to-day problems of economic survival and personal security.

The occupation of public spaces previously considered "off-limits" to women was perhaps most clearly exemplified by the mothers of the victims of state terror. The forced disappearance of thousands of people in the 1970s was meant not only to eliminate political opposition to military rule, but also to strike fear into the heart of the population. In fact, fear was central to the military's strategy of maintaining control. With virtually all the traditional actors imprisoned, killed, exiled, or forced into silence, women played a crucial part in denouncing human rights violations committed against their families. One of the ironies of this situation was that women were initially viewed as politically harmless by the military juntas. The dominant ideology portrayed women as essentially bound to the private sphere of the home. Furthermore, they were seen as upholding traditional values of loyalty to the family, the nation, and the state. Yet, by brutally destroying the integrity of families through its repressive tactics, the military itself violated such beliefs, exposing it to a critique from those who could still speak out: mothers who demanded the return of their disappeared sons and daughters.

Perhaps the best-known movement of this type is the Madres de la Plaza de Mayo in Argentina. As with other "new political actors," the Madres used innovative tactics to draw attention to their demands, while seeking to avoid repression. By staging weekly walks (or *rondas*) around the central square in Buenos Aires, these women contested the lies of the military regime and symbolized popular defence of the most basic human rights.[5] By occupying an important public place in this way, the Madres also challenged the dominant view that women should be confined to non-political tasks of providing for their families.

With the transition to democracy, the Madres continued to mobilize for their demands, although they tended to become more isolated from other struggles for economic, political, and social justice. This was due partly to their own style of mobilization, which some see as characteristic of popular movements in Latin America: their weak institutionalization, reliance on strong personal leaders, and an overly zealous concern with maintaining autonomy from all other actors. These features may have allowed the Madres and other movements to be very effective in crisis situations when they faced a clear and unified enemy. However, they are less conducive to stable and durable forms of participation in the more complex situations presented by democratization and the accompanying dispersal of demands and actors. In this context, popular movements may still express demands in street demonstrations and other arenas, but they are also obliged to negotiate with political parties and state institutions. In the case of the Madres, popular distrust of the party system is perhaps understandable since the democratic governments (particularly of Carlos Menem, 1989–99) decided to pardon some of the worst violators of human rights. However, the insistence by the Madres on fulfillment of their original demands has been criticized as unrealistic given the changing context of Argentine politics. Although the Madres have had a limited impact on the institutional form of the post-authoritarian state (as evidenced by the continued weakness of the rule of law and the pardoning of human rights violators), there is no doubt that they contributed to the downfall of the military regime by raising international awareness of the human rights situation. Furthermore, they transformed the position of women in political life by advocating a new form of feminism that does not negate motherhood, but empowers it in the public sphere.

The feminist nature of women's movements in Latin America has been an issue of great contention since the 1970s. The struggles for economic survival or human rights are not inevitably associated with feminist goals, but, in Latin America, they have been articulated in ways that suggest that feminism itself has been transformed. Thus, the third main area of women's activism, resistance to patriarchy, has been shaped by the particular contexts in which women live and act. In Latin America, it makes more sense to talk of "feminisms" in the plural, rather than the imposition of a single discourse modeled on experiences in North America or Europe. Nevertheless, the more self-consciously feminist groups have played a significant role in bringing out the ways in which gendered forms of discrimination are inseparable from economic and political forms of oppression. The International Women's Year Conference, held in Mexico City in 1975, was the catalyst for many groups that began to identify gender-specific problems of women in Latin America. These groups tended to be comprised of university-educated, middle-class women, many of whom had access to international networks of solidarity and feminist debates, a process which has expanded greatly with the development of new communications technologies such as the Internet.

In the 1980s, the promotion of feminist ideas often led to conflicts with existing popular organizations and political parties that had traditionally relegated women's demands to a secondary level. The meaning of social change and revolution was given a gendered perspective by feminists who criticized the male-dominated structures not only of oppressive regimes, but also of the traditional opposition movements, including industrial and rural unions and leftist parties (Sternbach et al. 1992). Although such tensions continue to exist, by the end of the 1990s women's movements had been largely successful in gaining acceptance for their own organizations and sectors within larger movements. This legitimacy derived not simply from a theoretical critique of patriarchy, but also from the insertion of feminist ideas into concrete day-to-day struggles. The most significant include efforts to combat domestic violence and rape, the struggle for the expansion of reproductive health rights, an end to discrimination, and respect for sexual orientation.

By affirming these issues in the public arena, feminists (in a manner similar to environmentalists) have created gender as a new political fact, one that all actors must respond to, although the nature of these responses inevitably varies. The transitions to democracy were in part shaped by women's movements, and the new governments were forced to recognize the political presence of new discourses on gender and equality. In some cases, this awareness led to the formal incorporation of women into new cabinet positions. For example, in Chile, the government of Patricio Aylwin in 1990 created the National Women's Service (*Servicio Nacional de la Mujer*, SERNAM), with an official mandate to address a variety of women's issues. However, feminists have noted the conservative bias of the pro-family discourse of the SERNAM, which appears to have become a vehicle for co-optation rather than an effective institutional expression of women's demands for equality and justice.[6] Furthermore, governments have sought to bypass more representative organizations in order to avoid having to implement reforms that would most likely antagonize conservative forces on the right. Institutionalization of women's demands through bodies such as the SERNAM may hurt feminism in the long run as it creates a privileged (and relatively weak) interlocutor for the government, while marginalizing calls for faster and more far-reaching reforms.

In addition, similar efforts to incorporate women in governmental agencies, such as the creation of Councils on the Status of Women in Brazil, are often contingent on the support of the president of the day, continuing rather than transcending the traditions of corporatism and clientelism noted in previous chapters. As a result, feminist organizations have tended to view the state as an important arena of struggle, but not to the exclusion of other strategies that focus more on building awareness and support within civil society. After a decade or more of democratic government, feminists, as well as other "new political actors," have developed a sharper awareness of the complexities of both state and civil society. Neither are simple, unified blocs, but rather contested and shifting terrains.[7]

In sum, the women's movement in Latin America illustrates well some of the ways in which new political actors have had an impact in the region. On the one hand, authoritarian governments were discredited partly through the ways in which women defied fear and spoke out against repression. In some cases, particularly in Chile, women also helped to coordinate opposition movements in the struggle to end dictatorship. However, the impact on the new democratic systems has been ambiguous to say the least. Co-optation of leaders has often led to demobilization at the grassroots. Conflicts have been depoliticized through an increasing emphasis on technical expertise and fear of being cut off from scarce funds. Nevertheless, at other, perhaps less visible levels, new actors have indeed created possibilities for participation that did not exist until recently. The incursion of previously marginalized actors into political life has altered people's views about themselves and legitimized issues that had traditionally been seen as taboo.

Future directions: global networks and NGOs

We have noted some of the novel and most significant features of new political actors. In general, we can say that popular participation has expanded to more arenas and has evolved in new ways, although traditional practices of clientelism and corporatism have not disappeared. The struggle to democratize political institutions has also been extended to social and cultural spheres, including those that were once seen as the apolitical, private domains of the home and the family. Given the great diversity of these struggles, it is impossible to characterize them in any one single way. However, it has become increasingly clear that they share a common concern with achieving voice in an infinite number of decision-making arenas. These new actors appear to have found a point of reference in the concept of "citizenship," understood as a political practice involving the right to participate as equal and valued members of a society. In this regard, very different kinds of demands are expressed in terms of rights and the search for more inclusive and participatory forms of democracy. This search is taking place not solely within Latin American nations, but also through global networks of international non-governmental organizations (INGOs) that have linkages with national level non-governmental organizations (NGOs). Such organizations and linkages have formed important "transnational advocacy networks" that mobilize national and international opinion around multiple policy arenas including economic development, the environment, women's issues, trade, and human rights (Keck and Sikkink 1998; Risse, Ropp, and Sikkink 1999).

International and national non-governmental organizations are private organizations funded by voluntary contributions through membership, donations from large funding organizations, and self-financing through publications and other activities. In some ways, NGOs can be viewed as a logical extension of earlier forms of social movement organizations (SMOs), which have become further institutionalized with formal offices, budgets, staff, membership, newsletters, and open accountability procedures. Other NGOs developed outside specific social movement sectors. Some of the first took the form of research institutes staffed by social scientists who had been expelled from the universities by military governments. They were initially funded by international agencies or foreign governments, but soon began to seek funding for consultation and advisory work. Such income-generating activities became their most salient feature following the debt and fiscal crises of the early 1980s, as they began to connect grassroots movements to the international funding community, and broker financial support for ground-level development projects. It was the funding by foundations, foreign aid programs and international NGOs in the US and Europe that fuelled the massive expansion of Latin American NGOs from some 250 in the early 1970s to some 25,000 by the end of the 1990s (Vetter 1995: 2).

Some NGOs are now large and self-sustaining organizations like GIA, the *Grupo de Investigación Agraria*, in Chile. Others are smaller and/or more specialized, and their own development priorities may be distorted by the changing funding fashions of the international agencies that support them. On the other hand, these agencies rely on information and advice from NGOs to disburse funding effectively, and NGOs may abuse their position as brokers to favor certain clienteles or monopolize resources. In other words, the agencies and their officers "not infrequently have their pet ideas, pet theories, and their pet partners," but NGOs are replete with managers and activists who are ready to pursue their own agendas (Lehmann and Bebbington 1998: 268). Recent research by the Inter-American Foundation – a supporter of the NGO sector in Latin America

for over twenty-five years – shows that international donors have
focused massively on just three programatic areas: the environment,
children at risk, and microenterprises (Vetter 1995: 3).

During the period of the democratic transitions in Latin America,
NGOs became protagonists in the development drama, and participated in meetings and forums sponsored by multilateral institutions
such as the World Bank and the Inter-American Development Bank.
But the foreign funding of NGOs has been dropping vertiginously,
by as much as 50 percent in some regions (Vetter 1995: 1). Indeed,
the grassroots movements and NGOs often received more such
funding prior to the democratic transitions. This was true of Chile,
where the annual US$100 million in international NGO income at
the end of the 1980s, comprising about 70 percent of total income,
subsequently suffered drastic cuts, with major international NGOs
like Christian Aid and Oxfam withdrawing completely. The rapid
reduction in external funds forced NGOs to turn towards the state at
a moment when newly democratic governments were seeking to
restore a developmental role, partly for reasons of legitimacy, and
beginning to deploy and involve NGOs in an array of community and
social welfare projects. In Chile, the switch to state funding was facilitated by technocratic elites who favored NGO-style management
methods, and by 1993 the state was funneling some US$35 million
into the NGO sector (Kirby 1996: 21).

It thus appears that the ambiguities that characterized popular
movements in their national arenas are now being played out at a
global level. The simultaneous search for representation and autonomy is creating dilemmas on how far to work within existing structures while maintaining contact with grassroots membership. Initially,
grassroots organizations were generated in and shaped by their
interaction with the state. But there is a significant change in emphasis in grassroots organization and strategy that can be characterized
as the change from grassroots *movement* to non-governmental
organization. The process of institutionalizing grassroots movements
is not new, but it has accelerated, where increasing institutionalization and diminishing autonomy may be two sides of the same coin.
Tensions between leaders and base, elite and mass, professionals
and volunteers tend to be resolved through more organization and
consequently less mobilization. The process is driven, on the one
hand, by the need for politically agile actors to prosper in a more
complex political environment, and, on the other, by the need for
financial survival. But "who says organisation, says oligarchy"
(Michels [1911] 1959), and the grassroots movements become less
rooted in the people they grew up to serve. Such a process of insti-

tutionalization can facilitate the operation of clientelism and the co-optation of leaderships.

If the movements described in this chapter are to avoid such a fate, they will need to remember that one of their conscious objectives is precisely the creation of more participatory forms of organization, in which leadership is rotated and information disseminated horizontally. Given the impact of globalization on policy-making, it is likely that access to informational networks and communication technologies will play an increasing role in the repertoire of social activists. However, this trend entails the danger that many people who lack such access or skills will be excluded from the development of oppositional discourses and strategies. In addition, the relationship between grassroots organizations and the state in the new democracies is characterized by both clientelism and "clientization." This does not mean that they can have no influence on social policy, but it does mean that this influence will be fragmentary and piecemeal, and that their main role will be in social service delivery rather than in shaping social policy. But, despite these constraints, their role can still be important, and so should be supported by international funding agencies. The agencies, for their part, should strive to be less selective in their funding agendas and more selective about the specific organizations they fund. The relevant criteria here are "organisational authenticity, legitimacy and voice" (Diamond 1999: 254). Are they an authentic response to community needs rather than a spurious response to international funding fashions? Are they the legitimate representative of indigent people or threatened nature rather than the narrow representatives of their own professional and pecuniary interests? And do they give voice to those who would otherwise be condemned to the "political silence" created by the combination of neoliberal policy and exclusionary democracy?

We can thus conclude that the main contribution of new political actors in Latin America has been in the area of expanding the possibilities for popular participation. This participation is increasingly tied into global networks that have been facilitated by new communications technologies and greater diffusion of movement ideas and practices. At another level, however, popular participation is intensely local in that it is often rooted in the affirmation of particular struggles and identities. Governments do not usually see such participation as overtly political because of its emphasis on daily life, cultural identities, or religious celebrations. However, these forms of participation also present a challenge to the dominant myth of homogeneous societies and effective national institutions. As noted earlier, state formation in Latin America was led by elites that failed to control large areas of national territory and tended to create a false image of governmental power and cultural unity. New political actors are revealing a different reality, one in which cultural diversity and sub-national politics represent important challenges for democratic development. As we shall see in the following chapter, this is particularly clear when examining the political impact of indigenous peoples' mobilization in the region.

9 | MINORITY AND INDIGENOUS RIGHTS

In the previous chapter we noted how new political actors have sought to expand arenas for political participation in Latin America. In doing so, they have challenged the dominance of political parties and corporatist organizations in the representation of citizen demands. Many of the new political actors mobilize around community-based needs and often reflect the diverse regional or ethnic characteristics of sub-national politics. Indigenous peoples in particular have become significant political actors in their own right, challenging governments to recognize the multicultural nature of Latin American societies and to carry out political reforms that improve the quality of democracy by being more inclusive of cultural diversity (Dandler 1999; Díaz Polanco 1997; González Casanova and Roitman, eds, 1996; Yashar 1999).[1]

In this chapter we discuss the status of minority rights in Latin America and examine the recent politicization of ethnicity in the region. The chapter is divided into four sections. We begin by providing a historical account of the concepts of "minority" and "indigenous rights," and emphasize the role played by international law in legitimizing minority and indigenous rights, thereby providing an important political weapon for indigenous organizations in Latin America. The second section explains the comparatively late politicization of ethnic cleavages in Latin America by referring to the impact of state formation and assimilationist policies during the twentieth century. The next section provides evidence of how, since the 1960s, indigenous movements in Latin America have resisted economic exploitation and assimilation by combining material and cultural struggles. The final section examines how governments have responded to these struggles by comparing the content of different types of constitutional reform. This section also notes some of the problems facing the implementation of recent reforms concerning indigenous peoples in the region.

Minority and indigenous rights

There is no universally accepted definition of minority and indigenous rights.[2] However, the main criteria for defining "minority" are implied in the title of the 1992 United Nations Declaration on the Rights of Persons Belonging to National or Ethnic, Religious and Linguistic Minorities. According to this document, a minority may be defined as a group which is numerically inferior to the rest of a state's population, occupies a non-dominant position, possesses distinctive national, ethnic, religious or linguistic characteristics, and seeks to ensure its survival and development as a culturally distinct population. In addition to these general criteria, indigenous peoples are defined as the descendants of the population of a country or region that underwent conquest and colonization, and that seeks to maintain indigenous cultural institutions as well as to achieve equality with the dominant groups in society.

The concepts of minority and indigenous rights can only be understood in the historical context of state formation and colonialism. In Europe, protests against religious orthodoxy led to the first type of minority right: the freedom of religious expression. This was followed by the formation of independent states in which a culturally distinct group, or "nation," claimed the right to self-determination. This right became the right of a centralized state rather than the right of all the sub-national groups residing within its borders. As a result, modern European nation-states attempted to centralize political authority and create a sense of cultural homogeneity. Only laws that were in theory equally applicable to all individual citizens protected members of minority groups. Minority groups as such were denied collective rights. This liberal, individualistic model was also used to deny the existence of national minorities in the United States.

Theorists of liberal democracy have been divided over the extent to which individual and group rights are compatible. John Stuart Mill, for example, believed that only a homogeneous population could understand and uphold the principles of representative government, implying the forced assimilation of national minorities in Great Britain. In this case, Mill argued that the effective extension of individual rights would be sufficient to protect minorities from the will of the majority. In contrast, Lord Acton believed that some degree of autonomous control by national minorities would provide a check against the abuse of centralized state power. For this reason, individual rights needed to be supplemented by recognition of group rights if they were to be meaningful. This latter argument led to the creation of a minority rights regime within the League of Nations. However, the Nazis, who mobilized ethnic Germans in Poland and Czechoslovakia against their governments, manipulated this regime. As a result, the concept of minority rights fell into disfavor after the Second World War, and was replaced by an almost exclusive focus on individual rights, which was enshrined in the United Nations Declaration on Human Rights in 1948 (Kymlicka 1995).

Whereas in Europe minority rights have evolved in the context of nation-state formation, in developing countries minorities and indigenous groups that preexist European conquest have had to respond to the legacies of colonial rule. In Africa, one of the most salient legacies is the rivalry between ethnic groups for control of state resources. Through divide-and-rule tactics, colonial powers pitted one group against another in order to maintain political control. In addition, the colonial administration of territories bore no relation to ethnic identities. When African states gained their political independence after 1945, existing borders were retained, creating an artificial sense of nationhood, one that was determined by colonial demarcations rather than social composition. Those groups that claim a majority have therefore tended to hold state power and use it to exclude rival minority groups.

Most African and Asian states have sought to constitute themselves as unified nations through the centralization of control over education policy, religious practices, and economic development, accompanied on occasion by the massive expulsion of minority populations from their lands and the systematic discrimination toward nomadic, peripheral, and mountain peoples. Whereas in Asia many of these efforts have enforced a significant degree of national conformity, in Africa they have usually failed, leading to almost permanent conflict between ethnically defined factions and a collapse of state authority amid civil war.

In Latin America minorities and indigenous peoples were not seen, until the 1990s, as a significant factor in national politics. This is due to the marked decline of the native population after the European conquest in the sixteenth century and the subsequent policies of extermination and assimilation that occurred under liberal, oligarchic, populist, and military regimes (see chapter 1). Official claims to the contrary, discrimination is widespread and is manifested in the extreme poverty and social exclusion of the majority of indigenous people in Latin America (Wearne 1996: 28). Since the 1970s, however, indigenous peoples have become more active in demanding material improvements as well as recognition of collective rights in the areas of land tenure, development, education, and internal governance (van Cott 1994). This has paralleled similar movements of indigenous peoples and minorities in the United States and Canada.

Struggles for minority and indigenous rights have been compounded by economic globalization and increasing competition for scarce resources. Minorities are particularly affected as they make up much of the migrant labor force that faces discrimination in receiving countries. Structural adjustment programs that aim to privatize landholdings and promote export-oriented agriculture and mining enterprises also affect the livelihoods of indigenous peasants. Scarcity of land and depletion of natural resources are often at the root of political conflicts involving ethnic minorities and dominant national and transnational elites.

In the 1990s the importance of minority and indigenous rights gained international recognition. Several European countries shifted away from centralist models of government authority and adopted greater formal recognition of group rights. The Council of Europe also developed the European Charter for Regional or Minority Languages (1992) and the Framework Convention for the Protection of Minorities (1994). The latter explicitly seeks to end assimilationist policies, especially in the states of Eastern Europe. In 1992 the UN General Assembly also adopted the United Nations Declaration on the Rights of Persons Belonging to National or Ethnic, Religious and Linguistic Minorities. Although this document still avoids recognition of collective rights, it does go beyond earlier UN documents by obliging states to tolerate and actively promote minority rights (Minority Rights Group 1997: 755).

With regard to indigenous rights, the main international documents have been developed by the UN International Labour Organization (ILO) in Conventions 107 (1957) and 169 (1989). The former convention was assimilationist in its intent and reflected the postwar rejection of minority rights in favor of universal individual rights and nation building. The latter convention is more supportive of the rights of indigenous peoples by recognizing them as collective subjects and obliging states to allow them greater participation in decision-making with regard to social, cultural, and economic development. In addition, states are obliged to recognize the right of indigenous peoples to practice customary law within their own jurisdictions.[3] For example, Article 7 of ILO 169 states that indigenous peoples should have the right to participate in the design, implementation, and evaluation of national and regional development plans that may directly affect them, while Article 8 upholds their right to preserve their own customs and governing institutions as long as they are not incompatible with the basic rights established by national and international law. This Article also recommended the creation of conflict-resolution mechanisms in order to mediate disputes arising from the application of customary law.

Given the significance of land tenure for the survival of indigenous cultures, Article 13 includes the concept of "territory" to refer not just to agricultural land but the entire habitat that indigenous peoples occupy or use. As we shall see below, these Articles are politically controversial since they imply a radical reform of the historical relations between states and indigenous peoples. For this reason, many indigenous movements in Latin America appeal to ILO 169 as one of their central legal and political weapons in the struggle for minority rights today. A draft declaration of the UN Working Group on Indigenous Populations (1995) went further than ILO Convention 169, calling for the right of indigenous peoples to self-determination. Members of the UN have not accepted this since national governments claim sole sovereignty over matters of domestic jurisdiction (Thornberry 1991: 31).

State formation: the denial of minorities

As with democratization and neoliberalism, Latin America is also a participant in the global concern with multiculturalism and the rights of minorities in nation-states. In many countries, the transitions from authoritarian rule have been followed by a weakening or even collapse of government authority and the emergence of ethnic nationalist movements seeking secession and the establishment of new states. This phenomenon was particularly evident in the former Yugoslavia. We can also point to the Chechnya struggle for independence from the Russian Federation, the civil wars in Central Africa and the demands for independence of several Indonesian provinces. In each case, state formation remained vulnerable to the strength of regionally based ethnic identities that did not disappear during long periods of centralized rule. In fact, it turned out that central governments were often much weaker than they appeared and failed to subdue regional resistance effectively or assimilate cultural differences into a more unified national identity. Even in countries with a longer history of state formation and comparatively strong governmental institutions (such as Great Britain, Canada, Belgium, and Spain), we still find the continuation of political conflicts between minorities and majorities which directly affect governability, national identity, and economic integration. In each case, state formation has involved some combination of violent repression, assimilation, and centralization of governmental authority. During the past twenty years, however, there has been a resurgence of ethnic conflict around the world that poses important dilemmas for reforming national governments in ways that allow for the recognition of sub-national differences while upholding the principles of democratic contestation, the rule of law, and citizen participation. Latin America shares in these dilemmas and an analysis of the region's own experiences with multiculturalism may provide useful lessons for understanding similar situations in other parts of the world.

From a comparative perspective, the politicization of ethnic cleavages in Latin America is a relatively recent phenomenon. The conquest of the region decimated the native population, permitting the colonial authorities to maintain tight political control over indigenous peoples for over three centuries.[4] During the colonial period, the Church and the Crown concentrated native peoples in new communities, thereby dismantling previous loyalties and alliances, and preventing the emergence of broader ethnic identities that could mount organized resistance (Wearne 1996: 95–8). Nevertheless, Indians were able to retain some important degrees of autonomy in relation to internal governance and the use of communal lands. Colonial courts often upheld these rights against the incursions of private landowners belonging to local elites. Such decisions resulted from the Crown's desire to limit the economic power of an independent Creole elite. In doing so, Indians continued to have access to a limited land base and relatively independent forms of community government until the onset of capitalist agriculture and liberal property laws in the mid-nineteenth century. Colonial rulers were largely successful in avoiding rebellion until the late eighteenth century when the Spanish Crown, seeking to finance its wars in Europe, began to exact increasing amounts of tribute from the colonies through a more centralized administrative bureaucracy. Indians participated in the wars of independence, believing that they would regain some measure of autonomy by overcoming the impositions of their colonial rulers.

Political independence did not liberate Indians from political and economic subordination. Instead, the new elites continued to exploit Indian land and labor for the purpose of national development and integration into world markets through the export of primary products (foods and minerals). The promulgation of liberal constitutions and the expansion of individual property rights affected indigenous communities directly as they were dispossessed of lands that they needed for economic survival. Former protections were dismantled as liberal elites sought to reduce the power of the Catholic Church by legislating the privatization of lands that the Church had controlled since the colonial period. The state also passed laws declaring the break-up of communal landholdings and promoted foreign investment in the development of export-oriented agricultural enterprises. Nineteenth-century elites tended to view indigenous peoples as an obstacle in the way of achieving progress and national prosperity. In Argentina, for example, military campaigns in the nineteenth century virtually wiped out the native population. Surviving groups were forced to resettle in remote locations, while colonists and European immigrants occupied the best lands.[5]

In countries with larger indigenous populations, such as Mexico, Guatemala, Bolivia, Peru, and Ecuador, the loss of land to capitalist agriculture was resisted through popular rebellion and political alliances with reformist governments. During the twentieth century each of these countries experienced rural-based revolts that fed into larger national political transformations (the Mexican revolution of 1910–17, the ten-year respite from oligarchic rule in Guatemala in 1944–54, the Bolivian revolution of 1952, and reformist military governments in Peru and Ecuador in the 1970s). In these cases, land reform was a key pillar of governmental legitimacy and served to integrate indigenous communities into state-led development programs and corporatist organizations. States and modern political parties tended to ignore the ethnic dimension of indigenous peoples, emphasizing instead their economic or class identity as peasants (*campesinos*). From the 1930s until the early 1990s, Latin American governments denied the existence of minorities and ethnic discrimination in their countries and sought to assimilate indigenous peoples into elite visions of unified nations. Bilingual education programs were designed not to promote native languages, but to incorporate Indians into Spanish-speaking society. This effort was particularly strong in those countries (such as Mexico) that had experienced a high level of interracial mixing, or *mestizaje*, during the colonial period (Wade 1997).

Besides indigenous peoples, several Latin American countries also have significant black populations, descendants of African slaves that were brought to areas where local native labor was unavailable or had already been depleted by disease. These mainly coastal areas are located in Colombia, Venezuela, Ecuador, Brazil, and the Caribbean Basin. Despite the common history of subordination of blacks and indigenous peoples, national elites have tended to view the two groups differently. Whereas Indians have always been treated as a special category to be studied and assimilated (as well as exploited), blacks have simply been seen as subordinate members of the nation. Wade (1997) explains this different treatment by noting how theologians, governments, and scholars have seen race in terms of physical traits (phenotype) and ethnicity in terms of cultural traits linked to place. This distinction meant that nation-building policies tended to be more directed toward Indians (in the belief that they eventually could be assimilated, for example, through land reform or bilingual education), whereas blacks were always members of a distinct black race.[6]

Unlike in other regions of the world where ethnicity has been an important factor in political conflict and civil war, in Latin America, ethnic cleavages were effectively depoliticized by the early suppression and isolation of native populations, the incorporation, via land reform, of indigenous peoples into a single category of "campesinos," the imposition of assimilationist policies in the areas of education, language, and culture, and the racial subordination of blacks. For the most part, between the 1930s and the 1980s, land tenure conflicts were also cast in terms of *campesinos* against landlords or government officials, rather than as ethnic conflicts or struggles against discrimination. This does not mean that ethnic identities disappeared. Instead, they often remained hidden to the state and continued to be a latent source for political mobilization. They also evolved as they came into contact with political parties, labor unions, Churches and guerrilla movements (Rubin 1997; Harvey 1998).

Until the 1990s, governments lacked the legal or institutional mechanisms to protect minority rights, since the very existence of minorities was denied. The rule of law was meant to apply equally to all citizens, although, as we have seen, it was manipulated through patrimonial forms of political control. As a result, the politicization of ethnic cleavages and the emergence of minority rights is a comparatively recent phenomenon in Latin America and coincides with the region-wide transitions to democracy and the adoption of the neoliberal development model. The reaffirmation of ethnic identities also reveals the mistaken assumption of states that indigenous peoples were destined to disappear in the face of economic modernization and national integration. It is important to note that, in contrast to separatist movements that are seeking statehood elsewhere in the world, indigenous movements in Latin America wish to reform existing states in ways that reflect and include ethnic diversity. As one Guatemalan Mayan activist put it, "We want a role in the states from which we have been so long excluded, rather than their overthrow or break-up" (cited in Wearne 1996: 19).

Indigenous movements, land, and cultural identity

Contrary to the expectations of modernizing elites, indigenous peoples have not disappeared. Today there are around 800 ethno-linguistic groups in Latin America. The largest are found in the same regions where pre-Hispanic civilizations flourished: the Quechua and Aymara in the central Andes, the Nahua in central Mexico, and the Maya in southern Mexico, Guatemala, Belize, Honduras, and El Salvador. Estimates vary greatly for the size of indigenous populations. For the sake of consistency table 9.1 refers to the figures provided by the Minority Rights Group (1997).

Mexico has the largest indigenous population of any Latin American country, comprised of 56 ethno-linguistic groups and estimated at between 10 and 20 million people (between 10.8 and 23.8 percent of the national population). Indigenous peoples are a numerical majority in two countries: Guatemala (5.8 million or 59 percent of the population), and Bolivia (4.1 million, or 65 percent of the population). Peru and Ecuador also have large indigenous populations (8.8 million and 2.1 million, respectively), while both Colombia and Brazil have relatively small indigenous populations (620,000 and 254,000 respectively).

In contrast to the highland areas of Mesoamerica and the Andes, in the lowland regions of the Amazon basin and the rainforests of Central America the indigenous population is much smaller but is also more diverse with hundreds of distinct ethno-linguistic groups. Highland Indians have had more contact with dominant society and a greater degree of incorporation into national political structures of government, whereas the lowland population has lived in more remote and inaccessible frontier regions traditionally beyond the reach of weakly centralized states. Their relative isolation was broken only recently with the expansion of the agricultural frontier and state-led development projects that simultaneously sought to secure national borders.

Despite the diversity of indigenous peoples, they share some similarities in terms of their relationship to land and territory. Their survival has depended on their continued access to communal land and the avoidance of ecological crises. However, the incursions of the military, the state, and the market have threatened security of land

Table 9.1 Indigenous and black population in Latin America

	Population (and % of national population)
Mexico	10–20 million (10.8–23.8%). 56 indigenous peoples, mostly in central and southern Mexico. Largest are Nahua in centre, and Maya in southeast. Afro-Mexicans number 460,000–4.7 million (0.5–5%)
Guatemala	5.8 million (59%). 21 indigenous peoples (Maya), mostly in northern highlands. 5,500 Garífuna in east
Honduras	141,000 (3%). Largest are Lenca (90,000) and Miskitu (35,000). Afro-Honduran minority numbers 100,000–320,000 (1.8–5.8%)
El Salvador	324,000–1,080,000 (6–20%). Largest are Pipil (related to Nahua), Pocomam (related to Maya) and Lenca
Nicaragua	111,000–204,000 (2.8–5.1%). Most are located in eastern rainforests. Largest are Miskitu (67,000–160,000), who live in the Atlantic coast region.
Costa Rica	25,000 (0.8%) live in isolated areas along Panamanian border. Afro-Costa Ricans number 64,000 (2%).
Panama	109,000–200,000 (4.2–8.2%). Largest are Ngobe-Bugle (54,000–145,000) and Kuna (30,000) who live on San Blas islands and Colombian border. Afro-Panamanians number 325,000 (13%).
Colombia	620,000 (1.7%). Largest are Paez and Guambiano, located in Cauca Valley in central region. Afro-Colombians number 4.9–15 million (14–42%).
Ecuador	2.6 million (25%). 12 indigenous peoples in highlands, Amazon lowlands and coast. Afro-Ecuadorians number 573,000–1.1 million
Peru	8.8 million (39%). Largest are Aymara and Quechua in highlands, Ashaninka in Amazon basin. Afro-Peruvians number 1.4–2.2 million
Bolivia	4.1 million (65%). Largest are Quechua (2.3 million) and Aymara (1.6 million) in highlands, and Chiquitano (40,000) in Amazon lowlands. Afro-Bolivians number 158,000 (2%).
Brazil	254,000 (0.16%), distributed among 197 peoples located in Amazon rainforest. Afro-Brazilians number 65–120 million (40–75%)
Venezuela	316,000 (1.5%), distributed among 28 peoples in Orinoco Delta region. Afro-Venezuelans number 1.9–14 million (9–67%)
Paraguay	95,000 (2.3%), distributed among 18 peoples, many nomadic, in Chaco and lowland rainforest regions. Guaraní spoken by 90% of the national population.
Uruguay	No indigenous peoples since nineteenth century, but recent return of some Guaraní Mbyá. Afro-Uruguayans number 38,000 (1.2%).
Argentina	373,000 (2%), mainly in northern Chaco and forest regions (Toba, Wichi and Guaraní Mbyá) or extreme south near Chilean border (Mapuche).
Chile	990,000 (7%). Largest are Mapuche in south and Rapanui (Easter Islanders).

Source: Minority Rights Group (1997)

tenure and led in many cases to environmental destruction. Examples include the loss of land to the construction of hydroelectricity dams, the contamination of land and groundwater due to mining, gold prospecting, and oil exploration, and the depletion of forests due to unsustainable logging and uncontrolled colonization (for the case of Brazil, see Wearne 1996: 123, 127).

The protection of land rights has therefore been at the center of indigenous peoples' movements throughout Latin America. This is not simply a struggle for material goals, since land is central to the survival and development of indigenous cultures. In all cases the struggle for land and cultural integrity have gone together. The following discussion provides evidence for this argument from Ecuador, Bolivia, Colombia, Mexico, and Guatemala.

The struggle for protection of land rights began in South America in the early 1960s. In these years state and transnational corporations began to exploit intensively the valuable forest resources of the Amazon basin (encompassing parts of Ecuador, Brazil, Peru, Colombia, Venezuela, and Bolivia). National governments, particularly in Brazil and Ecuador, promoted mining, logging, and oil exploration as they sought to boost national revenue and spur economic growth. These extractive industries were followed by the arrival of thousands of colonists and ranchers, who were encouraged to settle in the Amazon as a means of avoiding the politically controversial problem of implementing land redistribution elsewhere. The combined effect of the new development projects and colonization was a rapid increase in deforestation and the spread of new diseases among indigenous communities.

The first organized response came from Shuar Indians in the Ecuadorian Amazon. With support from Salesian missionaries, the Shuar organized local committees and a Shuar Federation in 1964. They mobilized to demand recognition of rights to their traditional territories and built regional coalitions with other Amazonian groups faced with similar pressures during the 1970s. In the 1980s these groups formed an Amazonian confederation (CONFENIAE) that focused primarily on defending indigenous territories against oil exploration, logging, and colonization. In the same year it joined forces with highland Indians and helped form the Ecuadorian National Indigenous Organization (CONAIE). Over the following decade both the Amazonian and the highland movements matured and gained national prominence. For example, the Amazonian movement led a successful march to the capital city, Quito, in 1991, which led to the titling of more than 1 million hectares of indigenous land (van Cott 2000a: 10).

The 1960s also saw the creation of the first organizations among highland Indians. As noted above, several countries adopted land reform programs as a means of modernizing rural economies and assimilating Indians into the dominant society. In the case of Guatemala, land reform was brought to a halt by the military coup that overthrew the reformist government of Jacobo Arbenz in 1954. Elsewhere, land reform continued well into the 1970s. This was particularly the case in Mexico, Bolivia, Peru, Ecuador, and Colombia. However, despite formal support for these programs, the implementation process was often manipulated by clientelism and in most cases failed to redistribute sufficient good-quality land. In addition to these limitations, the population of indigenous communities began to increase more rapidly in the 1960s. The combined effect was the increasing pressure on available land. In several countries, this situation led to a more intense struggle for land.

We noted on page 176, in the case of Ecuador, that highland Indians united in 1980 with the Amazon-based movement in a new national organization. In the highlands, indigenous people had a longer history of contact with the state, political parties, and labor unions. The Communist Party was the most influential force and created the Ecuadorian Indigenous Federation (FEI) in 1944. In the 1960s, the FEI took advantage of new legislation designed to break up the traditional system of large estates that the government viewed as unproductive and a source of social tension. Indians were able to gain access to land and establish community-level institutions that had been decreed by a 1937 law (*comunas*). In 1972, a new national organization of highland *comunas* (ECUARUNARI) was formed with the help of the Catholic Church. This organization was also able to draw on the skills of a new generation of indigenous leaders who benefited from bilingual education programs in the early 1980s. By the end of the 1980s, the highland movement had matured in tandem with its Amazonian counterpart. The new national organization, CONAIE, combined class and ethnic demands in its program and staged a nationwide uprising in 1990 that blocked transportation and forced the government to cede control over bilingual education to the indigenous movement. A similar protest in 1994 obliged the government to drop proposed legislation for the privatization of landholdings (van Cott 2000a: 11).

In Bolivia, where indigenous peoples constitute a majority (estimated at 65 percent of the population), a similar pattern of mobilization can be traced to the 1970s. In the highland regions, however, indigenous organizations have been weaker than in Ecuador, partly because of their incorporation into a larger labor confederation that has tended to privilege class over ethnic demands. When organized labor was severely weakened by structural adjustment programs in the mid-1980s, indigenous groups were also affected and proved unable to maintain a strong and independent movement. In contrast, the lowland Indians of the Bolivian Amazon have built a more autonomous organization, which, as in Ecuador, seeks to defend territorial rights from the encroachments of logging companies. This movement led a successful "March for Territory and Dignity" in 1990, which resulted in the titling of more than 2 million hectares of indigenous land (van Cott 2000a: 14). The government also passed an agrarian reform law in 1996 that allowed indigenous peoples to claim territorial rights. By 1997 the government had granted recognition to seven indigenous territories covering 2.6 million hectares and was processing a further thirty-four demands representing another 20 million hectares (Yashar 1999: 94).

In the case of Colombia, the first indigenous movement was born in the Cauca Valley in the early 1960s as an attempt to recuperate ancestral indigenous lands. This movement evolved in different ways over the next decade, with one current emphasizing land reform and another demanding recognition of traditional indigenous governance. These currents have been developed in different organizations, known as the National Indigenous Organization of Colombia (ONIC) and the Southwest Indigenous Authorities (AISO), respectively. Despite its comparatively small size,[7] Colombia's indigenous population has succeeded in making a political impact on national legislation (see p. 183). As in Ecuador, both currents view land reform not solely as a material goal, but as the basis on which indigenous cultures can be rebuilt and defended.

In Mexico, the struggle for land intensified in the early 1970s when the government promised to revive a flagging agrarian reform program. By the end of the decade, this promise had not been fulfilled and official policy shifted away from land distribution and towards the promotion of private investment to boost agricultural productivity. During the 1980s indigenous peoples in Mexico organized a series of protests and marches to demand the continuation of land reform, a demand that remained particularly strong in the heavily indigenous southern state of Chiapas. The failure of the government to respond to this demand was one of the reasons behind the armed indigenous uprising of the Zapatistas in January 1994. As in Ecuador and Colombia, the Zapatistas have also combined material goals with cultural aspirations. They have demanded land redistribution in Chiapas and Mexico, but they have also insisted on the need for constitutional reforms that would recognize the right of indigenous communities to govern themselves according to their own needs and traditions (Harvey 1998; Latin American Perspectives 2001).

Finally, in Guatemala, where, like Bolivia, indigenous people constitute a majority of the population (estimated at 59 percent), the struggles for land and cultural integrity have gone together. As in other countries, political parties, government agencies, and churches have influenced the organization of highland Indians. In the Guatemalan case, however, military governments that suspected the involvement of radical guerrilla movements often repressed grassroots organizing. During the early 1980s, the army was responsible for the destruction of hundreds of villages and the murder of thousands of Mayan Indians in the western highlands. The guerrilla movements proved unable to protect these communities from military repression. Internal changes within the Guatemalan regime allowed for a return to civilian rule in 1986 and the beginnings of peace talks with the main guerrilla organizations. Indigenous leaders sought to influence the negotiations, hoping to bring an end to the violence as well as gain recognition of ethnic rights in the context of Guatemala's democratization. A final peace accord was signed in late 1996 and included a set of agreements to support indigenous rights and culture, as well as provide land for refugees and those displaced by the violence of the 1980s. However, the accords were rejected in a referendum in 1999 in which only 18 percent of the electorate participated. One of the reasons for this result was the effective campaign of right-wing, non-indigenous groups that raised the specter of secession by autonomous indigenous regions. Although the accords were based on the principles of ILO Convention 169 that preclude the right of secession, this did not prevent the right wing from using the media to attack the accords and in effect prevent the implementation of indigenous rights.

From the above survey of several Latin American countries we can see that, for indigenous peoples, land and cultural identity are intertwined. The emergence of regional and national organizations can be explained in terms of the need to defend land rights against the incursions of oil exploration, logging, ranching, and colonization. Land is defended not solely as a material resource but also as the basis for maintaining and developing distinct cultural identities. As a result of these struggles, by the end of the 1980s indigenous rights were on the political agenda. The following section examines how Latin American governments have responded to this new challenge.

Constitutional reform and indigenous rights

The nature of the indigenous challenge to national government is distinct from other pressures by social groups such as labor and business. The demand for cultural recognition goes to the heart of state formation and national identity, issues which liberal, conservative, and populist elites thought they had largely resolved many decades ago. As argued in chapter 3, the form that states took in Latin America tended to obscure the absence or weakness of central government institutions in large areas of the national territory. This is especially true in rural and peripheral areas where the majority of indigenous people live.[8]

Indigenous peoples are demanding that they be recognized in national constitutions as "collective subjects", rather than as simply "ethnic groups" or "indigenous communities." The term "collective subjects" empowers indigenous peoples to govern themselves according to their own needs and customs. On a practical level, this would give indigenous government the same legal status as other subnational units of government such as municipalities. In contrast, the terms "ethnic groups" or "indigenous communities" do not imply such a degree of political empowerment. On the contrary, these terms correspond more closely to the maintenance of centralized governmental authority. Figures 9.1 and 9.2 depict protest and rebellion from "minorities at risk" (Gurr 1993) in the region for the 1980s and 1990s. The figures use standardized measures of protest and rebellion. The protest scale ranges from 0 for no protest to 5 for demonstrations with a participation greater than 100,000. The rebellion scale ranges from 0 for no rebellious activity to 6 for large-scale guerrilla activity. The figures show that peaceful protest was much more common than rebellion, and that the early 1980s saw more of both activities. Such levels of mobilization challenge governments to acknowledge minority demands, and in this section we discuss how governments have responded to indigenous demands, in some cases conceding rights to new "collective subjects" while, in others, reaffirming state control.

The first case of constitutional reform came in Nicaragua in the 1980s. During this time the leftist Sandinista National Liberation Front (FSLN) was in government following the revolution that ousted the Somoza dictatorship in 1979. The US government financed and equipped a rebel army of former Somoza supporters (the *Contras*) with the goal of overthrowing the Sandinistas and installing a government more friendly to US foreign policy and business inter-

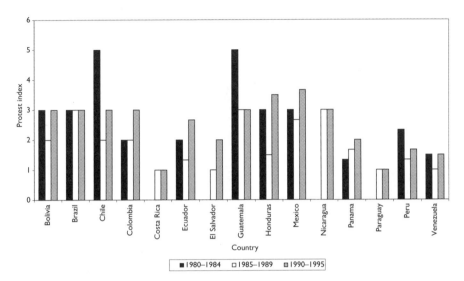

Figure 9.1   Minority protest in Latin America, 1980–1995
Protest index: none (0); verbal opposition (1); symbolic acts of resistance (2);
    demonstration <10,000 (3); demonstration <100,000; and demonstration
    >100,000
Source: Gurr (2000) and the *Minorities at Risk Data Set*
    (www.cidcm.umd.edu/inscr/mar/)

ests. The *Contras* were able to gain some support among Miskitu
Indians in the Atlantic coast region of Nicaragua, an area where the
Sandinistas had a limited presence. This region fell under British
domination during the colonial period and remained geographically
and culturally distinct from the Spanish-speaking and mestizo centers
of political power in the west and south of Nicaragua where the 1979
revolution was fought out. In an effort to undermine the influence of
the *Contras*, in 1987 the Sandinistas recognized the Miskitu people as
a collective subject and created two multiethnic autonomous regions
in the Atlantic coast, comprising almost half of the national territory.
Although this measure gained some legitimacy for the Sandinistas,
subsequent governments have restricted the autonomy of these two
regions and many of the supposed gains have not been fulfilled
(González Pérez 1997; Hale 1994).

The Nicaraguan case was exceptional because of the circumstances
in which the autonomous regions were created. Nevertheless, it also
reveals the more common problem of establishing legitimacy by recognizing ethnic rights. In this regard it is important to consider the

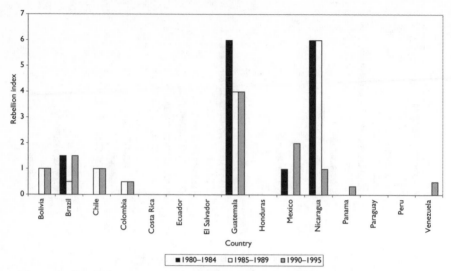

Figure 9.2   Minority rebellion in Latin America, 1980–1995
Minority rebellion: none (0); political banditry (1); campaigns of terrorism (2);
   local rebellion (3); small-scale guerrilla activity (4); intermediate-scale guerrilla activity (5); large-scale guerrilla activity (6)
Source: Gurr (2000) and the *Minorities at Risk Data Set*
   (www.cidcm.umd.edu/inscr/mar/)

broader contexts in which governments sought to respond to indigenous movements in the 1990s. We have already mentioned the significance of international law, particularly ILO Convention 169, in
legitimizing indigenous rights. Indigenous movements have consistently appealed to this document in their dealings with national governments. During the 1980s, leaders of indigenous organizations also
became closely involved in an international network of indigenous
rights advocates that helped formulate the ILO 169. International
attention was also raised by the protests against official celebrations
of the Quincentenary of European conquest in 1992. In the same year
the Nobel Peace Prize was awarded to Guatemalan Mayan activist
Rigoberta Menchú. The United Nations also declared 1993 the "Year
of Indigenous Peoples" and 1994–2004 the "Decade of Indigenous
Peoples" with the goal of developing and implementing laws to
protect indigenous rights. The growing international legitimacy of
indigenous rights coincided with the declining political legitimacy of
several Latin American governments in the 1990s. In some cases,

recognition of indigenous rights was seen as a means to reestablishing governmental legitimacy.

In Colombia and Ecuador, the crisis of legitimacy was so deep that reform through traditional means proved insufficient to secure stability. In both cases, legitimacy had been eroded by the clientelism and corruption of the dominant political parties, the exclusion of other political forces, and, particularly in the case of Colombia, the participation of the state in political violence. Special elections were held for new constituent assemblies that drafted new national Constitutions (in Colombia in 1991 and Ecuador in 1998). In both countries, indigenous movements capitalized on their prior history of mobilization and were able to insert their own demands into debates concerning their countries' new Constitutions. They were assisted in this by the presence of a firm bloc of allies from leftist parties in the respective constituent assemblies and were able to draw on the support of relatively unified national organizations in presenting their proposals. In both cases, indigenous movements expressed their goals in terms of the broadening of democracy and the establishment of a multicultural state rather than simply demanding land reform.

In the case of Colombia, the 1991 Constitution protected the inalienable nature of indigenous collective lands (*resguardos*), recognized indigenous peoples as collective subjects, and provided them with the same juridical status as Colombian municipalities. This means that *resguardos* receive the same proportion of funds as municipalities and are governed by indigenous authorities (*cabildos*). Further measures to increase indigenous participation in regional development planning through the establishment of Indigenous Territorial Entities (ETIs) have been blocked by landowners. The new indigenous authorities have also had to contend with constant threats and encroachments from the main sources of violent conflict in Colombia: drug-traffickers, guerrillas, paramilitary groups, and the government's own security forces. Implementation of the constitutional reforms has been most effective in the area of indigenous customary law, largely owing to the supportive role played by the Colombian Constitutional Court, itself a creation of the 1991 Constitution (van Cott 2000b: 110–18). Indigenous people were also guaranteed representation in the national congress through Article 171, which establishes a two-seat senatorial district for Indians. Black communities did not gain the same rights (due to the historical distinctions between race and ethnicity noted above). However, the Constitution did recognize the collective property rights of black communities in the Pacific coast Chocó region (van Cott 2000b: 85–7), even though implementation of these new rights has also been affected by the shifting political conjuncture. After 1992 newly elected presidents gave less attention to indigenous rights. For example, President Ernesto Samper (1994–8) was accused of having accepted money from the drug cartels during his election campaign. Samper's entire period in government was taken up with this issue, while the old vices of corruption and clientelism undermined the advances made by the constituent assembly.

In Ecuador, the 1998 Constitution was strongly influenced by the indigenous delegates of the Plurinational Pachakutik Unity Movement (MUPP), which had been founded prior to the 1996 elections by the CONAIE and other social movements. Given the fragmentation of the Ecuadorian party system (see chapter 6), the MUPP was able to form an important bloc with leftist parties and win approval of ILO Convention 169 as well as the inclusion of some of its own proposals within the new national Constitution. As a result, the 1998 Constitution recognized self-governing indigenous and Afro-Ecuadorian territories and corresponding electoral districts that guarantee representation in the national congress. The exact functions of these territories are dependent on implementing legislation but they may allow for the autonomous administration of indigenous justice systems and the design of economic development projects through greater local consultation. As in Colombia, the outcome is contingent on the shifting balance of forces within the legislature and between congress and the executive. In this respect it is important to note how the involvement of the MUPP in electoral and party politics has created tensions as well as opportunities for the broader indigenous movement in Ecuador.

Prior to 1995 the CONAIE had shunned the electoral arena and favored mass mobilization to press indigenous demands. Like most social movements in Ecuador, it criticized the lack of representativeness and corruption of the political parties. However, a shift occurred in 1996 when the MUPP was created to contest the presidential and congressional elections as a new kind of party, claiming to be more representative of the country's poor majority (especially the indigenous population) than the clientelistic parties that are dominated by non-indigenous elites. As noted on page 183, during late 1997 and early 1998 the MUPP delegates were able to influence the constituent assembly due to the fragmented nature of the party system and the divisions within the conservative bloc. However, divisions within the indigenous movement itself (over tactics and strategy) led to a decrease in its vote in the May 1998 elections. A conservative President, Jamil Mahuad, was elected and the new congress was dominated once more by conservative parties. A smaller bloc of MUPP deputies decided to support the latter in the naming of the president of the congress and engaged in negotiations and pacts in order to advance their positions within the new administration. This kind of deal-making is common in Ecuador's fragmented party system and is part of the price that social movements pay when participating in arenas that are still controlled by economic and political elites. However, this strategy of accommodation was severely criticized by rival leaders and grassroots organizations in CONAIE, who dubbed the MUPP tactics as "politics-as-usual." During 1999 the severe economic crisis, currency devaluation, and rising poverty (combined with allegations of corruption in the Mahuad government) created a political crisis from which the MUPP deputies could not escape. By the end of the year, opinion polls revealed that 90 percent of the population wanted Mahuad to resign. The means by which he was eventually removed from power surprised most observers and demonstrated the tensions and divisions within the indigenous movement (Beck and Mijeski 2001).

On January 21, 2000, a few thousand indigenous protesters, labor unions, leftist militants, and sympathetic elements of the military took control of congress, the Supreme Court, and the presidential palace, forcing Mahuad to resign. Each group had its own set of grievances, but all tended to share the belief that the government was corrupt and incapable of managing the economic crisis. However, the coup attempt was aborted when the military leader General Carlos Mendoza resigned from the newly created National Salvation Front just a few hours after forcing Mahuad from office. In accordance with the Constitution, the Vice-President was installed as President and the government continued to function while the parties engaged in a new set of alliances and negotiations. The impact on the indigenous movement was largely negative. Many grassroots activists, although also opposed to Mahuad, denounced the secret dealings between CONAIE leaders and the military as another example of "politics-as-usual."

The abortive coup also reveals longstanding tensions over tactics and strategy within Ecuador's indigenous movement, between pragmatists favoring negotiations with the parties and radicals favoring direct action. The recent incursions into party politics and the electoral arena have had mixed results. On the one hand, indigenous delegates were able to win important reforms in the context of the constituent assembly. On the other, once the composition of congress had shifted back to conservative dominance, the effectiveness of the

MUPP delegates was curtailed. The combination of economic crisis and rising frustrations within the indigenous movement led some leaders to try more dramatic means of removing the government from power, in turn provoking further dissent within an increasingly divided indigenous movement. The Ecuadorian case should serve as a reminder of the tensions and contradictions within indigenous movements, as well as the broader political context of party politics and elite pacts in which they are increasingly inserted.

In Bolivia, a new Constitution was also passed in 1994, although in this case the political crisis was less severe, allowing the government to maintain control of the reform process and avoid the election of a new Constituent assembly. The reforms corresponded more closely to the goals of President Gonzalo Sánchez de Losada (1993–7) and his supporters in congress, while indigenous organizations were more marginal than in Colombia or Ecuador. As a result, the 1994 Constitution does not recognize the territorial rights of indigenous peoples and the main reform is limited to permitting the administration of customary law (van Cott 2000a: 14). In this case, the election of a more conservative President, Hugo Banzer, in 1997 also limited the implementation of the Sánchez de Losada reforms. The Banzer government has replaced the emphasis on collective rights and political participation with a more welfarist focus on reducing poverty through microcredit programs. Indigenous peoples are being cast more as small-scale entrepreneurs than as collective subjects (van Cott 2000b: 213–18). In Peru, the outcome of constitutional reform was even less favorable for indigenous peoples. In the 1993 Constitution the Fujimori government effectively recentralized political power in the Executive branch and excluded indigenous representatives from the design of constitutional reforms.

In the above cases we can see how governments have taken steps to recognize minority and indigenous rights. According to van Cott (2000a), a comparative analysis of these cases reveals at least three factors that influence the scope of constitutional reform: the election of a new constituent assembly; the alliance of indigenous organizations with a strong leftist bloc in the assembly; and the relative unity of a national indigenous organization. Where these conditions existed (Colombia and Ecuador), indigenous peoples made the greatest gains. Where they were lacking (Bolivia and Peru), governments were able to limit the scope of indigenous rights.

This model is also useful when considering the case of Mexico, where the Zapatista uprising in 1994 challenged the state to reform its relations with indigenous peoples. Although the Zapatistas also called for the election of a constituent assembly and the drafting of a new Constitution, the PRI government was able to maintain control of the political reform process (as in Bolivia), although at the "cost" of reducing electoral fraud and democratizing the terms of contestation between political parties (leading to the eventual defeat of the PRI in the 2000 presidential elections). The Zapatistas were able to unite a national indigenous movement (known as the *Congreso Nacional Indígena*, CNI) behind a set of proposed reforms that were also accepted by the government within the framework of peace negotiations. These accords, known as the San Andrés Accords on Indigenous Rights and Culture (after the town where they were signed in February 1996) called for similar reforms to those entailed in ILO Convention 169.

The Mexican government failed to implement these accords, leading to a suspension of talks and a worsening of the conflict in Chiapas. In late 1996 a multiparty legislative body known as the Commission for Peace and Reconciliation in Chiapas (COCOPA) attempted to mediate and produced a revised document that met with the approval of the Zapatistas but failed to win the backing of the federal government and President Ernesto Zedillo (1994–2000). The historic defeat of the PRI in the 2000 presidential elections raised the hope that the new President, Vicente Fox Quesada of the center-right National Action Party (PAN), would fulfill his campaign promises and act to win approval for the COCOPA Law on Indigenous Rights and Culture, thereby allowing for a resumption of peace talks with the Zapatistas. However, the Zapatistas lacked strong allies in the new congress, where the PRI and the PAN made up the majority. President Fox did not apply much effort into convincing PAN legislators of the merits of the COCOPA law and the congress finally approved a much weaker and revised version in April 2001. This version restricted the degree of indigenous autonomy to communities within single municipalities, denied constitutional recognition of indigenous peoples as collective subjects with the right to decide upon their own forms of governance and development, and maintained a paternalistic relation in which the federal government would provide social services to indigenous communities.

The revisions to the COCOPA law met with predictable opposition from the Zapatistas and the CNI. Nevertheless, the constitutionally requisite number of state legislatures subsequently ratified the reforms, although, significantly, it was rejected in those states with the largest indigenous populations (including Chiapas, Oaxaca, and Guerrero). In addition, anomalies in the ratification process led to a series of legal appeals concerning the validity of the entire procedure. Despite the fact that these appeals were still awaiting a ruling from Mexico's Supreme Court, President Fox decided to promulgate the new law, which entered into effect on August 14, 2001.

In the case of Mexico, political reform was kept separate from the demands of the indigenous movement. No constituent assembly was elected and constitutional reforms concerning indigenous rights were at first delayed and then watered down. Indigenous peoples were not considered to be "collective subjects" but simply "indigenous communities." The end result was the reaffirmation of centralized state power and the continued denial of collective rights of indigenous peoples. Following van Cott's model, Mexico's indigenous movement has failed to win meaningful reforms because it was denied the opportunities provided by constituent assemblies and lacked a strong bloc of supporters in the national congress at the time when constitutional reforms were modified. The CNI has overcome many of the divisions between sectors of the indigenous movement and there was unified support for the COCOPA law. However, in the absence of the other two factors, the Mexican experience more closely resembles that of Bolivia, Guatemala, and Peru rather than that of Colombia or Ecuador.[9]

In this chapter we have traced the comparatively late politicization of ethnicity in Latin America and noted the importance of international law for legitimizing the claims of indigenous peoples in the 1990s. We have also shown how indigenous movements combine material and cultural demands in their opposition to economic marginalization and political exclusion. In several cases governments made concessions in the area of indigenous rights in order to regain political legitimacy. However, in other cases states continue to exercise centralized control and deny claims for the extension of collective rights.

Even in those cases where the most gains were made (Nicaragua, Colombia, Ecuador, and, to a lesser extent, Bolivia), serious problems remain in the implementation of indigenous rights. These include the desire of central governments to limit the scope of the reforms, the lack of protection for territorial rights, and legal ambiguities regarding the actual content of new legislation. Indeed, some observers are skeptical about the real impact of constitutional reforms alone since they were adopted under domestic and international pressures during acute periods of political crisis, but without real commitments for effective implementation. Once the crisis period passed and political control was reasserted, governments had less incentive to follow through with the requisite funds and political support for protecting the newly established rights (Wade, 1997:105–7). In addition, changes in the composition of governments following subsequent elections have displaced concern with indigenous rights. In sum, we need to keep in mind longer-term trends as well as the shifting nature of political conjunctures when evaluating the impact of recent reforms.

10 | UNEVEN DEMOCRATIC PERFORMANCE

The uneven performance of Latin American democracies

Democratic government may be defined in a minimal and procedural fashion as a political system where political parties compete for control of the government through relatively free and fair elections. Today there are some 120 such systems across the world, including all the countries of Latin America with the exception of Cuba.[1] But beyond this minimum benchmark it is recognized that the democratic performance of these governments varies widely (Diamond 1999: 24–63). In other words, the claim to be democratic serves to legitimate an increasing number of governments, but – in fact – some of these governments are far more democratic than others. Thirty years ago Dahl recognized that no government could be perfectly democratic, and so chose to refer to existing democratic governments as "polyarchies" (Dahl 1971). Nonetheless, some polyarchies are less perfect than others.

Most of the democratic governments of Latin America are numbered among the least perfect polyarchies in the world. They are seen to be imperfect because their democratic performance is so uneven. The uneven quality of democratic government in Latin America (though not uniquely in Latin America) has been characterized as electoral democracy without liberal democracy (see chapter 2). Electoral democracy advances, with political parties competing for control of the government through relatively free and fair elections (O'Donnell 1997). But liberal democracy remains absent without an effective rule of law that might underpin individual and minority freedoms and protections (Diamond 1999: 1–23). The democratic constitutions of Latin America all enshrine liberal democratic principles, but if these principles fail to operate in practice, the citizens will not enjoy democratic freedoms.

In chapter 2, democracy was defined by the presence of the three primary principles of contestation, constitutionalism, and inclusiveness. In the terms of this definition, the current unevenness of Latin American democracy is characterized by contestation and inclusiveness without constitutionalism. Contestation is assured through political party competition and an active political opposition, while a degree of formal inclusiveness is achieved through political participation in the electoral arena. But the absence of effective constitutionalism means that political and civil rights cannot be properly protected. In other words, although the institutional core of democratic government is affirmed by political party systems and electoral competition for both executive and legislature, individual and minority rights continue to languish.

It seems simple to characterize the unevenness of Latin American democracy in this way. But things are likely to be more complicated in the real political world where distinct institutional attributes of democratic government may coexist uncomfortably, as may different individual rights. By way of example, it is often observed that the *vertical* accountability implicit in electoral politics does not necessarily entail an equal degree of *horizontal* accountability between branches of government (O'Donnell 1997, 1999a; Schedler 1999), often because the latter is checked by military prerogatives and military influence over civilian government. Equally, the *political* rights required for electoral politics can promote more intense contestation, with *civil* rights suffering as a consequence.

Thus it is not quite accurate enough to characterize the uneven quality of democratic government in Latin America as the assertion of electoral democracy at the expense of liberal democracy, or even as the absence of effective constitutionalism. Electoral democracy certainly advances, but cannot become fully established if only because "free and fair" elections require entrenched civil liberties (Riker and Weimer 1993). Consequently, the boundaries between electoral politics and their broader democratic context can sometimes become overdrawn in theory and blurred in practice. Analogously, constitutionalism provides some protection for the basic rights and procedures of electoral politics (regular elections, universal suffrage, the right to form political parties), but much less against civil rights violations, despite their proven capacity to impair both the "freedom" and "fairness" of elections.

Exploring uneven performance

Democratic performance is different from the simple endurance or longevity of democratic government, though it is clearly important for democratic government to survive if democratic politics is to prosper (Przeworski et al. 2000). It is also different from government effectiveness in matters such as national security, macroeconomic management, or even social policy and welfare provision, since these concerns are common to all governments, whether democratic or not. It is, in contrast, a gauge of how well democratic governments are performing as democracies, or how well they fulfill in practice their democratic principles. In this perspective, democratic performance "refers to the degree to which a system meets such democratic norms as representativeness, accountability, equality and participation" (Lijphart 1993: 149).

There is a broad consensus on the foundational principles of liberal democracy. The intellectual grounds for the consensus were created by long traditions of both liberal and democratic thought, beginning in seventeenth-century England, and in the encounter and conversation between them. The classic statement of liberal principles is found in Locke's *Second Treatise*, and his defence of the constitutional protection of individual liberty and equality under the rule of law has remained central to liberal theory ever since (Locke 1924: 180–3). The first strands of modern democratic thought were skeptical of the ability of the law to protect liberty and equality unless each citizen could "exercise an equal right of participation in the making of the laws" (Skinner 1998: 69–70). By making government accountable to the people, self-rule provides a guarantee that it will uphold the law, so supplying the essential democratic link to liberal democracy.

Over time liberal democratic government has developed the institutional and legal means for achieving the rule of law and sovereignty of the people, and so defending the key principles of liberty and equality (Foweraker and Krznaric 2000). The institutional means include the party political competition and electoral participation that promote contestation and inclusiveness, while the legal means are mainly expressed through the panoply of rights (property rights, political rights, civil rights, and minority rights) that underpin constitutionalism. Modern forms of democratic government therefore have distinct dimensions, so it follows that any account of democratic performance must itself be multidimensional.

To assert that the performance of Latin American democracies is "uneven" is to recognize the multidimensionality of democratic government. Self-evidently, if governments perform well in some respects but poorly or erratically in others, then their performance can be judged as uneven. If these distinct dimensions can be measured in some way, then the measures may achieve meaningful comparisons of different democracies with different performance profiles. Yet this is not the approach of most "democratic indicators" that have come to constitute barometers of comparative democratic performance in academic, public policy, and business circles (Foweraker and Krznaric 2000). These indicators usually tend to focus on just one or two aspects of democratic government that only provide a rather partial picture (Hadenius 1992: 5; Gastil 1991: 26), even if this partiality is often disguised by single scales masquerading as summary performance measures.

Getting the measures right is important because they have practical policy implications. The governments of advanced industrial democracies and major international institutions like the World Bank and the International Monetary Fund have come to require democratic governance as a condition – severally – of diplomatic recognition, political and military support, and economic aid and restructuring. A key development in this regard was the World Bank's interpretation of "good governance" to include not just sound public finance but also civil and political rights (Kieley 1998). Good governance has become democratic and responsible governance. At the same time, it is alleged that policy conditionality or linkage to democratic governance derives from a "minimalist" conception of democracy that places "excessive emphasis" on "free and fair elections" (Diamond 1999: 59). Do the democratic governments of Latin America mirror this minimalist version of democracy, or do they truly achieve good governance?

Demonstrating uneven performance

The only way to respond to this question is to find ways of measuring the distinct dimensions of performance that are described as contestation (political party competition), constitutionalism (rights), and inclusiveness (electoral participation). At the same time it is best to use tried and tested measures to maximize reliability and economy of effort, and our measures have been used previously in mainstream comparative work on democracy and democratic institutions.[2] These measures reflect the democratic performance over time of nine Latin American governments, namely Argentina, Brazil, Chile, Colombia, Costa Rica, El Salvador, Guatemala, Nicaragua, and Venezuela. In

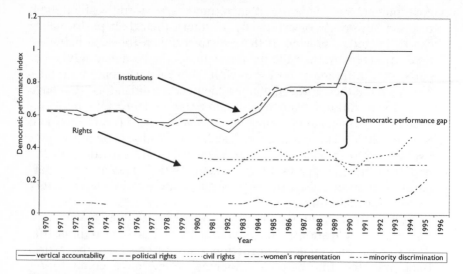

Figure 10.1 Democratic performance in Latin America (institutions and rights), 1970–1996

Countries include: Argentina, Brazil, Chile, Colombia, Costa Rica, El Salvador, Guatemala, Nicaragua, and Venezuela

Source: Foweraker and Krznaric (1999), *Database of Liberal Democratic Performance*

each case, the time period in question runs from 1970, or the first year that the government became democratic, until 1998. A minimal and procedural threshold for democracy is sufficient to warrant inclusion, with no prior attempt to distinguish "electoral" from "liberal" democracies, since the difference between the two is a matter of democratic performance – and this is what the measures are intended to establish.

As noted above, previous measures of democratic performance have tended to sum up distinct dimensions of performance into a single score, so obscuring the different ways that performance can vary across governments.[3] Our measures, in contrast, provide a differentiated picture of democratic performance in Latin America that succeeds in describing the particular performance profile of the continent. In short, they are designed to show not just whether this performance is uneven, but in what specific ways it is uneven.

As a first step, two measures were selected to capture competitive party politics and electoral participation (figure 10.1). Both measures show the same pattern of little change until 1982, with a marked rise

from the mid-1980s that accelerates in subsequent years before flat-
tening again in the 1990s. In effect, they reproduce the conventional
shape of the "third wave" of democratization that is familiar from
previous measures, and tell the same story of the spread of the formal
institutions of procedural democracy over this period.[4] But a different picture emerges from the three measures selected to reflect the
practical performance of civil and minority rights during the same
years (also figure 10.1). In stark contrast to the rising trajectory of
the "contestation" and "inclusiveness" measures, the "constitutional"
measures remain flat throughout the period. The particular twist to
these results is that political rights improve with the rapid dissemi-
nation of competitive electoral politics across Latin America, while
civil and minority rights remain fragile. The citizens of these democracies are enfranchised, but still unprotected and vulnerable.[5]

Uneven performance and democratic transition

This picture of democratic governments that enshrine competitive
politics at the expense of civil and minority rights can be seen to
match the mainstream accounts of democratic transition that focus
on "short-term maneuvering" and negotiation between elite actors
(Levine 1988: 385). In this perspective, the elites decide the terms of
the pacts and settlements that will found the new democratic regime
(e.g. Higley and Gunther 1992). Competitive electoral politics are
required to underpin the pacts by offering the different elites an
equal chance of access to power and the spoils of office, so assuaging
their uncertainty about the future (Przeworski 1986: 58–9).[6] These
accounts accurately reflect, wittingly or not, the contemporary profile
of Latin American democratic performance that tends to ignore "the
citizenry at large" and its "wish to be rid of tangible evils" (Rustow
1970: 354–7) – not least the widespread abuse of its civil rights.

The emphasis on elite calculation within processes of democratic
transition tends to demote the role of popular agency and underes-
timate the importance of the links between elites and mass publics
or popular organizations (see chapter 2). The consequence may be a
partial or distorted view of the real process of making democracy. But
the main point here is different. For democracy itself is a matter of
mass as well as elite, and it is only the effective presence and practice of civil liberties and minority rights that can deliver the substance
of democracy to the individuals who compose the polity. And this is
not just a moral but also a political question. Without some sense of

rights, what will win the support of the populace for the newly minted democratic arrangements? Without the rule of law – and its corollary, the elimination of arbitrary power – what will create the diffuse support for the emerging democratic system? These questions may remain unanswered so long as the uneven quality of these democracies divorces democratic constitutionalism from the lived experience of the citizens.

Uneven performance and democratic consolidation

The question of popular support for democracy is quite naturally understood to be important to the consolidation of democracy. This is said to occur when it "becomes routinized and deeply internalized in social, institutional and even psychological life," so that democracy has become the "only game in town" (Linz and Stepan 1996: 15–16). The perceived lack of democratic consolidation in Latin America is linked to the widespread experience of "lawlessness and distrust" that is reinforced by the "weakness of both state and the rule of law" (Diamond 1998: 55). The summary statement of these circumstances characterizes Latin American democracies as insufficiently institutionalized. The primary consequence is the lack of legitimation of democratic government. The notion of legitimacy serves as the most salient criterion of the elusive process of democratic consolidation.

One problem with this approach to democratic consolidation is that it takes as its "comparative yardstick, a generic and somewhat idealized view of the old polyarchies" (O'Donnell 1997: 44). In Latin America, by contrast with these established democracies, it is not always clear "who must accept formal democratic rules, and how deep must this acceptance run" (O'Donnell 1997: 48). Research into consolidation tends to focus on survey data that records the attitudes of the population at large, but the Latin American historical record demonstrates that "democracies are overthrown by elite conspiracies, not popular revolt", with loss of popular support neither "a necessary nor sufficient condition for democratic breakdown" (Remmer 1995: 113).

The survey data themselves are taken as conclusive evidence of the lack of consolidation. For the last several years an average of around 60 percent of the population of Latin America show support for democracy, dropping to some 50 percent in the first year of the new millennium (see figure 7.15). This compares with recent averages of 78 percent in Southern Europe and 79 percent in Eastern Europe (Diamond 1998: 10). In other words, support for democracy in Latin America does not reach "the two-thirds level" that is a "minimum threshold" for a "consolidated regime" (Diamond 1998: 12–13). But it is equally possible to argue that – in the conditions of uneven performance demonstrated above – this level of popular support for democracy in Latin America tends to exceed expectations.[7] In fact it may be rather difficult to argue that it is the lack of popular support that constitutes the main impediment to democratic consolidation in the continent.

An alternative approach to the question of consolidation denies that it is insufficient institutionalization that leads to a lack of legitimacy. Political life is certainly institutionalized – but through the informal rules that coalesce in clientelism and nepotism rather than the formal rules of the legal and constitutional framework. The democratic governments of Latin America are then deemed unconsolidated because of the lack of "fit between formal rules and actual behaviour" in polities where clientelism and patronage come to "vigorously inhabit most formal political institutions" (O'Donnell 1997: 47–9).[8] In large degree these informal rules hold sway because they are pervasive traits of the political culture since time immemorial. Contemporarily, however, the informal rules may simply facilitate corruption plain and simple, and corruption has tended to grow fat and bloated on the proceeds of the narcotics trade on the one hand and the privatization of state assets on the other. What is undeniable is that both traditional clientelism and modern corruption now affect the core institutions of the state in most Latin American countries.

Explaining uneven performance

The uneven performance of Latin American democracy reveals how political party competition through electoral politics can take hold even while civil and minority rights remain fragile and uncertain. This distorted democratic pattern may be explained in some degree by political culture as manifested in the "rule of informal rules" and of clientelism in particular. But the explanation must remain incomplete without addressing the question of political power, especially the unchanging nature of oligarchic power, and the constitutional and political prerogatives that render the military, and some police forces, largely unaccountable. It is oligarchic power that sanctions the political activities of military and police forces that lead directly to the abuse of civil and minority rights.[9] In these circumstances democratic government is nothing more than a set of "façade arrangements" that serve to disguise "traditional power relations" (Whitehead 1992: 158). It is the *combination* of oligarchic power with clientelist controls that can explain the patchy and imperfect rule of law and the failure to achieve a stable regime of individual and minority rights.

This combination is expressed in different ways in different places. In Brazil, for example, regional oligarchies have retained their traditional powers through deeply embedded systems of patronage, and clientelist political machines in national government (especially the national congress) have operated to protect both military autonomy and landed property. In Guatemala, party politics is patronage politics, where the traditional oligarchic families have continued to exert a powerful influence over the elected executive. In Colombia, national politics is divided between oligarchic domains that encompass local and regional politics and severely constrain the reach of political parties and political representation. Here and elsewhere oligarchic actors allied to powerful economic interests are able to target the executive and capture "benefits that flow more as patronage and privileges than as universal rights," while "operating through parties and legislatures only to defend achieved privileges" (Malloy 1987: 252).

Yet, oligarchic power is not abstract or invisible, but operates through the interrelationships among powerful political families. In Brazil, once again, the principal families of the political elite of Minas Gerais remain especially strong, and have been successful in colonizing political parties and maintaining control of local politics, in addition to preventing agrarian reform (Hagopian 1996: 247–9). Moreover, "no group or political party is today in a position to govern Brazil except by means of alliances with those traditional groups – and therefore, without large concessions to the needs of political clientelism" (Souza Martins 1996: 196). In Guatemala, the networks of the Castillo, Novella, Gutiérrez, and Herrera families enjoy government protection and incentives to their major economic enterprises, while family members and high-level employees frequently occupy government posts, including ministerial posts (Casaus Arzú 1992: 106). In Colombia, apart from the new "narco-oligarchy," traditional families dominate politics and the press, with "the sons of ex-presidents [appearing] as candidates for the presidency or other political posts in disproportionate numbers, [with the same applying] to the sons of senators and regional leaders" (Melo 1998: 66).

Thus, oligarchic power provides structural support to clientelist control and influence to produce an imperfect rule of law, and it does so in two main ways. First, it underpins what Weber called a patrimonial pattern of politics, where there is no clear and enduring distinction between the private and public spheres (Weber 1966: 347–9), and therefore no cultural or political defense of a *res publica* that requires the rule of law. Second, it assumes and promotes a particularistic style of politics that produces and reproduces power through *particular* relationships of favor and loyalty that are inimical to the *general* claims of individual rights. The tension between the *particularism* of clientelism and the *universalism* of an effective regime of individual rights characterizes the uneven performance of the Latin American democracies (Foweraker 1993: ch. 10; Foweraker 1995: 90–114; Foweraker and Landman 1997: 26–45).

Uneven performance and the rule of law

What is at issue here is the rule of law. In some degree this rule is imperfect because of the incomplete or contradictory nature of the law itself. The special immunities and protections of the military or police clearly contribute to damage the integrity of civil and minority rights.[10] But the main problem is simply that the law is bypassed or subverted, and this is a problem of accountability. In principle, democratic government is designed to safeguard the rule of law by making government accountable to the people. But in conditions of continuing oligarchic power and clientelistic controls the principles and practice of accountability are fractured or enfeebled. The result is freely elected governments that "either do not respect or do not maintain the state based on the rule of law" (Merkel 1999: 10). The governments enjoy the democratic legitimacy of popular election but the people are not sufficiently sovereign to defend the rule of law and prevent the violation of their liberties and protections.

As observed above, the mainstream accounts of democratic governments in Latin America argue that they will never be consolidated without an effective "rule of law to ensure legal guarantees for citizens' freedoms and independent associational life" (Linz and Stepan 1996: 7).[11] But the increasing longevity of Latin American democracies casts doubt on these assumptions. The evidence suggests, on the contrary, that these democracies can and do survive without a fully effective rule of law. They do so despite the merely formal presence of the law and its subversion by the informal rules that favor the oligarchy and discriminate systematically against the powerless. What survives is a form of democracy that is only partially constrained by a constitutional order (Linz 1964; Foweraker 2001a).

It has been argued throughout this chapter that the striking exception to this institutionalized informality (partial or complete depending on the country in question) is the electoral arena, which remains
protected or "ring-fenced" (O'Donnell 1997: 49). This relative
immunity may be achieved through the measure of accountability
implicit in political party competition. It may also be buttressed by
international monitoring and stimulated by the requirements of
international legitimacy and finance. (After all, membership of the
democratic club brings privileges and serves to assuage sanctions, and
governments can only claim membership so long as elections proceed
regularly and without let or hindrance). Consequently the citizens of
Latin America's democracies may enjoy the basic political freedoms
implicit in (relatively) free and fair elections, even while their civil
rights of personal integrity and equality before the law are infringed
or ignored.

Putting the people back in democracy

A competitive political party regime and electoral politics requires
parties and party leaders to appeal to a mass public, and, in some
degree, to organize this public for participation in public life. But this
does not mean to say that the people do not themselves organize and
participate of their own volition. It was noted on page 195 that the
elite-centered view of democratic transition tends to ignore the
popular contribution to the making of democracy, and, in particular,
the "many ties that bind leaders to mass publics, for example, through
political parties, trade unions, and secondary associations of all kinds"
(Levine 1988: 385). As a consequence "we are left with reified social
forces moving at one level, and leaders interacting at another"
(Levine 1988: 388). This lack of attention to popular agency in the
process of democratic transition also applies to contemporary char-
acterizations of democratic systems in Latin America. The common-
place perception of the uneven performance of the democratic
governments of the continent, and especially the recurrent violations
of civil and minority rights, pays little or no attention to the popular
response. This is strange to the point of becoming paradoxical,
since what motivated popular mobilization prior to and during the
democratic transitions of recent years was above all a sense of civil
and political rights, and a struggle for these rights (Foweraker and
Landman 1997).

Yet no analysis of Latin American government today can be complete – or sufficiently dynamic – without a proper appreciation of the

role of popular agency. The major works of political sociology that address the role of popular politics in Latin America have argued that the present conjuncture represents a sea change in the politics of the continent and in the import of popular agency in particular. Touraine interprets the half-century from 1930 to 1980 in terms of the dominance of the "national popular model," where the state is not clearly differentiated from the political system, and where social mobilization is mainly subordinated to political power (Touraine 1989: 185–92). In analogous fashion the Colliers define the same period in terms of the political incorporation of the labor movement, with social agency mainly expressed through the choices of national political elites (Collier and Collier 1991). Both works characterize the recent change as a consequence of attempts to achieve a more autonomous expression of "interests" by the labor movements and other popular actors. But, in our view, this key change is characterized not by the social mobilization of *interests* but by the historical encounter between social mobilization and the language of *rights*. It is certainly the case that the waves of mobilization that accompanied many processes of democratic transition in the continent have since subsided, but it cannot be assumed therefore that the mobilizing potential of the rights agenda has run its course.

Perceptions of uneven performance are expressed in a growing body of work on the "low intensity citizenship" (O'Donnell 1999a) and imperfect legal protections (Diamond 1999) of the illiberal (Zakaria 1997) or defective (Merkel 1999) democracies of the continent. This work, and that of O'Donnell in particular, is imaginative and important. But its strong emphasis on the absence or imperfections of the rule of law make the analysis more static than it should be. It is true that civil, political, and minority rights must be guaranteed by the state, and that their presence requires an effective rule of law. But historically these rights have nearly always had to be won by social and political struggles against the state, or against powerful actors in civil society. It may be readily admitted that the present conjuncture certainly does not favor and can actively discourage popular participation and popular struggle. Economically, a strong adherence to neoliberal policies precludes a political emphasis on social development. Politically, governments tend to remain "unconnected with the lived experience of the mass of the population" (Whitehead 1992: 154). But this cannot mean that popular mobilization has come to an historical full stop.

There is little doubt that popular political agency has changed. NGOs have multiplied while many more traditional social movements have disappeared or been transformed (Foweraker 2001b).

These changes cannot be reversed. But they can mean that civil society, however defined, is now more diverse and "resourceful." Despite their many weaknesses, NGOs can and do create new resources for popular mobilization, including education, leadership, know-how, and information. Even without a social base NGOs can promote popular mobilization, as the democratic transition in Chile demonstrated. This may not eventually be the *same* popular mobilization as before, but it will continue to express the impetus and invention of "society getting organized" (Monsiváis 1987). The last century of modern Mexican history, for example, has been marked by successive waves of popular mobilization. Is it at all plausible that this history has come to a halt? The experience of Chiapas suggests not. It follows that any informed analysis of Latin American democracy must look beyond the present conjuncture and consider developments over the long term. The initial focus of the historical encounter between popular mobilization and rights in Latin America was democratic transition. In the future, the popular struggle for rights may mainly seek to improve the quality and consistency of democratic government in the continent.

This perspective differs from the view of democracy as the historical result of good behavior in the form of the civic community (Putnam 1993). This view takes "civicness" as a functional prerequisite for democracy rather than exploring the popular agency that may achieve or improve it. If it is not an entirely static view, it is certainly rather slow moving. To the potential dismay of those peoples still aspiring to achieve or improve their democracy, "civicness" may take centuries to accumulate. In fact, no less than nine centuries in Northern Italy, the focus of Putnam's study. Unsurprisingly, "civicness" includes neither popular political struggle nor individual rights. An emphasis on popular political agency, in contrast, suggests that it is "bad behavior" in the form of the fight for rights that can do most to improve the quality of democracy and deliver its substance to the citizenry at large.

The future democratic performance of Latin America

What prospect is there that Latin American governments will achieve a less uneven, more consistent, and therefore more authentically democratic performance? If it is conjectured that their uneven performance is simply a consequence of being new, then *given time* they may come to fit the more even profile of the older and more established democracies. But in this regard the evidence is not yet in. Whether the electoral principle alone is sufficient to promote a fully effective rule of law over the longer term is an open question, and one that will no doubt receive different answers in different political contexts and different historical moments. For Putnam, more "civicness" will lead inexorably to better democracy. In our view, the historical outcome is less certain, if only because the historical relationship between the political activity of the people and the quality of democracy is indeterminate, depending in large degree on the variable success of popular struggle in achieving and exercising citizenship rights, and so defending and enhancing the rule of law. Such success is usually partial and always reversible. But it does mean that the quality of democracy can be improved generation on generation, and without waiting for the slow historical sedimentation of civic virtue.

There are encouraging signs. The political climate in many countries has become markedly more pragmatic and consequently less ideological. It would be absurd to suggest that all ideological divisions have disappeared, but they do not drive the political process as they did in the 1960s and 1970s. The political concerns of most governments have rather to do with governability, order, and "accommodation." In these circumstances, the supposedly negative aspects of the political culture that are simultaneously causes of uneven performance may have a positive role to play. The pervasive patterns of patronage and clientelism were seen to contaminate the pristine institutions of democratic government, leaving government practices a long way short of democratic principles. But such "unprincipled" traits may also promote and facilitate the practical democratic business of debate, negotiation, and bargaining, and sharpen perceptions of trade-offs and "satisfycing" solutions. None of this alters the current uneven performance of these democracies. Democratic government in Latin America is far from perfect, and is rarely as responsive, transparent, accountable, or just as popular sovereignty would require. It is certainly not yet "good government" (Torres Rivas 1995: 55). But there is political learning, and at least some governments are finding new ways of doing democratic politics. There is therefore some hope that democratic performance will improve, and that the current wave of democratization will endure.

▌ NOTES

CHAPTER I   AUTHORITARIANISM AND DEMOCRACY IN LATIN AMERICA

1   In the nineteenth century, the Spanish term "caudillo" was used to refer to a type of political and military leader who sought undisputed loyalty from the population in exchange for his protection.

2   A good example of caudillo government is that of General Porfírio Díaz, who ruled Mexico from 1876 through to 1911. His rule was justified by intellectuals in terms of the need for order and stability. As one contemporary writer, Francisco Cosmes (1850–1907) put it, rights had to come second to "bread, order, security and peace." Rights had only brought disorder and stress. "Now let us try a little tyranny," Cosmes wrote, "but honorable tyranny, and see what results it brings" (Hale 1996:154). The results in Mexico are well known: a social revolution which toppled the Díaz government and sent the caudillo into exile in 1911. However, the new revolutionary Constitution of 1917 retained a strong authoritarian bent and maintained the supremacy of the executive branch over all other branches of government, marking a clear continuity with this aspect of caudillo government.

3   In 1823 President James Monroe warned against attempts by the Holy Alliance to help Spain regain control of its former colonies in the Americas. In what would become known as the "Monroe Doctrine," he declared that "We owe it, therefore, to candor, and to the amicable relations existing between the United States and those powers, to declare that we should consider any attempt on their part to extend their political system to any portion of this hemisphere as dangerous to our peace and safety . . . We could not view any interposition for the purpose of oppressing (the newly independent nations), or controlling in any other manner their destiny, by any European power in any other light than as the manifestation of an unfriendly disposition toward the United States" (cited in Smith 1996:20).

4   A different kind of military regime came to power in Peru and Ecuador in the late 1960s and early 1970s. Although they similarly constrained democratic participation, these regimes embarked on reforms designed to modernize their countries through redistributive programs and government-led organization of the popular sectors. As such, they targeted the power of traditional oligarchies who were seen as an obstacle to achieving national integration and modernization. With mixed results in the area of social reforms, combined with economic instability and opposition to military rule, these regimes began their transitions to civilian, elected government in the late 1970s.

5   Horizontal accountability refers to the checks and balances that exist between the different branches of government (executive, legislature, and judiciary). In Latin America, the executive branch has traditionally imposed its will on the other branches such that many observers question the independence of the congress and the courts. The congress has often played the role of a "rubber-stamp" institution, simply validating the decisions of the president. One of the goals of democratization is therefore the establishment of stronger checks on executive decisions and actions through the empowerment of leglislative oversight and the strengthening of an independent judiciary and the rule of law.

6   As O'Donnell points out, "whether it is called culture, tradition, or historically-structured learning, the caudillista tendencies toward delegative democracy are detectable in most Latin American countries long before the present social and economic crisis" (O'Donnell 1994: 60).

7   As Peeler puts it, "what is left of democracy when candidates gain election by telling direct falsehoods and then vest policymaking power in officials beyond the reach of the people?" (Peeler 1998: 154).

CHAPTER 2   LATIN AMERICA AND THE DEMOCRATIC UNIVERSE

1   Venezuela suffered from failed military coup attempts in 1992, while Peru and Guatemala were subjected to "*autogolpes*," or self-coups at the hands of Presidents Fujimori and Serrano respectively. In Peru, Fujimori had the support of the military and popular sectors for his actions, which yielded a new Constitution with increased powers for the executive (see chapter 4 this volume). In Guatemala, the Supreme Court immediately condemned Serrano's actions as unconstitutional, forcing him to capitulate.

2   Such a formal and minimal definition of democracy "requires two consecutive 'free and fair' elections, and a plausible claim that the outcome of the election can change the government" (Foweraker 1998a: 651, fn. 2.).

CHAPTER 3   GOVERNMENT AND CITIZENS

1   For Weber, it was particularly important that the state be the only body capable of exercising legitimate force in order to ensure compliance with

its authority, arguing that "the state is a human community that (successfully) claims the monopoly of the legitimate use of physical force within a given territory." (Weber 1956: 78).

2   The salience of charismatic leaders in the twentieth century was not unique to Latin America. Europe clearly had its share, with Mussolini, Hitler, and Stalin representing only the most obvious examples. We could also mention the dictatorial rule of Franco in Spain (1939–75) and the decree powers assumed by Charles de Gaulle during his years as President of the Fifth Republic in France (1958–69).

3   As we noted in the previous chapters, the availability of social rights depended on the political balance of forces and economic doctrine during the period between 1945 and the early 1980s. In Latin America today, the concept of social rights has been dismantled by the break-up of earlier class compromises and the dominance of neoliberal thought. Democracy today entails a weak concept of the state's obligations to provide social services, favoring instead targeted anti-poverty programs and efforts to stimulate small-scale entrepreneurial activity.

4   During the first half of the 1960s, the US government sought to avert another revolution in the Americas as had occurred in Cuba. Drawing on some aspects of modernization theory (see chapter 2), foreign policy-makers sought to chart a middle course between revolution and authoritarianism. Recognizing that social exclusion and political repression could lead to uncontrolled revolutionary action and even communist-led revolution, the administration of John F. Kennedy (1961–3) designed a new policy, known as the Alliance for Progress, which sought to modernize the region's economic structures and demonstrate the viability of capitalism for achieving growth and development in Latin America. Politically, the success of this strategy depended on the availability of strong centrist political parties that could avoid ideological polarization between left- and right-wing groups and thereby lay the basis for political stability. The policy-makers believed that the urban-based, educated middle classes would be the natural constituency of moderate and centrist parties. The strategy failed, partly because the right wing was unprepared to make concessions on key areas of the reform package (particularly land reform) and ideological confrontation continued throughout the 1960s. The impetus behind the Alliance for Progress ended when Kennedy was assassinated in 1963. Subsequent administrations tended to focus more on the fight against communism and the strengthening of military alliances in the hemisphere (Smith 1996).

CHAPTER 4   CONSTITUTIONALISM AND THE RULE OF LAW

1   Path dependency in political science refers to the historical structuring of future outcomes based on previous sets of choices.

2   Divided government in the United States occurs when the president is from one political party, while another political party controls the

Congress. Recent examples of divided government in the United States include Ronald Reagan's term of office facing a Congress with a majority of Democrats, and the Republican electoral success in the 1994 mid-term elections. Political scientists have long debated whether divided government is a problem for the US political system (see McKay 1994).

3   A notable exception is Uruguay, which had been ruled by a collegial "presidency" and "quasi-presidential" system in 1830, 1934, 1942, 1966 (Sartori 1994: 99, n. 11).

4   Vargas was famous for his saying: *Aos meus amigos, tudo; aos meus inimigos, a lei*, which in English means, for my friends, anything they want, for my enemies, the law (see O'Donnell 1999a: 303).

5   In Peru, President Fujimori committed an *autogolpe*, or "self-coup" in 1992, which led to a new Constitution in 1993 with greater concentration of power in the executive. In 2000, he sought reelection for a third consecutive term even though the 1993 Constitution restricts the executive to two consecutive terms.

6   Other important international human rights instruments include the International Convention on the Prevention and Punishment of the Crime of Genocide (1948); the Convention Relating to the Status of Refugees (1951); the International Convention on the Elimination of all Forms of Racial Discrimination (1966); the Convention on the Elimination of All Forms of Discrimination against Women (1979); the Convention against Torture and other Cruel, Inhuman, or Degrading Treatment or Punishment (1984); and the Convention on the Rights of the Child (1989).

CHAPTER 5   POLITICAL PARTIES

1   The constitutional inducements to elite party pacts in Bolivia have already been noted. In Brazil, party pacts within the Constitutional Assembly of 1987 neutralized popular pressure for agrarian reform, despite the presence of the Workers' Party (PT) and its real responsiveness to grassroots organizations. In Chile the party elites agreed to play by the rules of the Pinochet Constitution that gave the parties of the right a systematic electoral advantage. The Socialist and Christian Democrat parties then succeeded in trumping these rules by "concerting" their electoral campaigns.

2   No doubt they were always heterogeneous, but this heterogeneity now finds more effective and sometimes more aggressive political expression.

CHAPTER 6   PRESIDENTS, LEGISLATURES, AND ELECTIONS

1   The claim that all these countries enjoyed elected and constitutional governments is not the same as claiming that all these governments were, in fact, democratic. A minimal definition of democracy requires

two consecutive "free and fair" elections, and a plausible claim that the outcome of the election can change the government. By this definition Mexico may need one more free and fair election before it can claim to be democratic.

2   Lijphart divides this compass into four main categories, which are presidential-plurality (US, Philippines), parliamentary-plurality (the United Kingdom, the old Commonwealth, India, and Malaysia), PR-parliamentary (Western Europe), and PR-presidential (Latin America).

3   Deviations from the pure model have been noted, severally, in Bolivia, Peru, and Chile, and, in lesser degree, in Ecuador, Uruguay, and Guatemala (Shugart and Carey 1992).

4   Most legislation in most Latin American countries is initiated by the executive, which also tends to have both total and line-item vetoes; and presidents tend to have both decree and extensive emergency powers, including that of the state-of-siege.

5   *Decretismo* was typical of Colombia during the National Front years and later, with the country being under state-of-siege for 75 percent of the time from 1958 to 1989. "Delegative democracy" has been used to characterize regimes as different as those of Menem in Argentina and (early) Fujimori in Peru.

6   *Autogolpe* refers to action by an elected president to curtail or dismantle democratic government, usually with the open collaboration or covert collusion of the military.

7   Without a straight majority or near-majority, the president needs to build either a stable coalition majority, or shifting coalition majorities on single issues and initiatives; and a near-majority will certainly facilitate such coalition-formation.

8   At the time of the *autogolpe* in Uruguay in 1973 the President Juan Maria Bordaberry controlled the smallest ever number of assembly seats of any Uruguayan president.

9   The "effective number of parties" in a party system is a technical measure developed by Laakso and Taagepera that today sets the industry standard for describing party systems.

10 It is therefore regrettable that all the countries that have drafted new electoral laws in recent years have adopted the majority runoff rule, including Chile, Colombia, Brazil, Dominican Republic, Ecuador, El Salvador, Guatemala, Peru, and Uruguay, so that it is just Honduras, Panama, Paraguay, Mexico, and Venezuela that now use a pure plurality formula. Costa Rica's low first-round threshold of 40 percent places it close to plurality, as does Argentina's first-round threshold of 45 percent, or a minimum of 40 percent with a 10 percent margin over the nearest rival.

11 The case of "segmented" party systems is different, especially if they are segmented by national or ethnic identities, and especially if such identities are regionally concentrated. Perhaps surprisingly, such national or ethnic identities are relatively unpoliticized in Latin

America (in contrast to Eastern Europe and the countries of the ex-Soviet Union).

CHAPTER 7   POLITICAL AND SOCIAL RIGHTS

1   Justiciability refers to the ability for a particular concept enshrined in law to be adjudicated by some form of judicial body. In other words, it is the degree to which an assembly of judges can provide a remedy for aggrieved individuals or groups that claim a violation of their rights (Steiner and Alston 1996: 298).
2   The measure of political rights comes from Freedom House, whose checklist for such rights includes: chief authority recently elected by a meaningful process; legislature recently elected by a meaningful process; fair election laws, campaigning opportunity, polling and tabulation; fair reflection of voter preference in the distribution of power; multiple political parties; recent shifts in power through elections; significant opposition vote; free of military or foreign control; major groups or groups allowed reasonable self-determination; decentralized political power; informal consensus, de facto opposition power (see Gastil 1987, 1990; Freedom House 1990).
3   Another popular indicator depicts the functional distribution of income, which measures the degree to which national income is distributed to labor, industry, and agriculture.

CHAPTER 8: NEW POLITICAL ACTORS

1   For a short and accessible introduction to the concept of "civil society" in the Latin American context, see Vilas (1992). There is a large literature on popular movements and political change since the 1970s. See, for example, Eckstein (1989), Foweraker (1995), Foweraker and Craig (1990), Foweraker and Landman (1997), Slater (1985), Escobar and Alvarez (1992) and Alvarez, Dagnino, and Escobar (1998). For a more theoretical and comparative discussion of civil society, see Cohen and Arato (1992).
2   As García argues for the case of Venezuela: "To achieve [their] political-environmental demands, new forms of articulation have emerged among popular organizations, neighborhood associations, grassroots Christian groups, women and environmentalists. The mistrust of the sociopolitical model, the rejection of the political parties, and the deepening of the economic crisis have gradually delegitimized the 'political' space as a privileged space to address the national problems. *These very factors have displaced the party-state system as the only realm in which to create shared meanings about a desirable society.* And in response to these challenges, the government created the Commission for the Reform of the State in 1984" (García-Guadilla 1992: 152)(emphasis added).

3   As Burdick argues: "we should not begin by examining a particular social movement but by considering how, for example, women, youth, the unemployed, blacks, or the formal proletariat . . . encounter a field of ideological, discursive, and practical options. Only then, I suggest, can we identify the processes through which people become involved in some options and not others, as well as the circumstances under which they desist and distance themselves from a given movement – a process that is perhaps as common as participation itself" (Burdick 1992: 183–4).

4   Chuchryk 1994:67. As Chuchryk states: "Generally speaking, the military's new economic model left massive poverty, a disproportionately large unemployed and demoralized labor force, and deteriorating wage levels in its wake."

5   In this regard, the Madres de la Plaza de Mayo illustrate several of the novel aspects of what we have been calling "new political actors." As Feijoó and Nari argue: 'The Madres showed a capacity for innovation in the cultural dimension of 'doing politics'. Their originality was evident in their development of new forms of mobilization, such as the walk (*ronda*) around the plaza; the assignment of new meanings to old symbols (e.g. the white handkerchiefs); and their capacity to resignify a public space (the plaza); and their capability of sustaining a political agenda outside the realm of the political parties" (Feijoó and Nari 1994:113).

6   See, for example, Chuchryk (1994) and Schild (1998).

7   In the case of feminist movements in Brazil, Alvarez has noted how these lessons have been debated with regard to dealing with state institutions: "Many Brazilian feminists are again reassessing their relationship to the State. Some of the vexing questions confronting them include How can feminists continue to depend on an increasingly undependable State? Which aspects of feminist politics might still be launched from the State? And where in the State (i.e., the executive, the bureaucracy, the legislatures, the judiciary) should feminist advocacy efforts be focused? What strategies would be necessary to secure the implementation and enforcement of the rights women conquered in theory during the 1970s and 1980s? How can women of all ethnic groups, social classes, and sexual orientations come to enjoy more meaningful political, social, cultural and sexual citizenship?" (Alvarez 1994: 54).

CHAPTER 9   MINORITY AND INDIGENOUS RIGHTS

1   The relationship between indigenous peoples and the state is a central issue in assessing the quality of democracy in Latin America. As van Cott argues: "the systematic exclusion of indigenous people from democratic institutions in Latin American societies has perpetuated conflict between ethnic groups – in itself a problem for democratizing countries. More importantly, it has postponed the creation of a broadly democratic society in Latin America, founded in law, embracing cultural diversity, and encouraging wide participation in decision-making and consensual governance." (van Cott 1994: 2).

2 This section is taken from Harvey (2001).
3 The following Latin American countries have ratified ILO Convention 169: Argentina, Bolivia, Colombia, Costa Rica, Ecuador, Guatemala, Honduras, Mexico, Paraguay, and Peru. ILO 169 has also been ratified by Denmark, Fiji, the Netherlands, and Norway.
4 The estimated population of the Latin American region at the time of conquest was 100 million people. This population was reduced to less than 20 million just sixty years after contact, and to just 2 million forty years later (van Cott 2000a: 3; Wearne 1996:3). The main causes of population decline were the effects of European diseases for which native people lacked immunities, violent conquest, and forced labor (Wearne 1996: 75–9). The impact was felt most in lowland areas where diseases spread more rapidly and among smaller island and coastal populations of the Caribbean Basin. The relative isolation and dispersal of lowland Indians in the Amazon region delayed contact in some cases until the mid-twentieth century. Survival rates were higher in regions with more developed civilizations and larger populations, such as the Aztecs and Maya of Mesoamerica (extending from the central plateau of modern-day Mexico as far south as El Salvador) and the Inca Empire of the Andean region (the mountainous areas of Colombia, Ecuador, Peru, Bolivia, and Chile). These differences are reflected in the relative size of indigenous populations in Latin American countries today (see table 9.1). The estimated indigenous population in the region today is 40 million, or 10 percent of total population (van Cott 2000a: 2).
5 For these reasons several authors believe that the liberal land reforms of the nineteenth century were more destructive of indigenous communities than the impositions of colonial rule. See, for example, Wearne 1996: 108–11; van Cott 1994:4; Wade 1997: 30–2; Stavenhagen 1996: 142; and Díaz Polanco, 1997: 65–8.
6 On blacks in Latin America, see Graham (1990), Marx (1998), Minority Rights Group (1995), NACLA (1992), and Wade (1993).
7 According to the Minority Rights Group (1997) Colombia's indigenous population numbers 620,000 people or 1.7 percent of the national population. Van Cott, citing the 1993 census, gives the higher figure of 972,000 or 2.7 percent of the population (van Cott 2000b: 44).
8 As Yashar argues, "Latin America remains very much in the throes of state formation, where the identities, borders and legitimacy of the state are highly politicized and contested processes, particularly in the countryside" (Yashar 1999: 87).
9 For a comparative overview of the status of indigenous rights in Latin American constitutions see van Cott (2000b: 257–80).

CHAPTER 10 UNEVEN DEMOCRATIC PERFORMANCE

1 Just a quarter of a century ago there were some 35 democracies in the world, most of them rich and industrialized nations in the Western hemisphere. Today this number has grown to some 120. Huntington argues

that at least thirty countries turned democratic between 1974 and 1990 (Huntington 1993: 3), while Diamond takes Freedom House data to show that the number of democracies increased from 39 in 1974 to 118 in 1996 (Diamond 1997: 22). Consequently democratic governments now outnumber all others.

2   A full account of the decisions governing the selection and rejection of measures can be found in Foweraker and Krznaric (2001).

3   The Polity III Democracy Scale (Jaggers and Gurr 1995) and the Freedom House Index of Political Freedom (Freedom House 1997) are the standard aggregate indices of democracy, and both of them place country cases on a single, ordinal scale. In principle, the Polity III Scale encompasses electoral and representative institutions, while the Freedom House Index reflects both institutions and political rights, such as freedom of opposition and association.

4   The annual average scores from Polity III (1970–94) and Freedom House (1972–98) were plotted for the same nine Latin American cases. They show a third wave that builds slowly in the 1970s, gains momentum in the 1980s, and accelerates rapidly in the late 1980s and early 1990s. This reflects the "global trend in the direction of democratisation" (Jaggers and Gurr 1995: 477) that reaches a "high-water mark" in the early 1990s (Diamond 1997a: 23).

5   To check the validity of the results, the same measures were applied to seventeen old and established democracies over the same period. In these cases both the institutional variables and the rights variables remain flat and constant over time. Since these are all liberal democracies where individual and minority rights are mainly protected under the rule of law, this picture of "no change" (not shown here) conforms to our expectations.

6   Elite actors must be convinced of the institutional guarantees that minimize the threat to their longer-term interests: in the reiterative game of electoral democracy, today's losers must be able to think of themselves as tomorrow's winners.

7   Note that "political factors – especially relating to how democratically the regime is performing or being seen to perform – are much more important than economic ones in shaping perceptions of legitimacy," especially those relating to "increased freedom, responsiveness and transparency" (Diamond 1998: 62).

8   Note that by this criterion the democratic governments of India, Japan, or even Italy might also be deemed unconsolidated.

9   In some cases the military police and paramilitary organizations act directly to protect oligarchic power, especially in the form of private property in land.

10   The residual problem here is the (often long-term) suspension of constitutional guarantees in specious conditions of domestic strife or national emergency (compare the discussion of "reserve domains" of military power in chapter 2).

11   It is the rule of law that underpins consolidated democracy by its specific effects on political attitudes and political behavior. Moreover, in
Linz and Stepan's analysis, it emerges that the rule of law is also central
to the other four "arenas" of consolidated democracy. On the one hand,
"the necessary degree of autonomy and independence of civil and political society must be embedded in and supported by the rule of law." On
the other, the rule of law is integral to a "useable state bureaucracy"
and a regulated "economic society" (Linz and Stepan 1996: 10–11).

▍ References

Alvarez, S. 1994: The (Trans)formations of Feminism(s) and Gender Politics in Democratizing Brazil, in J. S. Jaquette (ed.), *The Women's Movement in Latin America: Participation and Democracy*. Boulder, CO: Westview Press.

Alvarez, S., Dagnino, E., and Escobar, E. (eds) 1998: *Cultures of Politics/Politics of Cultures: Re-visioning Latin American Social Movements*. Boulder, CO: Westview Press.

Anderson, B. 1983: *Imagined Communities: Reflections on the Origins and Spread of Nationalism*. London: Verso.

Anglade, C. 1994: Democracy and the Rule of Law in Latin America, in I. Budge and D. McKay (eds), *Developing Democracy: Comparative Research in Honour of J. F. P. Blondel*. London and Thousand Oaks: Sage Publications, 233–52.

Asociación Latinoamericana de Organizaciones de Promoción (ALOP) 1999: *Qué Role Cabe a ALOP y a las ONG en la América Latina de Hoy? Retos y Perspectivas*, report of the workshop on Cambios Institucionales de las ONG de América Latina.

Barbalet, J. M. 1988: *Citizenship: Rights, Struggle and Class Inequality*. Milton Keynes: Open University Press.

Barnes, S. 1997: Electoral Behaviour and Comparative Politics, in M. Lichbach and A. Zuckerman (eds), *Comparative Politics: Rationality, Culture and Structure*. Cambridge: Cambridge University Press, 115–41.

Beck, S. H. and Mijeski, K. 2001: Barricades and Ballots: Ecuador's Indians and the Pachacutik Political Movement. *Ecuadorian Studies/Estudios Ecuatorianos*, 1.

Beetham, D. 1999: *Democracy and Human Rights*. Cambridge: Polity.

Bell, D. 1960: *The End of Ideology: On the Exhaustion of Political Ideas in the 1950s*. New York: Free Press.

Blondel, J. 1998: Democracy and Constitutionalism, in T. Inoguchi, E. Newman, and J. Keane (eds), *The Changing Nature of Democracy*. Tokyo, New York, and Paris: United Nations University Press.

Brohman, J. 1996: *Popular Development*. Oxford: Blackwell.

Bulmer-Thomas, V. 1996: *The New Economic Model in Latin America and its Impact on Income Distribution and Poverty*. London: Macmillan.

Bunster, X. 1988: Watch Out for the Little Nazi Man That All of Us Have Inside: The Mobilization and Demobilization of Women in Militarized Chile. *Women's Studies International Forum*, 11 (5): 485–91.

Burdick, J. 1992: Rethinking the Study of Social Movements: The Case of Christian Base Communities in Urban Brazil, in A. Escobar and S. Alvarez (eds), *The Making of Social Movements in Latin America: Identity, Strategy and Democracy*. Boulder, CO: Westview Press, 171–84.

Burgenthal, T., Norris, R., and Shelton, D., 1990: *Protecting Human Rights in the Americas*. Kehl-am-Rhem: Engel.

Burke, E. 1955: *Reflections on the Revolution in France*. Chicago: Henry Regnery.

Burkhart, R. and Lewis-Beck, M. 1994: Comparative Democracy: The Economic Development Thesis. *American Political Science Review*, 88 (4): 903–10.

Calvert, P. and Calvert, S. 1993: *Latin America in the Twentieth Century*. London: Macmillan.

Cammack, P. 1996: Democracy and Dictatorship in Latin America, 1930–1980, in D. Potter, D. Goldblatt, M. Kiloh, and P. Lewis (eds), *Democratization*. Cambridge: Polity Press, 152–73.

Casaus Arzú, M. 1992: *Guatemala: Linaje y Racismo*. Guatemala City: FLACSO.

Castañeda, J. 1994: *Utopia Unarmed: The Latin American Left after the Cold War*. New York: Vintage Books.

Cavarozzi, M. and Garretón, M. 1989: *Muerte y Resurrección: Los Partidos Políticos en el Autoritarismo y las Transiciones en el Cono Sur*. Santiago, Chile: Facultad Latinoamericana de Ciencias Sociales.

Chalmers, D. A., Martin, S. B., and Piester, K. 1997: Associative Networks: New Structures of Representation for the Popular Sectors?, in D. A. Chalmers, C. M., Vilas, K. Hite, S. B. Martin, K. Piester, and M. Segarra (eds), *The New Politics of Inequality in Latin America: Rethinking Participation and Representation*. Oxford: Oxford University Press, 543–82.

Chuchryk, P. M. 1994: From Dictatorship to Democracy: The Women's Movement in Chile, in J. S. Jaquette (ed.), *The Women's Movement in Latin America: Participation and Democracy*. Boulder, CO: Westview Press, 65–107.

Cohen, J. and Arato, A. 1992: *Civil Society and Political Theory*. Cambridge, MA: MIT Press.

Cohen, Y. 1987: Democracy from Above: The Origins of Military Dictatorship in Brazil. *World Politics*: 30–54.

——1994: *Radicals, Reformers, and Reactionaries: The Prisoner's Dilemma and the Collapse of Democracy in Latin America*. Chicago: University of Chicago Press.

Collier, D. S. and Collier, R. B. 1991: *Shaping the Political Arena: Critical Junctures, the Labor Movement, and Regime Dynamics*. Princeton: Princeton University Press.

Collinson, H. (ed.) 1996: *Green Guerrillas: Environmental Conflicts and Initiatives in Latin America and the Caribbean*. London: Latin American Bureau.

Conger Lind, A. 1992: Power, Gender and Development: Popular Women's Organizations and the Politics of Needs in Ecuador, in A. Escobar and S. Alvarez (eds), *The Making of Social Movements in Latin America: Identity, Strategy and Democracy*. Boulder, CO: Westview Press, 134–49.

Cornelius, W., Eisenstadt, T., and Hindley, J. (eds) 1999: *Subnational Politics and Democratization in Mexico*. La Jolla: Center for US-Mexican Studies, University of California-San Diego.

Crapotta, J. F. 1994: Hispanic Gay and Lesbian Issues, *Community News*. New York: Gay, Bisexual and Lesbian Staff and Supporters at Columbia University (GABLES-CU), April.

Dahl, R. 1971: *Polyarchy: Participation and Opposition*. New Haven, CT: Yale University Press.

Dandler, J. 1999: Indigenous Peoples and the Rule of Law in Latin America: Do They Have a Chance?, in J. Méndez, G. O'Donnell, and P. Sérgio Pinheiro (eds), *The (Un) Rule of Law and the Underprivileged in Latin America*. South Bend, IN: Notre Dame University Press.

Davidson, S. 1992: *The Inter-American Court of Human Rights*. Aldershot: Dartmouth.

——1993: *Human Rights*. Buckingham and Philadelphia: Open University Press.

Dehesa, G. I. 1997: *Gobiernos de Coalición en el Sistema Presidencial: América del Sur*, Doctoral Thesis. European University Institute, Florence.

Diamond, L. 1997: The End of the Third Wave and the Global Future of Democracy. Reihe Politikwissenschaft/Political Science Series No. 45, Institute for Advanced Studies, Vienna.

——1998: Political Culture and Democratic Consolidation. Working Paper 118 (June). Madrid: Juan March Institute.

——1999: *Developing Democracy: Toward Consolidation*. Baltimore: Johns Hopkins University Press.

Diamond, L., Linz, J. J., and Lipset, S. M. (eds) 1989: *Democracy in Developing Countries: Latin America*, vol. 4. Boulder, CO: Lynne Rienner Publishers.

Díaz Polanco, H. 1997: *Indigenous Peoples in Latin America: The Quest for Self-determination*. Boulder, CO: Westview Press.

Donnelly, J. 1999: Human Rights, Democracy, and Development. *Human Rights Quarterly*, 21 (3): 608–32.

Eckstein, S. (ed.) 1989: *Power and Popular Protest: Latin American Social Movements*. Berkeley and Los Angeles, CA: University of California Press.

Economic Commission for Latin America 2000: *Statistical Yearbook for Latin America and the Caribbean 2000*. Santiago, Chile: ECLA.

Elster, J. and Slagstad, R. (eds) 1988: *Constitutionalism and Democracy*. Cambridge: Cambridge University Press.

Escobar, A. and Alvarez, S. (eds) 1992: *The Making of Social Movements in Latin America: Identity, Strategy and Democracy*. Boulder, CO: Westview Press.

Evans, P. 1979: *Dependent Development: The Alliance of Multinational, State, and Local Capital in Brazil*. Princeton: Princeton University Press.

EZLN. Ejército Zapatista de Liberación Nacional. 1996. Fourth Declaration of the Lacandon Forest (January 1, 1996). Translation in *Dark Night Field Notes*. Chicago: Dark Night Press, 4: 33–40.

Faure, A. M. 1994: Some Methodological Problems in Comparative Politics. *Journal of Theoretical Politics*, 6 (3): 307–22.

Feijoó, M. and Nari, M. 1994: Women and Democracy in Argentina, in J. S. Jaquette (ed), *The Women's Movement in Latin America: Participation and Democracy*. Boulder, CO: Westview Press, 109–29.

Figueiredo, A. C. and Limongi, F. 2000: Presidential Power, Legislative Organization, and Party Behaviour in Brazil. *Comparative Politics*, 32 (2): 151–70.

Fisher, J. 1993: *Out of the Shadows: Women, Resistance and Politics in Latin America*. London: Latin America Bureau.

Fitch, J. S. 1998: *The Armed Forces and Democracy in Latin America*. Baltimore: Johns Hopkins University Press.

Food and Agriculture Organization of the United Nations (FAO) 2000: *The State of Food Insecurity in the World*. New York: United Nations.

Foweraker, J. 1981: *The Struggle for Land: A Political Economy of the Pioneer Frontier in Brazil from 1930 to the Present Day*. Cambridge: Cambridge University Press.

—— 1993: *Popular Mobilization in Mexico: The Teachers' Movement, 1977–87*. Cambridge: Cambridge University Press.

—— 1995: *Theorizing Social Movements*. London: Pluto Press.

—— 1998a: Review Article: Institutional Design, Party Systems and Governability – Differentiating the Presidential Regimes of Latin America. *British Journal of Political Science*, 28: 651–76.

—— 1998b: Ten Theses on Women in the Political Life of Latin America, in V. E. Rodriguez (ed.), *Women's Participation in Mexican Political Life*. Boulder, CO: Westview Press.

—— 2001a: Transformation, Transition, Consolidation: Democratization in Latin America, in K. Nash and A. Scott (eds), *Blackwell Companion to Political Sociology*. Oxford: Blackwell Publishers.

—— 2001b: Grassroots Movements and Political Activism in Latin America: A Critical Comparison of Chile and Brazil. *Journal of Latin American Studies*, 33: 4.

Foweraker, J. and Craig, A. (eds) 1990: *Popular Movements and Political Change in Mexico*. Boulder, CO: Lynne Rienner Publishers.

Foweraker, J. and Krznaric, R. 1999: Database of Liberal Democratic Performance (computer file and codebook), Study Number 4046. Essex: National Data Archive, University of Essex (www.data-archive.ac.uk).

—— 2000: Measuring Liberal Democratic Performance: An Empirical and Conceptual Critique. *Political Studies*, 48: 759–87.

Foweraker, J. and Krznaric, R. 2001: How to Construct a Database of Liberal Democratic Performance. *Democratization*, 8: 1–25.

Foweraker, J. and Landman, T. 1997: *Citizenship Rights and Social Movements: A Comparative and Statistical Analysis*. Oxford: Oxford University Press.

Fox, J. (ed.) 1990: *The Challenge of Rural Democratisation: Perspectives from Latin America and the Philippines*. London: Frank Cass.

Frade, C. 2001: Poder Global y Sociedad Civil: El Foro Social Mundial de Porto Alegre, in Bernard Cassen et al. (eds), *Attac: Contra la Dictadura de los Mercados*. Barcelona: Icaria Editorial.

Freedom House. 1990: *Freedom in the World: Political and Civil Liberties, 1989–1990*. New York: Freedom House.

——1997: *Comparative Survey of Freedom*. New York: Freedom House.

——2002: *Freedom in the World 2001–2002*, New York: Freedom House.

Fuentes, M. and Gunder Frank, A. 1989: Ten Theses on Social Movements. *World Development*, 17 (2): 179–91.

Fukuyama, F. 1992: *The End of History and the Last Man*. Harmondsworth: Penguin.

Galbaldón, A. J. 1992: From the Bruntland Report to Our Own Agenda. *International Journal of Sociology and Social Policy*, 12 (4–7): 23–39.

García-Guadilla, M. P. 1992: The Venezuelan Ecology Movement: Symbolic Effectiveness, Social Practices, and Political Strategies, in A. Escobar and S. Alvarez (eds), *The Making of Social Movements in Latin America: Identity, Strategy and Democracy*. Boulder, CO: Westview Press, 150–70.

García-Guadilla, M. P. and Blauert, J. (eds) 1992: Environmental Social Movements in Latin America and Europe: Challenging Development and Democracy. *International Journal of Sociology and Social Policy*, 12 (4–7): Special Issue.

Gastil, R. D. 1987: *Freedom in the World: Political and Civil Liberties, 1986–1987*. New York: Freedom House.

——1990: *Freedom in the World: Political and Civil Liberties, 1986–1987*. New York: Freedom House.

——1991: The Comparative Survey of Freedom: Experiences and Suggestions, in A. Inkeles (ed.), *On Measuring Democracy: Its Consequences and Concomitants*. New Brunswick: Transaction.

Geddes, B. 1996: Initiation of New Democratic Institutions in Eastern Europe and Latin America, in A. Lijphart and C. H. Waisman (eds), *Institutional Design in New Democracies: Eastern Europe and Latin America*. Boulder, CO: Westview Press, 15–41.

González Casanova, P. and Roitman, M. (eds) 1996: *Democracia y Estado Multiétnico en América Latina*. Mexico: Universidad Nacional Autónoma de México y La Jornada Ediciones.

González Pérez, M. 1997: *Gobiernos Pluriétnicos: La Constitución de Regiones Autónomas en Nicaragua*. Mexico: Editorial Plaza y Valdés.

Graham, R. (ed.) 1990: *The Idea of Race in Latin America, 1870–1940*. Austin: University of Texas Press.

Green, D. 1995: *Silent Revolution: The Rise of Market Economics in Latin America*. London: Latin America Bureau and Cassell.

Greenberg, D. and Katz, S. N. (eds) 1993. *Constitutionalism and Democracy.* Oxford: Oxford University Press.

Gurr, T. 1993: Why Minorities Rebel: A Cross National Analysis of Communal Mobilization and Conflict since 1945. *International Political Science Review,* 14 (2): 161–201.

——2000: *Peoples Versus States: Minorities at Risk in The New Century.* Washington, DC: United States Institute of Peace Press.

Gutiérrez, G. 1973: *A Theology of Liberation.* New York: Orbis.

Hadenius, A. 1992: *Democracy and Development.* Cambridge: Cambridge University Press.

Haggard, S. and Kaufman, R. 1995: *The Political Economy of Democratic Transitions.* Princeton: Princeton University Press.

Hagopian, F. 1990: Democracy by Undemocratic Means? Elites, Political Pacts and Regime Transition in Brazil. *Comparative Political Studies,* 23 (2): 147–70.

——1996: *Traditional Politics and Regime Change in Brazil.* Cambridge: Cambridge University Press.

Hale, C. A. 1996: Political Ideas and Ideologies in Latin America, 1870–1930, in L. Bethell (ed.), *Ideas and Ideologies in Twentieth-Century Latin America.* Cambridge: Cambridge University Press.

Hale, R. 1994: *Resistance and Contradiction: Miskitu Indians and the Nicaraguan State, 1894–1987.* Stanford, CA: Stanford University Press.

Harris, D. 1998: Regional Protection of Human Rights: The Inter-American Achievement, in D. Harris and S. Livingstone (eds), *The Inter-American System of Human Rights.* Oxford: Oxford University Press.

Hartlyn, J. and Valenzuela, A. 1994: Democracy in Latin America since 1930, in L. Bethell (ed.), *The Cambridge History of Latin America,* vol. VI, part 2: *Politics and Society.* Cambridge: Cambridge University Press, 99–162.

Harvey, N. 1998: *The Chiapas Rebellion: The Struggle for Land and Democracy.* Durham, NC: Duke University Press.

——2001: Rights, Minority and Indigenous, in J. Foweraker and P. B. Clarke, *Encyclopedia of Democratic Thought.* London and New York: Routledge.

Held, D. 1996. *Models of Democracy.* Cambridge: Polity Press.

Helliwell, J. F. 1994: Empirical Linkages between Democracy and Economic Growth, *British Journal of Political Science,* 24: 225–48.

Higley, J. and Gunther, R. (eds) 1992: *Elites and Democratic Consolidation in Latin America and Southen Europe.* Cambridge: Cambridge University Press.

Huber, J. D. and Bingham Powell, G. 1994: Congruence between Citizens and Policymakers in Two Visions of Liberal Democracy. *World Politics,* 46: 291–326.

Hunt, P. 1996. *Reclaiming Social Rights: International and Comparative Perspectives.* Aldershot: Dartmouth Publishing.

Hunter, W. 1997: *Eroding Military Influence in Brazil.* Chapel Hill: University of North Carolina Press.

Huntington, S. P. 1991: *The Third Wave: Democratization in the Late Twentieth Century.* Norman: University of Oklahoma Press.

Huntington, S. P. 1993: Democracy's Third Wave, in L. Diamond and M. Plattner (eds), *The Global Resurgence of Democracy*. Baltimore: John Hopkins University Press, 3–25.

Jaggers, K. and Gurr, T. R. 1995: Tracking Democracy's Third Wave with the Polity III data. *Journal of Peace Research*, 32 (4): 469–82.

Jaquette, J. S. 1994: Introduction: From Transition to Participation – Women's Movements and Democratic Politics, in J. S. Jaquette (ed.), *The Women's Movement in Latin America: Participation and Democracy*. Boulder, CO: Westview Press, 1–11.

Jones, M. 1995: *Electoral Laws and the Survival of Presidential Democracies*. South Bend, IN: University of Notre Dame Press.

Jones, P. 1994: *Rights*. London: Macmillan.

Kaimowitz, D. 1996: Social Pressure for Environmental Reform in Latin America, in H. Collinson (ed.), *Green Guerrillas: Environmental Conflicts and Initiatives in Latin America and the Caribbean*. London: Latin American Bureau, 8–20.

Keck, M. and Sikkink, K. 1998: *Activists Beyond Borders: Advocacy Networks in International Politics*. Ithaca: Cornell University Press.

Kieley, R. 1998: Neoliberalism Revised? A Critical Account of World Bank Conceptions of Good Governance and Market Friendly Interventions. *International Journal of Health Services*, 28 (4): 683–702.

Kingstone, P. R. and Power, T. J. 2000: *Democratic Brazil: Actors, Institutions and Processes*. Pittsburgh: University of Pittsburgh Press.

Kirby, P. 1996: *The Impact of Neo-liberalism on Chilean Society: A Report for Trócaire School of Communications*. Dublin: Dublin City University.

Klingemann, H., Hofferbert, R. I., Budge, I. with Keman, H. 1994: *Parties, Policies, and Democracy*. Boulder, CO: Westview Press.

Kymlicka, W. 1995: *Multicultural Citizenship*. Oxford: Oxford University Press.

Laakso, M. and Taagepera, R. 1979: Effective Number of Parties: A Measure with Application to Western Europe. *Comparative Political Studies*, 12 (1): 3–27.

Landman, T. 1999: Economic Development and Democracy: The View from Latin America. *Political Studies*, 47 (4): 607–26.

——2000: *Issues and Methods in Comparative Politics: An Introduction*. London: Routledge.

Lasswell, H. D. 1950: *Politics: Who Gets What When and How*. New York: P. Smith.

Latin American Perspectives 2001: The Indigenous Peoples of Chiapas and the State in the Time of Zapatismo: Remaking Culture, Renegotiating Power. *Latin American Perspectives*, 28 (2).

Leff, E. 1992: The Environment Movement and Prospects for Democracy in Latin America. *International Journal of Sociology and Social Policy*, 12 (4–7): 41–60.

Lehmann, D. 1990: *Democracy and Development in Latin America: Economics, Politics and Religion in the Post-War Period*. Philadelphia: Temple University Press.

Lehmann, D. and Bebbington, A. 1998: NGOs, the State, and the Development Process: The Dilemmas of Institutionalisation, in M. Vellinga (ed.),

The Changing Role of the State in Latin America. Boulder, CO: Westview Press.

Levine, D. 1988: Paradigm Lost: Dependency to Democracy. *World Politics,* 40 (3): 377–94.

Lijphart, A. 1984: *Democracies: Patterns of Majoritarian and Consensus Government in Twenty-One Countries.* New Haven: Yale University Press.

——1993: Constitutional Choices for New Democracies, in L. Diamond and M. Plattner (eds), *The Global Resurgence of Democracy.* Baltimore: John Hopkins University Press, 162–74.

——1994: *Electoral Systems and Party Systems: A Study of 27 Democracies 1945–1990.* New York: Oxford University Press.

Limongi, F. and Figueiredo, A. C. 1995: Partidos políticos na Câmara dos Deputados: 1989–1994. *Dados,* 38 (3): 497–523.

Linz, J. 1964: An Authoritarian Regime: Spain, in E. Allardt and Y. Littunen (eds), *Cleavages, Ideologies and Party Systems.* New York: The Academic Bookstore.

——1994: Presidential or Parliamentary Democracy: Does it Make a Difference?, in J. Linz and A. Valenzuela (eds), *The Failure of Presidential Democracy.* Baltimore: Johns Hopkins University Press, 3–87.

Linz, J. and Stepan, A. (eds) 1978: *The Breakdown of Democratic Regimes.* Baltimore: Johns Hopkins University Press.

——1996: *Problems of Democratic Transition and Consolidation: Southern Europe, South America, and Post-Communist Europe.* Baltimore: John Hopkins University Press.

Locke, J. 1924: *Of Civil Government: Two Treatises.* Everyman Library No. 751, London: J. M. Dent.

Loveman, B. 1993: *The Constitution of Tyranny: Regimes of Exception in Spanish America.* Pittsburgh: Pittsburgh University Press.

McAdam, D. and Rucht, D. 1993: The Cross-national Diffusion of Movement Ideas. ANNALS. *AAPSS,* 528: 56–74.

McKay, D. 1994: Review Article: Divided and Governed? Recent Research on Divided Government in the United States, *British Journal of Political Science,* 24: 517–34.

MacRae, E. 1992: Homosexual Identities in Transitional Brazilian Politics, in A. Escobar and S. Alvarez (eds), *The Making of Social Movements in Latin America: Identity, Strategy and Democracy.* Boulder, CO: Westview Press, 185–203.

McSherry, J. P. 1998: The Emergence of "Guardian Democracy": *NACLA Report on the Americas,* special issue: Militarized Democracy in the Americas: Faces of Law and Order, 32 (3): 16–24.

Mainwaring, S. 1990: Presidentialism in Latin America. *Latin American Research Review,* 25 (1): 157–79.

——1992: Transitions to Democracy and Democratic Consolidation: Theoretical and Comparative Issues, in S. Mainwaring, G. O'Donnell, and J. Samuel Valenzuela (eds), *Issues in Democratic Consolidation: The New South American Democracies in Comparative Perspective.* South Bend: IN: University of Notre Dame Press, 294–341.

Mainwaring, S. 1993: Presidentialism, Multipartism, and Democracy: The Difficult Combination. *Comparative Political Studies*, 26 (2): 198–228.

Mainwaring, S. and Scully, T. R. 1995: Introduction: Party Systems in Latin America, in S. Mainwaring and T. R. Scully (eds), *Building Democratic Institutions: Party Systems in Latin America*. Stanford: Stanford University Press, 1–34.

Mainwaring, S. and Shugart, M. S. (eds) 1997: *Presidentialism and Democracy in Latin America*. Cambridge: Cambridge University Press.

Mainwaring, S. and Wilde, A. 1989: *The Progressive Church in Latin America*. South Bend, IN: Notre Dame University Press.

Malloy, J. 1987: The Politics of Transition in Latin America, in J. M. Malloy and M. A. Seligson (eds), *Authoritarians and Democrats: Regime Transition in Latin America*. Pittsburgh: University of Pittsburgh Press.

Markoff, J. 1997: Really Existing Democracy: Learning from Latin America in the Late 1990s. *New Left Review*, 223: 48–68.

Marshall, T. H. 1964: *Citizenship and Social Democracy*. New York: Doubleday.

Martínez, A. G. 1992: Socio-ecological Struggles in Mexico – the Prospects. *International Journal of Sociology and Social Policy*, 12 (4–7): 113–50.

Marx, A. W. 1998: *Making Race and Nation*. Cambridge: Cambridge University Press.

Melo, J. O. 1998: The Drugs Trade, Politics and the Economy: The Colombian Experience, in E. Joyce and C. Malamud (eds), *Latin America and the Multinational Drugs Trade*. London: Macmillan and Institute of Latin American Studies.

Melucci, A. 1985: The Symbolic Challenge of Contemporary Social Movements. *Social Research*, 52 (4): 789–816.

Méndez, J. E., O'Donnell, G., and Pinheiro, P. S. (eds) 1999: *The (Un) Rule of Law and the Underprivileged in Latin America*. South Bend, IN: Notre Dame University Press.

Merkel, W. 1999: Defective Democracies. Estudio/Working Paper 1999/132 March 1999, Centro de Estudios Avanzados en Ciencias Sociales, Instituto Juan March de Estudios e Investigaciones (Madrid).

Michels, R. [1911] 1959: *Political Parties*. New York: Dover.

Migdal, J., Kohli, A., and Shue, V. (eds) 1994: *State Power and Social Forces: Domination and Transformation in the Third World*. Cambridge: Cambridge University Press.

Minority Rights Group 1995: *No Longer Invisible*. London: Minority Rights Group International.

——1997: *World Directory of Minorities*. London: Minority Rights Group International.

Molyneux, M. 1985: Mobilization without Emancipation? Women's Interests, the State, and Revolution in Nicaragua. *Feminist Studies*, 11 (2): 232–3.

Monsiváis, C. 1987: *Entrada Libre: Crónicas de la Sociedad que se Organiza*. Mexico: ERA.

Moore, B. 1966: *Social Origins of Dictatorship and Democracy: Lord and Peasant in the Making of the Modern World*. Boston: Beacon Press.

NACLA (North American Congress on Latin America) 1992: The Black Americas, 1492–1992. *Report on the Americas*, 25.

O'Donnell, G. 1973: *Modernization and Bureaucratic-Authoritarianism*. Berkeley: University of California.

——1978: Reflections on the Patterns of Change in the Bureaucratic-authoritarian State. *Latin American Research Review*, 13 (1): 3–38.

——1979: Tensions in the bureaucratic-authoritarian State and the Question of Democracy, in D. Collier (ed.), *The New Authoritarianism in Latin America*. Princeton: Princeton University Press, 285–318.

——1992: Delegative Democracy? Working Paper 172, Helen Kellogg Institute. South Bend, IN: University of Notre Dame.

——1994: Delegative Democracy. *Journal of Democracy*, 5: 55–69.

——1997: Illusions About Consolidation, in L. Diamond, M. F. Plattner, Y. Chu, and H. Tien (eds), *Consolidating the Third Wave Democracies: Themes and Perspectives*. Baltimore: John Hopkins University Press.

——1999a: *Counterpoints: Selected Essays on Authoritarianism and Democratization*. South Bend, IN: Notre Dame Press.

——1999b: Polyarchies and The (Un) rule of Law in Latin America: A Partial Conclusion, in J. E. Mendez, G. O'Donnell, and P. S. Pinheiro (eds), *The (Un) Rule of Law and the Underprivileged in Latin America*. South Bend, IN: Notre Dame University Press, 303–38.

O' Donnell, G. and Schmitter, P. 1986: *Transitions from Authoritarian Rule: Tentative Conclusions about Uncertain Democracies*. Baltimore: Johns Hopkins University Press.

O'Donnell, G., Schmitter, P., and Whitehead, L. (eds), 1986: *Transitions from Authoritarian Rule: Comparative Perspectives*. Baltimore: John Hopkins University Press.

Ogle, K. 1998: Guatemala's REMHI Project: Memory from Below. *NACLA Report*, 32 (2): 33–4.

Patrón, P. 1998: Peru: Civil Society and the Autocratic Challenge, in Alison Van Rooy (ed.), *Civil Society and the Aid Industry*. London: Earthscan.

Payne, L. 2000: *Uncivil Movements: The Armed Right Wing and Democracy in Latin America*. Baltimore: Johns Hopkins University Press.

Peeler, J. 1998: *Building Democracy in Latin America*. Boulder, CO, and London: Lynne Rienner Publishers.

Petras, J. and Morley, M. 1992: *Latin America in the Time of Cholera: Electoral Politics, Market Economy and Permanent Crisis*. New York: Routledge.

Potter, D., Goldblatt, D., Kiloh, M., and Lewis, P. (eds) 1997: *Democratization*. Cambridge: Polity Press.

Przeworski, A. 1986: Some Problems in the Study of the Transition to Democracy, in O' Donnell, G., Schmitter, P. C., and Whitehead, L. (eds), *Transitions from Authoritarian Rule: Comparative Perspectives*. Baltimore: Johns Hopkins University Press, 47–64.

——1991: *Democracy and the Market*. Cambridge: Cambridge University Press.

Przeworski, A. and Limongi, F. 1997: Modernization: Theory and Facts. *World Politics*, 49: 158.

Przeworski, A., Alvarez, M. E., Cheibub, J. A., and Limongi, F. 2000: *Democracy and Development: Political Institutions and Well-Being in the World, 1950–1990*. Cambridge: Cambridge University Press.

Putnam, R. 1993: *Making Democracy Work: Civic Traditions in Modern Italy*. Princeton: Princeton University Press.

Radcliffe, S. and Westwood, S. (eds) 1993: *Viva! Women and Popular Protest in Latin America*. London: Routledge.

Redclift, M. 1987: Mexico's Green Movement. *The Ecologist*, 17 (1): 41–3.

Remmer, K. L. 1995: New Theoretical Perspectives on Democratization. *Comparative Politics* (October): 103–22.

Riker, W. H. and Weimer, D. L. 1993: The Economic and Political Liberalization of Socialism: The Fundamental Problem of Property Rights. *Social Philosophy and Policy*, 10 (2): 79–102.

Risse, T., Ropp, S. C., and Sikkink, K. 1999: *The Power of Human Rights: International Norms and Domestic Change*. Cambridge: Cambridge University Press.

Rubin, J. 1997: *Decentering the Regime: Ethnicity, Radicalism and Democracy in Juchitán, Mexico*. Durham, NC: Duke University Press.

Rueschemeyer, D., Stephens, E. H., and Stephens, J. 1992: *Capitalist Development and Democracy*. Cambridge: Polity Press.

Rustow, D. A. 1970: Transitions to Democracy: Toward a Dynamic Model. *Comparative Politics*, 2: 337–64.

Sartori, G. 1976: *Parties and Party Systems: A Framework for Analysis*. Cambridge: Cambridge University Press.

Sartori, G. 1994: *Comparative Constitutional Engineering: An Inquiry into Structures, Incentives, and Outcomes*. London: Macmillan.

Schedler, A. 1999: Conceptualizing Accountability, in A. Schedler, L. Diamond, and M. F. Plattner (eds), *The Self-Restraining State: Power and Accountability in New Democracies*. Boulder, CO: Lynne Rienner Publishers, 13–28.

Schedler, A., Diamond, L., and Plattner, M. F. (eds) 1999: *The Self-Restraining State: Power and Accountability in New Democracies*. Boulder, CO: Lynne Rienner Publishers.

Schild, V. 1998: New Subjects of Rights? Women's Movements and the Construction of Citizenship in the "New Democracies", in S. Alvarez, E. Dagnino, and A. Escobar (eds), *Cultures of Politics/Politics of Cultures: Revisioning Latin American Social Movements*. Boulder, CO: Westview Press, 93–117.

Schumpeter, J. (1942/1996): *Capitalism, Socialism, and Democracy*. London: Routledge.

Sejersted, F. 1993: Democracy and the Rule of Law: Some Historical Experiences of Contradictions in the Striving for Good Government, in J. Elster and R. Slagstad (eds), *Constitutionalism and Democracy*. Cambridge: Cambridge University Press, 131–52.

Shugart, M. S. and Carey, J. M. 1992: *Presidents and Assemblies: Constitutional Design and Electoral Dynamics*. Cambridge: Cambridge University Press.

Siavelis, P. 2000: *The President and Congress in Postauthoritarian Chile: Institutional Constraints to Democratic Consolidation*. University Park: Pennsylvania State University Press.

Silva, P. 1999: The New Political Order in Latin America: Toward Technocratic Democracies?, in R. N. Gwynne and C. Kay (eds), *Latin America Transformed: Globalization and Modernity*. London: Arnold, 51–65.

Skidmore, T. E. 1967: *Politics in Brazil, 1930–1964: An Experiment in Democracy*. Oxford: Oxford University Press.

—— 1988: *The Politics of Military Rule in Brazil 1964–1985*. New York: Oxford University Press.

—— 1989: Brazil's Slow Road to Democratization: 1974–1985, in A. Stepan (ed.), *Democratizing Brazil: Problems of Transition and Consolidation*. New York: Oxford University Press, 5–42.

Skidmore, T. E. and Smith, P. 1992: *Modern Latin America*. Oxford: Oxford University Press.

Skinner, Q. 1998: *Liberty before Liberalism*. Cambridge: Cambridge University Press.

Skocpol, T. 1979: *States and Social Revolutions*. Cambridge: Cambridge University Press.

Slater, D. (ed.) 1985: *New Social Movements and the State in Latin America*. Amsterdam: CEDLA.

Smith, P. 1996: *Talons of the Eagle: Dynamics of US–Latin American Relations*. Oxford: Oxford University Press.

Souza Martins, J. 1996: Clientelism and Corruption in Contemporary Brazil, in W. Little and E. Posada-Carbó (eds), *Political Corruption in Europe and Latin America*. London: Macmillan and Institute of Latin America Studies, University of London.

Stavenhagen, Rodolfo (1968) Seven Fallacies about Latin America, in James Petras and Maurice Zeitlin (eds), *Latin America: Reform or Revolution?* Greenwich, CT: Fawcett Premier.

—— 1996: Indigenous Rights: Some Conceptual Problems, in E. Jelin and E. Hershberg (eds), *Constructing Democracy: Human Rights, Citizenship and Society in Latin America*. Boulder, CO: Westview Press, 141–60.

Steiner, H. J. and Alston, P. 1996: *International Human Rights in Context: Law, Politics, Morals*. Oxford: Oxford University Press.

Stepan, A. and Skach, C. 1994: Presidentialism and Parliamentarism in Comparative Perspective, in J. Linz and A. Valenzuela (eds), *The Failure of Presidential Democracy*. Baltimore: Johns Hopkins University Press, 119–36.

Stephen, L. 1996: Democracy for Whom? Women's Grassroots Political Activism in the 1990s: Mexico City and Chiapas, in G. Otero (ed.), *Neoliberalism Revisited: Economic Restructuring and Mexico's Political Future*. Boulder, CO: Westview Press, 167–85.

—— 1997: *Women and Social Movements in Latin America: Power from Below*. Austin, TX: University of Texas Press.

Sternbach, N. S., Navarro-Aranguren, M., Chuchryk, P., and Alvarez, S. 1992: Feminisms in Latin America: From Bogotá to San Bernardo, in A. Escobar and S. Alvarez (eds), *The Making of Social Movements in Latin*

America: Identity, Strategy and Democracy. Boulder, CO: Westview Press, 207–39.

Stiglitz, J. 2002: *Globalization and Its Discontents*. London: Penguin.

Tarrow, S. 1994: *Power in Movement: Social Movements, Collective Action and Politics*. Cambridge: Cambridge University Press.

Thornberry, P. 1991: *Minorities and Human Rights Law*. London: Minority Rights Group.

Tilly, C. 1998: Where Do Rights Come From?, in T. Skocpol (ed.), *Democracy, Revolution and History*. Ithaca and London: Cornell University Press, 55–72.

Torres Rivas, E. 1995: Democracy and the Metaphor of Good Government, in J. S. Tulchin with B. Romero (eds), *The Consolidation of Democracy in Latin America*. Boulder, CO, and London: Lynne Rienner Publishers, 45–57.

Touraine, A. 1989: *Palavra e Sangue: Política e Sociedade na América Latina*. São Paulo: Universidade Estadual de Campinas.

Trevisan, J. 1986: *Perverts in Paradise*. London: GMP Publishers Ltd.

UNDP 1999: *Human Development Report 1999*. New York: Oxford University Press.

Valderrama, M. 1998: *El Fortalecimiento Institucional y los Acelerados Cambios en las ONG Latinoamericanas*. Lima: ALOP-CEPES.

Valenzuela, A. 1993: Latin America: Presidentialism in Crisis. *Journal of Democracy*. 4 (4): 3–16.

van Cott, D. L. (ed.) 1994: *Indigenous Peoples and Democracy in Latin America*. New York: St Martin's Press.

——2000a: Explaining Ethnic Autonomy Regimes in Latin America. Paper presented at the XXII International Congress of the Latin American Studies Association, March 16–18, Miami, Florida.

——2000b: *The Friendly Liquidation of the Past: The Politics of Diversity in Latin America*. Pittsburgh: University of Pittsburgh Press.

Vetter, S. 1995: Mobilizing Resources: The Business of Grassroots Development. *Grassroots Development*, 19 (2). www.iaf.gov.

Vilas, C. M. 1992: The Hour of Civil Society. *NACLA Report on the Americas*, 27 (2): 38–43.

——1997: Introduction: Participation, Inequality, and the Whereabouts of Democracy, in D. A. Chalmers, C. M., Vilas, K. Hite, S. B. Martin, K. Piester, and M. Segarra (eds), *The New Politics of Inequality in Latin America: Rethinking Participation and Representation*. Oxford: Oxford University Press, 3–42.

Viola, E. J. 1988: Ecologist Movement in Brazil (1974–1986), from Environmentalism to Ecopolitics. *International Journal of Urban and Regional Research*, 12 (2): 211–36.

Wade, P. 1993: *Blackness and Race Mixture: The Dynamics of Racial Identity in Colombia*. Baltimore: Johns Hopkins University Press.

——1997: *Race and Ethnicity in Latin America*. London: Pluto Press.

Warren, K. 1998: *Indigenous Movements and their Critics: Pan-Maya Activism in Guatemala*. Princeton: Princeton University Press.

Wearne, P. 1996: *The Return of the Indian*. London: Latin America Bureau.

Weber, M. 1956: Politics as Vocation, in H. H. Gurth and C. Wright Mills (eds), *From Max Weber: Essays in Sociology*. London: Routledge, 77–128.

——1966: *The Theory of Social and Economic Organization*, T. Parsons (ed.), New York: Free Press.

Whitehead, L. 1992: The Alternatives to Liberal Democracy: A Latin American Perspective, in D. Held (ed.), *Political Studies*, 40. Special Edition on 'Prospects for Democracy.'

——1994: State Organization in Latin America since 1930, in L. Bethell (ed.), *The Cambridge History of Latin America*, vol. VI, part 2: *Politics and Society*. Cambridge: Cambridge University Press, 3–98.

Womack, J. 1999: *Rebellion in Chiapas: An Historical Reader*. New York: New Press.

World Bank. 1992: *Governance and Development*. Washington, DC: World Bank.

Yashar, D. J. 1999: Democracy, Indigenous Movements, and the Postliberal Challenge in Latin America. *World Politics*, 52 (1): 76–104.

Zagorski, P. W. 1992: *Democracy vs. National Security: Civil–Military Relations in Latin America*, Boulder, CO: Lynne Rienner Publishers.

Zakaria, F. 1997: The Rise of Illiberal Democracy. *Foreign Affairs*, Nov/Dec: 22–43.

INDEX

accountability 2, 4, 35, 59, 62–3, 147, 192; delegative democracy and 30, 55; Latin America and 65, 66, 67, 68, 69, 71, 72, 75, 199, 200, 205; "new political actors" and 154, 156; presidential models and 45; vertical/horizontal 63, 71, 109, 191, 205

Africa: democratization 34, 150; human rights 85; minority rights 168, 170

agriculture 138, 169; *see also* food provision and nutrition

Alemán, A. 23

Alfonsín, R. 47

Allende, S. 80

Alvarez, M. E. 36

Alvarez, S. 152, 160, 209, 210

Amazon: exploitation of 151, 174, 176, 177, 178; indigenous people and social movements 174, 176, 177, 178, 211

anarchism 15

Anglade, C. 45

Arbenz, J. 177

Argentina 3, 15, 16, 21, 23; bureaucratic-authoritarianism in 47; Constitution 81–2, 83, 86; democracy and democratic performance 14, 16, 30, 32, 68, 142, 159, 193, 194, 208; democratic transition 41, 128, 158; economy 29, 30, 32–3, 34, 52, 53, 107, 133, 137; governability 122; indigenous communities 172, 175; industry 134; Madres de la Plaza de Mayo 148, 158–9, 210; military 47–8, 157; neoliberalism 32; Peronist movement 17, 40, 67, 96, 97, 100, 103, 104, 106–7, 108; political parties and participation 16, 96, 97, 103, 108, 114, 115, 117, 129, 130; populism 17, 32, 68; presidentialism in 112, 117, 121; Radical party 16, 96, 97; revolutionary movements in 51; rights, human, political and social 87, 91, 127, 128; social development 134, 135, 137, 139, 140; social mobilization 141–2, 148; women's movements 158–9

Asia 134; democratization 34, 150

authoritarianism 12, 13, 33, 34, 38–9, 45, 74, 80, 111, 126–7; bureaucratic 4 , 21–2, 47; delegative democracy and 30;

democratic transition from 3, 17, 22, 34, 37, 38–9, 44, 47, 130, 149, 170; human rights violations and 89; new social movements and 147, 153, 156
authority 2, 4, 11; state 11–12, 15; *see also* legitimacy
autogolpe 113, 205, 207, 208; *see also* military, the
Aylwin, P. 48, 160

Banzer, H. 186
Barnes, S. 64
behaviour, political 61, 153, 213; *see also* participation, political culture, social movements
Belize 136, 137, 174
Bell, D. 104
Berlusconi, S. 105
Blair, T. 105
Blondel, J. 76
Bolaños, E. 23
Bolivia 29, 46, 118, 177–8; coalitions 117, 118; Constitution and reform 82, 186; democracy and transition 41, 108, 128, 142; electoral rules 117; governability 116; minority and indigenous communities 151, 172, 174, 175, 176, 177–8, 179, 181, 182, 188; participation and political parties 96, 99, 102, 109, 115, 116, 130, 207; presidentialism 99, 112, 115, 121, 208; rights, human, social and political 87, 88, 127, 128; social movements 148, 151; 1985 strike 29
Bordaberry, J. M. 208
Brazil 15, 21, 23, 35, 45, 80, 106, 108, 111; authoritarianism 80, 127; civil–military relations 47, 48, 108; clientelism 198; Constitution and reform 80–1, 82, 83, 86, 118; democracy, and performance of 17, 21, 34, 142, 193, 194; democratic breakdown 113, 116; democratic transition 41, 48, 81, 108, 128, 151; economy

52, 53, 91, 102, 132, 133, 137, 140; elections and participation 117, 129, 130; governability 113, 122; military rule 70, 71, 80, 81, 82, 98, 127, 157, 198; minority and indigenous communities 151, 172, 174, 175, 176, 181, 182; oligarchic power in 198; patronage in 198–9; political parties 40, 45, 46, 96, 97, 98, 102, 103, 104, 108, 114, 116, 117, 118, 119, 156, 198, 207; populism 17; presidentialism 112, 115, 118, 121; revolutionary movements 51; rights, human, social and political 87, 90, 126, 127, 128; social development 135, 137, 139; social movements 148, 151, 153–4, 210; women 160, 210
Brohman, J. 52, 54, 134
Burdick, J. 153, 210
bureaucracy 35, 61, 62, 66; authoritarian 4, 21–2; Weber's theory of 62
Burke, E. 13

camarillas 99
Calvert, P. 41
Calvert, S. 41
Cammach, P. 41, 43
Canada 25, 75, 169
capitalism 27–8, 75, 206
Cardosó, F. H. 48, 82, 118
Carey, J. M. 112, 208
Carribean 14, 131, 172
Castro, F. 26
Catholic Church 79, 152, 172, 177; Ecclesiastical Base Communities (CEBs) 152–3; Liberation Theology 152–3
caudillo governments 4, 13, 15, 33, 204, 205
censorship 71, 127
Central America 4, 14; democratization 22–4; dictatorship 22–3
charisma 62, 68, 206

Chávez, H. 19, 47, 50, 82, 98, 105, 106, 107, 113
Cheibub, J. A. 36
Chile 21, 23, 35, 80–1, 111; authoritarianism 80, 111; civil–military relations 47, 48; coalitions 117, 119; Constitution and reform of 80–1, 82, 207; democracy, and performance of 142, 193, 194; democratic breakdown 113; democratic transition 14, 15, 30, 34, 39, 41, 81, 128, 151; economy 52, 53, 71, 133, 137, 157, 163; governability 122; human rights and abuses of 48, 87, 88; liberty, political, social and cultural 91; military rule and 70, 71, 80–1, 157, 210; minority and indigenous communities 175, 181, 182; neoliberalism 28; non-governmental organizations and 162, 163; Pinochet regime 157, 210; political parties and participation 40, 46, 96, 97, 98, 100, 102, 103, 104, 108, 114, 115, 119, 130, 162, 207; president, authority of 113, 114; presidentialism 115, 119, 121, 208; rights, political and social 126, 127, 128; social development 135, 137, 138, 139, 140; Truth Commission 48; women's social movements 157, 160, 161
Chamorro, V. 23
Chuchryk, P. M. 210
Church, State and 13, 79
CIA 18, 70
citizenship: "active" 149; concept of 161; democratic 72–3, 74; "low-intensity" 201; see also social movements, "new political actors" and
citizenship rights 4, 11, 42, 59, 60, 77, 203; language of 153, 201; Latin America and 65, 68, 148–9, 150, 199; see also civil rights, participation, minority and

indigenous rights, women, rights of
civic virtue 203
civil associations 6
civil liberties 12, 90–1, 110, 191; Freedom House Index 90–1
civil rights 2, 3, 6, 36, 54, 62–3, 64, 68, 78, 83–4, 140, 192, 201; Latin America and 6, 43, 54, 66, 68, 109, 154, 195, 197–8, 199, 200; political rights and 63, 83, 84; see also political rights, social rights
civil society 5, 29, 37, 44, 50–1, 74, 75, 148, 201, 209; new social movements and 148, 149; "resurrection" of 156; "uncivil movements" 50–1, 110, 148; women's movements 157–61; see also social movements
civil war 4, 13, 39, 67
class and class relations 53–4, 63, 70, 154; compromise 63, 68, 206; democratization and 16, 20; export economy and 15; new social movements and 152, 154; representation and participation in government 63–4, 65, 142; see also social movements, polarization – social, revolution, unions
clientelism 6, 65–6, 68, 69, 72, 99–101, 106, 115, 141, 147, 153, 160, 161, 177, 183, 184, 197, 203; grassroots organizations and 164; oligarchic power and 198–9; tension with individual rights 199
Clinton, B. 105
coalitions 117–18, 119, 121–2
Cohen, J. 45, 113, 209
Cold War 17–18, 22, 71; see also Cuba
Collier, D. S. 201
Collier, R. B. 201
Collinson, H. 151
Collor de Mello, F. 34, 45, 48, 106, 107, 108

Colombia 3, 18–19, 82, 110,
178, 208; clientelism 183, 184;
coalitions 117; Constitution and
reform 82, 183–4, 186; democracy
18–19, 142, 193, 194, 198;
democratic transition 39; drug
cartels 18, 183, 184, 198; economy
133, 198; elites and oligarchic
power in 198; governability 122;
guerilla revolution 18–19, 51,
183; human rights 87, 88; "la
Violencia" 18, 100, 183;
legitimacy, crises in 183–4;
minorities and indigenous
communities 172, 174, 175, 176,
177, 178, 181, 182, 183–4, 186,
188, 211; political parties and
participation 96, 97–8, 100, 103,
105, 108, 115, 116, 119, 129, 130,
183, 198; presidentialism 114,
121; rights, human, political and
social 87, 88, 127, 135; social
development 135, 137, 139;
US involvement 19
colonial rule 12–13, 167, 168, 171,
176
communism 17, 22, 206
comparative political science 1, 2;
democracy and 37–40, 59;
democratic transition and 74;
Latin America and 2–3, 158;
social movements 154
consociationalism 18
consolidation, democratic 3, 60,
76–7, 89, 196–7, 212, 213; lack of
in Latin America 196–7
constitutionalism and constitutional
reform 4–5, 12–13, 36, 76–83, 130,
191, 193, 195, 196–7; minority and
indigenous rights and 167, 180–9;
political rights and 125;
principles of 77, 83
constitutions 191; as critical
dimension of democracy 76; role
of 77
contestation, political 2, 5, 147, 191,
193, 195

corporatism 17, 149, 150, 161;
societal 64; state 69, 141, 147, 160
corruption, political 2, 7, 19, 102–3,
106, 183, 197
Costa Rica 14, 18, 20; democracy in
20, 142, 193, 194; democratic
transition 39; economy 133, 136,
137; military 136, 138, 139;
minority and indigenous
communities 175, 181, 182;
political parties and participation
108, 115, 129, 130; presidentialism
113, 114, 117; rights, human,
political and social 87, 127; social
development 136, 137, 138; US
involvement 20
Cuba 4, 26–7, 90, 111; Castro
regime 36, 69; democratization
26; participation 130; relations
with US 26, 27, 69, 70;
Revolution (1959) 18, 69–70, 71;
social development 136; USSR
and 26, 69
Cuban Liberty and Democratic
Solidarity Act 1996 (Helms-
Burton) 27
culture: homogeneity of 164, 167–8;
see also minority and indigenous
communities, political culture

Dahl, R. 14, 190
Davidson, S. 77, 84, 85, 86
de Gaulle, C. 78, 206
de la Rúa, F. 32–3, 142
decolonization 76
democracy 2–3, 4, 34, 36, 126, 140,
190–203, 211–12; assessment of
54–5, 140; authoritarianism in 13;
basic requirements of 59; civic
community and 202, 203; "critical
dimensions"/primary principles
of 36, 191, 193; definitions of 5,
12, 35–7, 59, 123, 190, 191, 205,
207–8; discourses of 153–5;
economic determinants see
modernization theory; electoral
fallacy and 43; Freedom House

democracy (cont'd)
Index of Political Freedom 212;
grassroots organizations and 164;
human development and support
for 142–4; indicators of 193;
military "reserve domains" and
47–50, 110, 191; "new political
actors" and 147–65; normative
political theory 124, 125; Polity
III Democracy Scale 212;
"rights" protection and 140–1,
195–6, 202; social movements and
147–65; support for 142–4, 196–7;
"third wave" 4, 34, 41, 73, 74,
129, 130, 149, 195, 212; threats to
44–7; waves of 73, 128; see also
consolidation – democratic:
democratic transition –
democratization, economic
development and democracy,
legitimacy, neoliberalism,
participation
democracy, types of; delegative
30–3, 44, 54–5, 113, 205, 208;
electoral and liberal, gap between
40–4, 140, 190–1, 194; liberal 4,
13, 37–8, 39, 140, 190–1, 192;
oligarchical 4, 14, 16, 20, 33, 126;
polyarchy 190, 196; procedural
36, 37, 40, 42, 54, 123, 140, 195;
social 36, 123
democratic breakdown 5, 113
democratic performance 192–203;
Latin America and 6, 190–203;
measures of 193–5, 212; uneven
performance 193–200
democratic transition 3, 34–5,
38–40, 44, 110, 111, 127–8, 195,
200; authoritarian rule and 21–2,
60; average longevity of 113–14;
civil–military relations 47–50,
51; cycle of elections and 40–4;
economic crises 29; human
rights and 89; military
intervention and 45, 110;
minority and indigenous
communities and 173; new social

movements and 156–7; non-
governmental organizations and
163; "pacted" 23, 104; parties,
political and 95, 107–8;
revolutionary movements and
51; social mobilization and
39–40, 42, 50, 200, 201; transition
theory 37, 38–40, 74; uneven
democratic performance in
195–6; women's role in 160; see
also democratization, elites
democratization 3, 34, 37, 38, 60, 72,
141, 203, 205; index of 38; "third
wave" of 34, 41, 73, 74; see also
democracy, democratic transition,
economic development,
modernization
deregulation 29, 31
development see economic
development, human
development, modernization,
social development
Diamond, L. 14, 34, 43, 44, 74, 110,
128, 164, 190, 191, 193, 196, 197,
201, 212
Díaz, P. 14, 204
dictatorship 4, 74, 150; military
157; personalist 15, 33; see also
elites
"disappeared, the" 158–9
discrimination, racial 168–9, 172–3,
183–4; see also minority and
indigenous rights
dissent, political see political
violence, revolution, social
movements
Dominican Republic 15, 29, 137;
drug cartel 18, 31; human rights
87
Donnelly, J. 54, 124
drug trade 18, 183, 184, 197
Duvalier, F. 15

ecological issues 174, 176; see also
environmental politics
economic development 37–8, 51–4,
67, 69, 131–4, 140, 162; crash of

1929 16; democracy and 37–8,
140–4; environmental groups
and 150–1; food provision and
nutrition 138–40; healthcare and
education expenditure 136–8;
income and income distribution
123, 131–4, 141; indicators of 131,
134–40; industrialization 67, 103;
modernization theory and 37–8;
social rights and 125, 131;
state-led 27, 28; see also
democratization, human
development, modernization,
social development
economy: banks, national and
foreign 71, 73, 163; see also
International Monetary Fund,
World Bank; crash of 1929 16, 28;
foreign debt 28, 52–4, 100, 106,
162; foreign interests, role of
14–15, 21, 67, 71, 157; regional
integration 75; stabilization
policy 52–3, 141–2; state
intervention in 51–4; structural
adjustment programs 52, 53–4,
72, 169; trade and markets 13, 15,
67, 69, 75; transnationalization of
21, 71, 73, 75; US role of in Latin
American 14–15, 70, 73, 74; see
also globalization, neoliberalism
Ecuador 29, 34, 109, 118, 130, 177;
coalitions 117; democracy in 34,
142, 205; democratic transition
41, 128, 205; economy 133, 137,
205; Ecuadorian National
Indigenous Organisation
(CONAIE) 176, 184–6; electoral
rules 117, 208; governability 113,
116, 117, 122; legitimacy crises in
183, 184–6; military, role of 47,
49, 205; minority and indigenous
communities 172, 175, 176, 177,
178, 181, 182, 183, 184–6, 188; new
social movements 151; political
parties and participation 46, 97,
102, 108, 114, 116, 130, 184, 185;
presidentialism 115, 118, 121,

208; rights, human, political and
social 87, 91, 127, 128; social
development 135, 137, 139
education 84, 90, 107, 124, 126, 131,
134, 136–8, 149, 150; see also
social rights
El Salvador 23–4; civil war 1979–89
23; democracy in 142, 193, 194;
democratic transition 41, 108,
110, 128; economy 133, 137; elites
133; minority and indigenous
communities 174, 175, 181, 182;
political parties and participation
96, 104, 130; revolutionary
movements 51; rights, human,
political and social 87, 127, 128;
social development 137, 139
elections 12, 29–30, 42, 43, 64, 75,
97, 109; "free and fair" 125, 126,
191, 193, 200, 205, 208, 209; "ring-
fencing" 200; voter turnout
128–30; see also electoral
systems, participation, parties –
political
electoral rules 116, 120, 208; see
also party systems
electoral systems 5, 114, 116–17,
208; liberal democracy and 51;
presidentialism and 40–4, 112–17;
proportional representation 5,
35, 44–5, 46, 112, 116, 120; see also
party systems
elites 15, 18–20, 21, 22, 23, 61, 66,
98, 133, 196; democratic transition
and 38–9, 41, 44, 75, 104, 195,
200; intellectual 13–14; natural
resources and 169; pacts 6,
18–20, 22, 104, 186; political
parties and 98, 100; power of 14,
196; US support of 14–15, 22, 23;
see also caudillo government,
oligarchy
employment rights 149
environmental politics 84–5,
150–1, 162; see also Amazon,
minority and indigenous
communities

equality: political 3, 54, 63, 109,
123–6, 140–1, 192; social 123; *see
also* exclusion – social, minority
and indigenous rights, political
rights, social rights, women's
rights
ethnicity 124, 170–1, 173, 180;
politicization of 166; *see also*
minority and indigenous rights
Europe 11, 22, 66, 68, 83, 103, 120,
197; human rights 85, 167, 168
Europe, Eastern 208;
democratization of 34, 111, 169,
197; 1989 revolution 2, 111
European Union 85
exclusion, social 2, 35, 44, 53–4, 55,
91, 141, 142, 147, 169, 206;
inclusiveness 36, 63, 191, 195; *see
also* human rights, minority and
indigenous rights
executive, the 205, 208; presidential
systems and 116–17
executive–legislative relations 35,
44–7, 54, 63, 112–13, 115–16, 118,
184; institutional design and
44–7; military intervention and
47; *see also* constitutionalism and
constitutional reform, legislature,
presidentialism

Falklands/Malvinas War 41, 47
fascism 73, 83
feminism 159–61, 210; *see also*
women, rights of
Figueiredo, A. C. 102, 118
Fitch, J. S. 47, 48, 49
food and nutrition 138–40, 141, 157;
"food security" 138; measures of
138
Fox Quesada, V. 105, 107, 187–8
France 78, 116, 206; Revolution
78–9, 103
Franco, F. 206
freedom 109, 124; assembly 63, 88,
91, 128; association 63, 88, 91,
109, 128; press 12, 63, 88; *see also*
civil rights; political rights

Frei, E. 48
Foweraker, J. 39, 42, 50, 76, 79, 91,
96, 115, 125, 148, 192, 193, 194,
199, 200, 201, 205, 209, 212
Fujimori, A. 31–2, 45, 46, 49, 105,
106, 118, 186, 205, 208
Fukuyama, F. 104

García, A. 104
García-Guadilla, M. P. 151, 209
gender 159, 160; *see also* feminism,
women
Germany 73, 78, 116
globalization 3, 72, 73–5, 105, 141,
162, 163, 169; human rights and
84–5, 162; International Non-
Governmental Organizations
(INGOs) 162–3, minority and
indigenous rights and 169
governability 5, 13, 112, 115–16,
117, 119, 120, 122, 203
governance 1–2; constitutions and
77–83; "good" 105, 110, 193, 203;
see also constitutionalism and
constitutional reform, legitimacy,
rule of law, stability – political
Goulart, J. 80
Greece 33
green movement 150–1; *see also*
environmentalism
gridlock 112, 113, 114, 118, 120, 177,
179
Guatemala 17–18, 24, 110, 179;
democracy in 142, 179, 193, 194,
198; democratic breakdown 113;
democratic transition 24, 41, 128;
economy 133, 137, 198; electoral
rules 117, 208; elites and
oligarchic power 198; human
rights and abuses 24, 41, 87;
military repression 1980s 179;
minority and indigenous
communities 172, 173–4, 175,
176, 177, 179, 181, 182, 188; new
social movements 151;
participation 129, 130, 179, 198;
political and social rights 127,

128; presidentialism 115, 208; social development 134, 135, 137, 139, 140
Gunther, R. 22, 100, 195
Gurr, T. 180, 182, 212

Hadenius, A. 193
Haiti 15; democratic transition 41, 128; human rights 87, 88; political and social rights 128; revolutionary movements 51
Hale, C. 13, 181, 204
Harris, D. 89
Hartlyn, J. 36, 76, 79, 80, 126
Harvey, N. 154, 173, 179, 211
health and healthcare 124, 131, 134, 136, 138; indicators of 136; see also social rights
Held, D. 35
Higley, J. 22, 100, 195
Hitler, A. 206
Holocaust 83
Honduras: democratic transition and democracy in 41, 128, 142; economy 133, 137; human rights 87, 88; minority and indigenous communities 174, 175, 181, 182; participation 130; political and social rights 127, 128; social development 135, 137, 138, 139, 140
human development 131, 134–5, 143, 144; Human Development Index (HDI) 134, 135 136, 143, 144; support for democracy and 142–4; United Nations Development Program (UNDP) 134, 135; see also education, health and healthcare, literacy, social rights
human rights 3, 5, 77, 83–6, 123, 147; charters and declarations 83, 168; Constitutions and constitutional reform 77, 83, 86; Inter-American Court 85, 88; Inter-American System of Human Rights 77, 85, 88–9;
international instruments 87–9, 207; International System for Human Rights 88; Latin America and 5, 71, 77, 85–91, 124, 149; "negative" rights 76; non-governmental organizations (NGOs) 86; social, economic and cultural 84, 90; transnational advocacy networks 86, 162; women's movement and 157, 158–9; see also civil rights, political rights, minority and indigenous rights, social rights
Hunt, P. 125
Huntington, S. 73, 211–12

identity, political 3, 67, 149, 151, 208–9; difference and 151; "new" 149
ideological polarization 44, 46, 114, 119–20, 121–2, 206
ideology 103–4; "end of" 104
immigration 15, 105
imperialism 76; US in Latin America 14–15, 69, 70
inclusiveness 36, 63, 191, 195; see also social exclusion, minority and indigenous rights
income and income distribution 131–4, 209; Gini coefficient 132–3
India 208, 212
Indians, Latin American 70, 171, 173, 174, 181, 183, 211; exploitation of 171–2, 176; mobilization of 176–9; see also minority and indigenous communities, minority and indigenous rights
Indonesia 170
industry and industrialization 21, 67, 103, 105, 134, 176; import-substitution industrialization (ISI) 67, 69, 134
institutional design and democratic performance 44–7, 197; checks and balances 62, 63, 113, 205;

institutional design and (cont'd)
electoral systems and 44–5;
executive–legislative conflict and
35, 44–7; political party systems
and 44–5; presidential
democracies and 79; *see also*
consolidation – democratic,
constitutionalism and
constitutional reform, democratic
performance, executive–
legislative relations
Inter-American Development Bank
163
interest groups 61, 64–5, 150, 198
International Labour Organization
(ILO) 169–70, 179, 182, 184, 211
International Monetary Fund
(IMF) 25, 28, 29, 31, 51, 52, 71,
100–1; democratic governance
and 193; structural-adjustment
programs 52, 53–4, 72, 169
Italy 73, 212

Japan 51, 73, 212
Jones, M. 46, 79, 116, 124
judiciary 35, 45–6, 63; power of and
democracy 45–6, 55, 205
justiciability 125, 209

Keck, M. 86, 162
Kennedy, J. F. 206
Krznaric, R. 192, 193, 194, 212

Laakso, M. 121, 208
labor mobilization *see* social
movements, unions
land redistribution and rights *see*
minority and indigenous rights
Landman, T. 38, 39, 41, 42, 50, 76,
91, 125, 199, 200, 209
Latin America; authoritarianism
12, 80, 126–7, 130; civil society
148–65; constitutionalism in 77,
78, 79, 83; democracy and
democratic performance 2–3, 6,
16, 26, 29, 34, 37, 38, 43–4, 126,
128–30, 142–4, 190–203, 212;
democratic consolidation in
196–7, 199; economic
development and democracy 38,
140–4; GDP 131–2, 134;
governance 2–3, 7, 111–22;
Human Development Index
(HDI) 134, 135, 136, 143, 144;
human rights 3, 5, 22, 77, 85–91,
124, 149; income and income
distribution 123, 131–4, 141, 209;
military rule in 21–2, 27, 127, 152,
153, 167; minority and indigenous
communities 168–89;
mobilization and rights in 200–3;
Non-Governmental
Organizations, role of 162–3,
201–2; parties, political 95–110,
200; political and social rights
123–44; population and
population growth 134, 211;
populism 80, 96, 105–7, 168;
presidentialism 5, 35, 40, 44–7,
54, 66, 111–22, 207, 208; rule of
law and 77, 141, 198–200, 203; US
involvement 14–15, 17, 204, 206;
women's movement 157–61, 210;
see also names of individual
countries
leadership: charismatic/populist
105–7, 110, 206
legislature 112–13, 114–15, 116–17;
see also executive–legislative
relations, presidentialism,
political stability
legitimacy 2, 4, 5, 12, 30, 59, 60–2,
196, 197, 212; civil–military
relations and 47–50; ethnic rights
and 181–2, 188; Latin America
and 65, 66, 67, 109, 182–3, 196,
199; military rule and 70–1;
revolutionary movements and
69–70; theories of 60–1
legitimacy crises 18, 183, 188–9
Lehmann, D. 153–4, 162
Levine, D. 100, 195, 200
liberalism 15, 27, 62, 63;
conservative 14, 66; economic

27–8; principles of 192; *see also* democracy, neoliberalism
Liberation Theology 152
liberty 76, 192
life expectancy 134, 141
Lijphart, A. 192, 208
Limongi, F. 36, 38, 102, 118
Linz, J. J. 11, 14, 47, 77, 102, 111, 114, 196, 199, 213
Lipset, S. M. 14
literacy 127, 134, 136, 137, 141; *see also* education
Livingstone, S. 89
Locke, J. 192
log-rolling 102, 115
Loveman, B. 79

Mahaud, J. 49, 185
Mainwaring, S. 22, 42, 46, 97, 106, 109, 111, 113, 114, 115, 117, 118, 119, 121, 152
Malaysia 208
Malvinas/Falklands war 41, 47
markets and trade 25, 27; debt crises and 29, 106
Maya Indians 173–4, 179
McKay, D. 207
McSherry, J. P. 32
media, political participation and 64, 105, 106
Menchú, R. 182
Méndez, J. E. 89, 91
Mendoza, C. 185
Menem, C. 31, 32, 47–8, 82, 105, 106–7, 141–2, 159, 208
Merkel, W. 199, 201
Mexico 4, 14, 24–6, 35, 110; agrarian reform 178–9; civil society 154–6; Commission for Peace and Reconciliation in Chiapas (COCOPA) 187–8, 202; Constitution 82, 204; debt crises and 51, 101; democracy in 24–6, 34, 142, 208; democratic transition 41, 47–50, 51, 104, 108; economy 25, 26, 51, 53, 101, 133, 137; elections and participation 42, 130; human rights 87, 88; military 47–50, 55, 61; minority and indigenous communities 172, 174, 175, 176, 177, 178, 181, 182, 187–8; party system 25, 26; political parties 96, 97, 98, 100, 101, 102, 103, 104–5, 107; populism in 17, 68; Revolution 1910–17, 67–8, 172, 204; social development 135, 137, 138, 139, 140; social movements 148, 154–6, 202; social revolution in 14, 24–5, 29; trade and markets 75; US involvement and 6; Zapatista Army of National Liberation (EZLN) 148, 154–6, 178–9, 186–7
migration, rural–urban 105
military, the 110, 197–8, 199, 205; civilian control of 47–50, 55; democratic breakdown and 113; economic policies under rule 157; golpes/autogolpes 113, 205, 207, 208; guardian democracy and 32; repression and terror in 158–9; reserve domains of and democracy 47–50, 110, 191; rule of 4, 15, 18–19, 21–2, 27, 28, 47–50, 70–1, 72, 73
Mill, J. S. 167–8
minority and indigenous communities 70, 174–80, 211; as "collective subjects" 180, 187; as "new political actors" 166; assimilationist policies 166, 167, 169, 170–1, 172, 173; colonial rule and 168, 171–2, 211; economic exploitation of 166, 171–2, 173, 174–9; land dispossession of 171–2, 211; national identity and 166, 167, 169, 170–1, 173, 180; state formation and 170–4, 210, 211; *see also* Indians, Latin America
minority and indigenous rights 3, 6, 42, 54, 70, 84, 90, 167–70, 173, 176–9, 181–9, 192, 195, 197–8, 201;

minority and indigenous rights
(cont'd).
constitutional reform and 167,
180–9; customary law and 170,
186; definitions of 167;
globalization and 169; land rights
170, 175, 176, 177–9, 183;
Minority Rights Group 174, 175
mobilization, political and social
39–40, 42, 141, 142, 147, 148, 156,
163, 200–3; characteristics of
popular Latin American
movements 150–1, 201; language
of rights and 201; protest and
rebellion scale 180–4; see also
social movements
modernization 13, 71; Latin
America and 37–8, 205; military
and 205; theory of 37–8, 39, 206;
see also democratization,
economic development
Monroe Doctrine 204
Moore, B. 11
Mussolini, B. 206

nationalism 61–2, 67, 76; minorities
and national identity and 166,
167, 169, 170–1, 173, 180
natural resources, exploitation of
174, 176–9; see also
environmentalism
Navarro-Aranguren, M. 152, 160
neoliberalism 6, 25, 27–30, 44, 51–2,
54, 60, 104, 149, 164, 206; reforms
1980s and 1990s 28, 31, 51–2, 54,
73–5, 134, 150, 173; resistance to
154
Nicaragua 22–3; democracy in 142,
193, 194; democratic transition
41, 108, 128, 181–2; economy 133,
136, 137, 138; elites 133; human
rights 87; minority and
indigenous communities 175,
180–1, 182; Miskitu Indians 70,
180–1; participation 130; political
and social rights 127, 128;
Sandinista Front for National

Liberation (FSLN) 96, 98, 102,
138, 180–1; Sandinista Revolution
1979 15, 20, 23, 26, 51, 69–70, 133,
180–1; social development 135,
136, 137, 138, 139, 140
Noboa, G. 49
Non-Governmental Organizations
(NGOs) 86, 147, 148, 162, 201–2;
grassroots movements changing
to 163–4; International Non-
Governmental Organizations
(INGOs) 162; role of in Latin
American politics 162–3
Noriega, M. 41
North American Free Trade
Agreement (NAFTA) 25, 75

O'Donnell, G. 21, 22, 30, 38, 44, 54,
72, 90, 91, 109, 113, 156, 190, 191,
196, 197, 200, 201, 205, 207
oligarchy 2, 67, 69, 110, 197–9;
clientelism and 198–9; oligarchic
democracies 4, 14, 16, 20, 33;
power of 197–9, 205, 212
O'Neill, T. 101
Organization of American States 5

pacts see elites, pacts
Panama 15; democratic support in
142; democratic transition 41,
128; economy 133, 137; human
rights 87, 88; minority and
indigenous communities 175,
181, 182; participation 130;
political and social rights 127,
128; social development 135, 137,
139
Paraguay 128; democracy in 142;
human rights 87, 88; income
distribution 133; minority and
indigenous communities 175,
181, 182; participation 130;
political and social rights 127,
128; social development 135, 137,
139
parliamentary systems 102, 111,
112, 116, 119; see also
presidentialism

participation 2, 5, 16, 33, 36, 54, 55, 59, 60, 63–5, 68–72, 109, 127–31, 147, 153, 158, 200; equality and 141; grassroots and new democracies 163–4; Latin America and 65, 66, 67, 158, 200–3; media, role of 64; minorities and indigenous people, inclusion of 170–4; neoliberal reforms 31, 54; partisan mobilization and 64; political rights and 123–31, 140–4; revolutionary movements and 69–70; social movements, effect of 158–9, 161; voter turnout 128–30; *see also* exclusion – social, inclusiveness, legitimacy, social movements, suffrage

parties, political 40–4, 46, 61, 63–4, 65, 95–110, 197, 200, 206; authoritarian 104; coalitions and factions 117–18, 119; democracy and democratic stability 96, 97, 98–9, 109–10; discipline within 96, 101–3; duration of 96, 107–9; elitism and 98; formation of new 40, 156; general characteristics of Latin American 95–7, 200; ideology and 101, 119–20, 206; left–right spectrum and 96, 110, 103–5, 206; patronage and clientelism in 96, 99–100, 103; populism and 96, 105–7; presidential support of 115–16, 117; "ring-fencing" 200; "rootedness" of 96, 97, 99; *see also* ideological polarization

party systems 42, 63, 108–10, 114, 115–22; coalitions 117–20, 121; dominant party rule 24; effective number of parties in 208; institutional design and 46–7; legislative politics and 6; majority run-off rule 208; multipartism 115, 116, 117, 118, 119–20, 121; single-party rule 24, 117; two-party 119, 121

path dependency 206
patrimonialism 6, 61, 65, 72, 141, 147, 149–50, 173, 198–9
patronage 96, 99–100, 103, 106, 197, 198–9, 203
Payne, L. 50, 51, 89
Peeler, J. 28, 29, 205
Pérez, C. A. 34, 50
Peru 29, 30, 31–2, 35, 49, 130; Constitution and reform 81, 82, 186, 207; democracy and democratic transition 31, 127, 128, 142, 205, 208; democratic breakdown 113; economy 133, 137, 205; electoral rules 117, 208; governability of 122; human rights and abuses 32, 49, 87; liberty, political 91; military, role of 31–2, 49, 205; minority and indigenous communities 172, 174, 175, 176, 177, 181, 182, 186, 188; neoliberal reforms of Fujimori 31, 45, 47, 105, 106, 118, 186, 205, 207; participation 130; political parties 46, 96, 97, 103, 104, 105, 106, 115, 116, 119; presidentialism 121, 208; political and social rights 126, 127, 128; social development 135, 137, 139, 140; *see also* Shining Path

Philippines, the 154, 208
Pinochet, A. 41, 48, 52, 80–1, 108, 157
pluralism 65, 69
plurality, segmented 208–9
Poland, democratic transition in 39, 107
polarization, social 53–4, 70, 134
police, human rights and 89–90, 91, 110, 197–8, 199
political culture 82, 101–3, 111, 149, 197, 203; identity and 149, 164; "new political actors" and 156–61, 164–5; women's movements and 158–9; *see also* clientelism, patronage, populism

Political Database of the Americas,
    The 41
political liberties, Freedom House
    Index of 90–1
political mobilization *see*
    mobilization
political rights 5, 63, 83, 84, 90, 109,
    123–31, 140–4, 191, 192, 195,
    198–200, 201, 209, 212;
    democratic discourse of 153–5;
    rules and procedures to
    guarantee 140–1; *see also* civil
    rights
political violence 44, 50–1, 55, 82,
    91, 149, 183
polyarchy 190, 196
population growth 134, 211
populism 4, 16–18, 31, 33, 67, 68–9,
    70, 72, 74, 80, 96, 105–7, 141, 153;
    consumer populism 107; political
    parties and 96, 105–7
pork-barrel politics 101–2
Portugal 22, 34, 73, 78
positivism 13
poverty 51–4, 55, 69, 105, 106, 123,
    134, 141, 149, 150, 152, 157, 186,
    206; *see also* human development
power 4, 140–1, 196, 197–8;
    governmental types of 11;
    governmental, sources of 11–12;
    oligarchic 197–8, 199;
    presidential 112, 113, 114;
    relations 140–1, 142, 198–9
president: authority of 112, 113,
    114; party support of 114–15,
    117, 122
presidentialism 78, 111–22, 207,
    208; coalitions and 117–18,
    119–20, 208; electoral system and
    40, 116–17; executive–legislative
    conflict 35, 44–7, 54, 63, 112–13,
    115–16, 118; Latin America and
    5, 35, 40, 44–7, 54, 66, 111–22, 207,
    208; parliamentarianism and 111,
    113; United States and 78, 207,
    208
privatization 20, 28, 29, 31, 157, 197

procedural democracy 36, 37, 40,
    42, 54, 123, 140, 195; *see also*
    democracy
property rights 133–4, 192;
    indigenous people and 171–2
proportional representation *see*
    electoral systems, proportional
    representation
Przeworski, A. 22, 36, 38, 100, 128,
    131, 192, 195
Putnam, R. 202, 203

Reagan, R. 54, 207
religion *see* Catholic Church;
    Church, State and
representation 2, 5, 30, 102; *see also*
    electoral systems, participation,
    parties – political
republicanism 12, 79
revolution 4, 18–19, 33, 69–70, 206;
    see also social movements
rights, individual and group 167,
    169, 196, 198; democracy and the
    fight for 202; language of and
    social mobilization 201; *see also*
    civil rights, human rights,
    minority and indigenous rights,
    political rights
Roosevelt, F. 82–3
Rueschemeyer, D. 16, 38, 39, 63
rule of law 4, 5, 55, 66, 73, 76–7, 80,
    109, 192, 198–200, 203, 213;
    democracy and 76–7, 91, 141,
    147, 196–200, 205; ethnic
    minorities and 173; "imperfect"
    198–9; institutional weaknesses of
    6; uneven democratic
    performance and 199–200
Russia 170
Rustow, D. A. 39, 195

Salinas de Gortari, C. 25
Samper, E. 184
Sánchez de Losada, G. 186
Sarney, J. 48
Sartori, G. 119, 207
Schmitter, P. 22, 38, 156

Scully, T. R. 42, 46, 97, 106, 109, 114, 115, 119, 121
separation of powers model 5, 78
Shining Path 31, 49, 51
Shugart, M. S. 112, 117, 118, 208
Sikkink, K. 86, 162
Singapore 51
Skach, C. 45, 102, 113
Skidmore, T. E. 80, 81, 127
Skocpol, T. 11
Smith, A. 27–8
Smith, P. 204, 206
social capital 148
social democracy 36, 123
social development 131, 134; see also human development, social rights
social justice 72
social movement organizations (SMOs) 147, 162
social movements 5, 6, 50–1, 71, 141, 147–65, 200–3, 210; against poverty 147, 150; citizenship rights and 148–9, 150; debt crises 1980s and 1990s 28–9; democratic discourse of 153–5; democratization and 39–40, 42, 72, 141, 147; environmental 150; gay and lesbian 148, 152; grassroots organizations and 150, 153, 162–3; green 150–1; human rights 71, 86, 150; impact of 156–61; indigenous people's and 147, 151, 174–89; labor movements 39, 72, 148, 201; Liberation Theology 152–3; "new political actors" and 147–65, 210; protest and rebellion scale 180–4; women's 147, 150, 151, 152, 156, 157–61, 210; see also mobilization, political and social
social rights 68, 84, 123–7, 131–44; human development programs 134–5; International Covenant on Economic, Social and Cultural Rights (CESCR) 125; measures of 131; support for democracy and 142–4; UN Committee on Economic, Social and Cultural Rights 125; see also mobilization, political and social
social welfare 20, 53–4, 55, 74, 84, 105, 107, 123–4, 125, 131, 138–40, 141; see also human development
socialism 15, 104
solidarity rights 2, 5, 84
Somoza, A. 133
South Korea 51
Spain 22, 78, 107, 206; democratization 34, 39
state, the: checks and balances 62, 63; Church and 13, 79; dominant party 24, 25–6; formation of 61–2, 166, 167, 170–4, 180; foundation of power in 11, 61; repression 69, 84; single party 26–7; terrorism 71; use of force 205–6; see also accountability, constitutionalism and constitutional reform, electoral systems, governance, legitimacy, party systems, presidentialism
stability, political 3, 13, 20, 21, 31, 42, 70, 77, 112, 114; civil–military relations and 47–50; coalitions and 118; political parties and 109–10; social welfare provision and 124; trade-off with political participation 6, 100; uncivil movements and 50–1
Stalin, J. 206
Stepan, A. 11, 45, 47, 77, 102, 113, 196, 199, 213
Stephens, E. H. 16, 38, 39, 63
Stephens, J. 16, 38, 39, 63
Sternbach, N. S. 152, 160
Stroessner, A. 41
suffrage 84, 126, 129, 191; see also women, rights of

Taagepera, R. 121, 208
Taiwan 51
Tarrow, S. 156, 157
Thatcher, M. 54

Tilly, C. 11
Toledo, A. 32
totalitarianism 73
transformation theory 37, 39–40
transition, democratic; *see*
    democratic transition
transition theory 37, 38–40
transnational advocacy networks
    86, 162
transparency 35, 212
Trujillo, R. 15

unemployment 53, 157
Union of Soviet Socialist Republics
    (USSR) 73; collapse of 2, 26,
    104; Cuba and 26
unions 17, 21, 23, 29, 39, 64, 68, 69,
    148, 177–8, 201; clientelism and
    106, 200; debt crises and 29;
    suppression of 21, 69, 72
United Kingdom 54; minority
    rights and 167–8; parliamentary
    system 116, 208
United Nations 83, 125, 134, 135,
    138, 167; minority and indigenous
    rights and 169–70
United States of America: Alliance
    for Progress Policy 206; Carter
    administration 22; Clinton
    administration 27; Constitution
    78, 82–3; Cuba 18, 26–7, 206;
    divided government in 206–7;
    economic development 25;
    elections 2000 125; human rights
    and 85, 87, 88, 89; interest groups
    64–5; military intervention in
    Latin America 14–15; minorities
    167, 169; Monroe Doctrine 204;
    participation, political 129–30;
    parties, political 96, 99, 100, 102;
    political and social rights 127;
    presidentialism in 114, 206–7,
    208; Reagan administration 23,
    54; Revolution 78–9; separation
    of powers 5; trade and markets
    75; Washington Consensus 28, 74,
    104, 106

Uribe, A. 19
Uruguay 14, 15, 21; civilian–
    military relations 47, 48;
    coalitions 117; Constitution
    80–1; democracy and democratic
    transition 16, 30, 41, 46, 128, 142;
    democratic breakdown 113;
    economy 133, 137; governability
    113, 122; human rights 87, 88;
    minority and indigenous
    communities 175; parties,
    political 97, 108, 114, 115, 116,
    119; president, authority of 113,
    114; presidentialism in 121, 207,
    208; rights, political and social
    127, 128, 135; social development
    135, 137, 138, 139

Valenzuela, A. 36, 76, 79, 80, 111,
    112, 126
van Cott, D. L. 18, 79, 82, 169, 176,
    177, 178, 183, 184, 186, 188, 210,
    211
Vargas, G. 80, 207
Venezuela 17, 29, 106, 108;
    constitutional reform 82, 113;
    democracy and democratization
    18, 19–20, 39, 46, 82, 118, 142, 193,
    194; executive/legislative conflict
    in 47; governability 113, 122;
    human rights 87; military, role of
    50, 205; minority and indigenous
    communities 172, 175, 176, 181,
    182; participation and political
    parties 96, 98–9, 103, 105, 114,
    115, 118, 129; presidentialism in
    114, 117, 121; revolutionary
    movements 51; social
    development 135, 137, 139, 140;
    social mobilization in 141–2, 209
Vetter, S. 162, 163
Vilas, C. M. 134, 140, 141, 209
Viola, E. J. 151
violence, political *see* political
    violence; revolution; social
    movements
voting *see* participation

Wade, P. 172, 173, 189, 211
Washington Consensus 28, 74, 104, 106
waves of democracy *see* democracy, waves of
wealth *see* income and income distribution
Wearne, P. 169, 171, 174, 176, 211
Weber, M. 61, 62, 67, 198–9, 205–6
welfare 124, 131, 134; state 36, 54, 68; *see also* social rights, social welfare
Whitehead L. 22, 38, 198, 201
women: as "new political actors" 147, 150, 151, 152; development of movement in Latin America 157–61, 210; employment of 157; rights of 54, 63, 78, 87, 89, 90, 124, 126, 160, 162; *see also* feminism
World Bank 1, 28, 29, 51, 53, 71, 105, 132, 136, 163, 193; good governance requirement of 193

Yashar, D. J. 166, 178, 211
Yugoslavia 170

Zagorski, P. W. 47, 48, 49
Zapatista Army of National Liberation (EZLN) 148, 154–6
Zedillo, E. 187